More Praise for *The Bridge at the Edge of the World:*

"Gus Speth's critique of unbridled capitalism is riveting and haunting, and his solutions are poetic and inspiring."
—Devra Davis, author of *The Secret History of the War on Cancer* and *When Smoke Ran Like Water*

"In *The Bridge at the Edge of the World,* James Gustave Speth gives us new lenses with which to see what we have done to our environment and, more important, to see what we can do to restore it. He challenges us all to act not for ourselves but for our children and grandchildren. In particular, he takes on the most powerful guardians of the status quo—our mindsets. The bridge he hopes to construct has its bridgehead firmly based in today, because Speth asks us to think about it and then to use our creativity, imagination, and the power of common purpose to act to restore the environment and create a healthier world."
—Honourable Gordon Campbell, premier, Province of British Columbia

"Gus Speth is one of the leaders in trying to steer humanity on a course to sustainability, and this is his most important book to date. Read it, and then take some action."
—Paul R. Ehrlich, author with Anne Ehrlich of *The Dominant Animal: Human Evolution and the Environment*

"An extremely important book both for what it says and for who is saying it. The steady transformation of a solid, pragmatic, progressive negotiator into a 'radical and unrealistic' oracle concerned with the fundamental nature of modern economies is an important event."
—Richard Norgaard, University of California, Berkeley

"What a delight to read Gus Speth's new book, which no one else could write but all will admire, stunned by his remarkable talents. The book opens vast new opportunities for thought and discussion in science and public affairs and will undoubtedly long stand as the classic that it is."
—George M. Woodwell, founder, director emeritus, and senior scientist, Woods Hole Research Center

"One can scarcely choose a more important or timely subject than this one. Speth writes about it with passion and conviction, and a touch of humor."
—J. R. McNeill, Georgetown University

The Bridge at the Edge of the World

James Gustave Speth

The Bridge
of the

YALE UNIVERSITY PRESS

at the Edge
World

Capitalism, the Environment, and
Crossing from Crisis to Sustainability

NEW HAVEN AND LONDON

Set in Monotype Fournier type by Duke & Company, Devon, Pennsylvania. Printed in the United States of America.

"Manifesto" is reprinted from *Selected Poems of Wendell Berry* by Wendell Berry. Copyright 1999 by Wendell Berry. Reprinted by permission of the publisher. First published in *The Country of Marriage*, Harcourt Brace Jovanovich, Inc., 1973.

Illustrations on pages xx–xxi are redrawn with kind permission of Springer Science and Business Media from W. Steffen et al., *Global Change and the Earth System* (2005)

Figure 5 is redrawn from Marque-Luisa Miringoff and Sandra Opdycke, *America's Social Health: Putting Social Issues Back on the Public Agenda* (Armonk, N.Y.: M. E. Sharpe, 2008), p. 71. Copyright © 2008 by M. E. Sharpe, Inc. Reprinted with Permission.

Library of Congress Cataloging-in-Publication Data

Speth, James Gustave.

The bridge at the edge of the world : capitalism, the environment, and crossing from crisis to sustainability / James Gustave Speth.

    p.   cm.

"A Caravan book"—T.p. verso.

Includes bibliographical references and index.

ISBN 978-0-300-13611-1 (clothbound : alk. paper) 1. Environmental economics. 2. Capitalism—Environmental aspects. 3. Environmental policy. I. Title.

HC79.E5S6652 2008

333.7—dc22   2007043584

A catalogue record for this book is available from the British Library.

This book was printed with vegetable-based ink on acid-free recycled paper that contains postconsumer fiber. The case was manufactured using acid-free recycled paper that contains postconsumer pulps and colors that are lignin- and carbon-free.

10 9 8 7 6 5 4 3 2 1

For Cece
and her grandchildren

Contents

Preface

The Edisto River glides gracefully through the South Carolina low country, its dark, tannin-stained waters spreading over both banks into beautiful hardwood bottomlands—a swamp of tall cypress, tupelo, and sweet gum draped with Spanish moss and populated by sunfish, heron, and the occasional alligator and water moccasin.

I grew up in a small town on the Edisto in the 1940s and 1950s. Our house was about a mile from a swimming area the town had established down from a high bluff along the river. We swam there every summer. The area from the bluff's top down to the water had been terraced, and the girls put blankets on the grass and worked on their (one-piece) tans. At the bottom, along the riverbank, benches ran between the large cypresses where the mothers sat watching their children play in the shallow water near the edge. A pavilion atop the bluff served RCs and hot dogs. We racked up points on the pinball machines there and listened to the jukebox play "Sixty Minute Man," a song to fuel a boy's fantasy if ever there was one.

Childhood memories like this tumble out of deep storage as I get older. Thoughts of swimming in the Edisto occurred to me particularly often as I wrote this book. For many years I could not buck the river's current, but as I grew older and stronger, I was able to make good headway against it. In my environmental work for close to four decades, I've always assumed America's environmental community would do the same—get stronger and prevail against the current pushing in the opposite direction. But in the past few years I have been forced to think hard about whether this assumption is correct. I have concluded it is not. The environmental community has grown in strength and sophistication, but the environment has continued to deteriorate. This book seeks to explain why the current is too swift and what must be done instead of always swimming against it.

The need for a new approach on the environment would not be so urgent if environmental conditions were not so urgent. America is a comfortable place for many of us, myself included. But our comforts deceive us. The mounting threats recounted in the chapters that follow point to an emerging environmental tragedy of unprecedented proportions. I wrote this book because I am very worried. We should all be.

How serious is the threat to the environment? Here is one measure of the problem: all we have to do to destroy the planet's climate and biota and leave a ruined world to our children and grandchildren is to keep doing exactly what we are doing today, with no growth in the human population or the world economy. Just continue to release greenhouse gases at current rates, just continue to impoverish ecosystems and release toxic chemicals at current rates, and the world in the latter part of this century won't be fit to live in. But, of course, human activities are not holding at current levels—they are accelerating, dramatically. It took all of history to build the seven-trillion-dollar world economy of 1950; today economic activity grows by that amount every decade. At current rates of growth, the world economy will double in size in a mere fourteen years. We are thus facing the possibility of an enormous increase in environmental deterioration, just when we need to move strongly in the opposite direction.

My point of departure in this book is the momentous environmental challenge we face. But today's environmental reality is linked powerfully with other realities, including growing social inequality and neglect and the erosion of democratic governance and popular control. I have tried to show in the pages that follow how these three seemingly separate areas of public concern come together and how we as citizens must now mobilize our spiritual and political resources for transformative change on all three fronts.

In medicine, a crisis is a turning point where the patient either recovers or declines. America is at a crisis point now, and I hope this book will contribute to finding the path to recovery. The book's premise is one of hope, not despair, and of faith in the American people, especially the young people returning to campuses across America as I write.

Today's Environmentalism

The principal approaches to date for controlling the economy's impacts on the natural world can be thought of as today's environmentalism. This arena is where I have worked throughout my professional career. Like many others, I have helped launch environmental organizations, have been in court litigating to secure stronger implementation of federal environmental laws, and have lobbied Congress and testified there. I have led a large environmental think tank that turned out a steady stream of recommendations for government and other action. I have globe-trotted to any number of international summits and treaty negotiations. And, along the way, I served as President Jimmy Carter's White House environmental adviser and as head of the United Nations' largest agency for international development. In reviewing my book *Red Sky at Morning: America and the Crisis of the Global Environment*, *Time* magazine called me the "ultimate insider."[1] Inside today's environmentalism, I guess.

Now, near the end of my career, I find it impossible to be happy with the results. Important gains have been made, of course, and I will review some of them, including the progress we have made on local environmental problems like air and water pollution. But, all in all, today's environmentalism has not been succeeding. We have been winning battles, including some critical ones, but losing the war.

With the American public's heightened interest in climate change, things finally look hopeful again. It is a joy to see. America has passed a crucial tipping point on the politics of the climate issue. From now on it will be difficult to impossible to ignore. Since the 2006 elections and Al Gore's remarkable documentary, *An Inconvenient Truth*, Congress has been flooded with legislative proposals to address climate change, some of them impressive in their ambition. Our states and cities are stepping up to the plate on climate and energy issues as never before; renewable energy is taking off; citizens are mobilizing; businesses are showing environmental leadership, first in their own activities and more recently in joining with environmentalists in calling for national climate legislation.[2] America's industrial and financial sectors are going green at a pace not previously witnessed.

Having sought this moment for many years, I would not want to diminish its importance. I am elated. But it is easy to be caught up in the moment. It is critical to remember how far the United States still has to go to forge both an effective national climate program and a framework for a sustainable energy future, and how far the international community has to go to agree internationally on an effective post-Kyoto climate regime. The practical effort to reduce greenhouse gas emissions has hardly begun. It is also worth remembering what it has taken to build the current momentum: after a quarter century of neglect, societies now risk ruining the planet. And although the threat of disastrous climate disruption does seem to be motivational at last, many other environmental risks continue to be largely ignored.

It follows, I submit, that something is wrong. Most of us with environmental concerns have worked within the system, but the system has not delivered. The mainstream environmental community as a whole has been the "ultimate insider." But it is time for the environmental community—indeed, everyone—to step outside the system and develop a deeper critique of what is going on.

We all live lives powerfully shaped by a complex system that rewards as well as destroys. As I will describe, that system is giving rise to an undesirable reality—environmentally, socially, and politically. If we want to transform that system for the better, we should stop being predictable and become agents of change. And to do that we need to understand the structures that influence us, identify the new directions needed, and build the strengths to pursue them. George Bernard Shaw famously said that all progress depends on not being reasonable. It's time for a large amount of civic unreasonableness.

Guideposts

Before launching into what I believe is required and why, I should relate some thoughts that guided me in writing this book. First, I recognize that many of the proposals offered in these chapters may be controversial, especially with those favoring minimalist government. But our country is in deep trouble on several fronts, and if we want to cure these ills, some strong medicine must be taken. That points to effective government intervention as a big part of the answer. It makes no sense to deprive ourselves of the democratic means to correct harmful environmental and social consequences. Smart government does not mean wasteful, bloated government, but it does mean government.

Similarly, since today's environmental policy and politics offer too weak a medicine, the proper perspective on environmental business as usual must be critical and must offer proposals for deeper change. If someone says these proposals are impractical, or politically naive, then I would respond that we need impractical answers. That is merely a reflection of the condition in which we find ourselves. And if some of these answers seem radical or far-fetched today, then I say wait until tomorrow. Soon it will be abundantly clear that it is business as usual that is utopian, whereas creating something very new and different is a practical necessity.[3]

Often books are written by those who are deeply learned across the full range of their subject. I hasten to say that I make no such claim. I am searching for answers, and I hope my readers will join me in this effort. The young, in particular, may be well suited to the subject. The issues require a fresh conceptualization and a new way of thinking, even a new vocabulary.

The scope of this volume is broad. I doubt that there is anyone truly expert in all the areas covered in it. I have opted for breadth over depth. I know of no other way to provide the perspective the subject demands. But it is a challenge, for me at least, to achieve a reasonable command over so large an area. I have undoubtedly failed at points, and I hope the reader will bear with me when I have. I am consoled by Robert Browning: "Ah, but a man's reach should exceed his grasp / Or what's a heaven for?"

I have drawn on the writings of many people and have let them speak for themselves. It might be said that to search for answers in the writings of academics and other observers is a fool's errand—that answers are more likely to be found in the world of practical affairs. This is true to a degree, but it neglects a key point. In general, the world of practical affairs does not truly appreciate how much negative change is coming at us, nor how fast. As a result, it has yet to develop the needed answers, except partially in small experiments across the landscape. So we must look beyond the world of practical affairs to those who are thinking difficult and unconventional thoughts and proposing transformative change.

And, in any case, one must never forget the power of ideas. Remember the delightful point made by John Maynard Keynes in his *General Theory:* "The ideas of economists and political philosophers, both when they are right and when they are wrong, are more powerful than is commonly understood. Indeed, the world is ruled by little else. Practical men, who believe themselves to be quite exempt from any intellectual influence, are usually the slaves of some defunct economist."[4]

Milton Friedman was a great economist and a fierce advocate. I did not agree with many of his positions, but I believe he was right to point to the importance of ideas and the way crises can bring them to the fore: "Only a crisis—actual or perceived—produces real change," he wrote. "When that crisis occurs, the actions that are taken depend on the ideas that are lying around. That, I believe, is our basic function: to develop alternatives to existing policies, to keep them alive and available until the politically impossible becomes politically inevitable."[5] Today's young people are inheriting this world. My favorite lapel button says simply: "The meek are getting ready." I'm not sure the meek will inherit the earth, but I am sure young people will. I hope this book will help them get ready.

A book cannot cover everything, and this one is far, far more about the problems facing the affluent countries than those challenging the developing world. I spent much of my life working on international development and poverty alleviation through the United Nations and elsewhere, and my heart is with the developing countries as much as the developed. But this book is not. In *Red Sky at Morning*, I addressed the developing world's desperate need for sustainable, people-centered development and the alleviation of both poverty and population pressures, and I explored the links between addressing these needs and making progress on environmental challenges. But here, when I take up consumption, for example, the focus will be on the excessive consumption of the rich not the underconsumption of the poor. And when I ask, as I will, whether we have arrived at the point Lord Keynes foresaw when the "economic problem" is solved, I will be asking that question of the rich, not the poor.[6]

Indeed, this book focuses heavily on the very rich United States. America is large and influential. The U.S. government and U.S. corporations are leading forces in international trade and the globalization of the world economy. The United States and other developed countries are setting the terms for much of the world, spreading cultural and other norms, and driving much of the economic growth occurring abroad as well as at home. The world needs America to be a leading part of the answer, but we Americans have a long way to go to claim that role. Moreover, for many of the topics reviewed here, the United States is an extreme case among the developed countries. In America's individualism, consumerism, acceptance of market forces, commitment to capitalism and globalization, lack of social and public services, and in many other ways, the country tends consistently toward one end of the spectrum of the well-to-do. If answers can be found here, perhaps they can be found anywhere.

Red Sky at Morning addressed the issue of global-scale environmental threats with a focus on what the international community needs to do and, in particular, what the United States should do to be a responsible part of that community. It urged stronger treaties and international environmental institutions, such as a World Environment Organization. This book had its origins in the need to go beyond *Red Sky at Morning* and take a deeper and harder look at underlying forces and needed corrections. Although many of the solutions lie in international agreements and cooperation, many others are to be found at the national or local levels. Global-scale environmental threats have national and local roots.

Finally, people are guided inevitably by their values, and I should be explicit about mine, even though I often do not live up to them. In social dealings, it is hard to improve on the Golden Rule, and, extended, it provides a basis for an environmental ethic, too, specifically our duties both to future generations and to the life that evolved here with us. Society's duty to future generations is aptly captured in the expression, We have not inherited the earth from our parents, we have borrowed it from our children. And the duty to other life was captured forcefully by the best-known graduate of the school where I am dean, Aldo Leopold. "A thing is right," he wrote in *A Sand County Almanac,* "when it tends to preserve the integrity, stability and beauty of the biotic community. It is wrong when it tends otherwise."[7] To leave a ruined world to our children and grandchildren and ruin the world for other life would violate the two central precepts of environmental ethics. Our duty lies in precisely the opposite directions, to struggle against the contempocentrism and anthropocentrism that dominate modern life.

Acknowledgments

I am heavily indebted to the insights of many people and to the reviews of friends and colleagues, all of which I acknowledge with gratitude. The list of those who provided constructive comments and contributions to the manuscript is long indeed: Dean Abrahamson, Paul Anastas, William Baumol, Seth Binder, Jean Thomson Black, Jessica Boehland, Alan Brewster, Peter Brown, Benjamin Cashore, Roger Cohn, Robert Dahl, Herman Daly, John Donatich, Laura Jones Dooley, William Ellis, Rhead Enion, Laura Frye-Levine, John Grim, Jacob Hacker, Noel Hanf, Harry Haskell, Zeke Hausfather, Jack Hitt, Jed Holtzman, Jon Isham, Stephen Kellert, Donald Kennedy, Nathaniel Keohane, Pushker Kharecha, Jennifer Krencicki, Jonathan Lash, Kathrin Lassila, Anthony Leiserowitz, Kelly Levin, Paul Lussier, Victoria Manders, J. R. McNeill, Pilar Montalvo, John Nixon, William Nordhaus, Richard Norgaard, Sheila Olmstead, Robert Repetto, Laura Robb, Jonathan Rose, Heather Ross, Sherry Ryan, Cameron Speth, Fred Strebeigh, Lawrence Susskind, Betsy Taylor, Mary Evelyn Tucker, Immanuel Wallerstein, and Dahvi Wilson. And, of course, there are those on whose research and writings I have drawn and, I hope, appropriately referenced. I thank them all, abundantly. Finally, I express appreciation to Peter Haas, my coauthor in our book *Global Environmental Governance* (2006), and to the students in my fall 2006 seminar, Modern Capitalism and the Environment, at the Yale School of Forestry and Environmental Studies.

J. G. S.
New Haven

The Great Collision

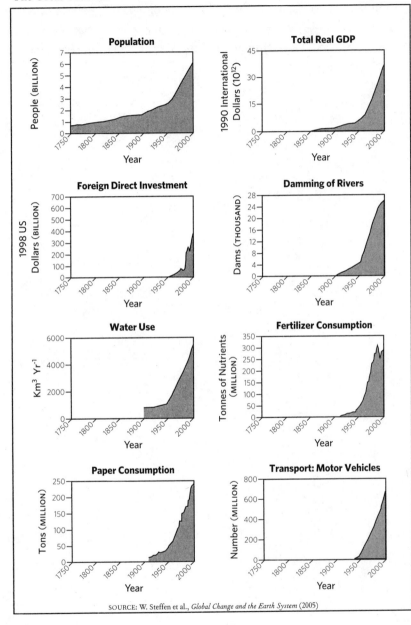

SOURCE: W. Steffen et al., *Global Change and the Earth System* (2005)

1750-2000

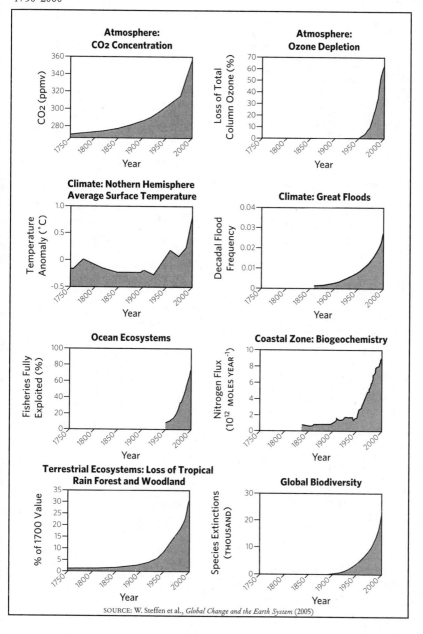

SOURCE: W. Steffen et al., *Global Change and the Earth System* (2005)

Introduction:
Between Two Worlds

The remarkable charts that introduce this book reveal the story of humanity's impact on the natural earth.[1] The pattern is clear: if we could speed up time, it would seem as if the global economy is crashing against the earth—the Great Collision. And like the crash of an asteroid, the damage is enormous. For all the material blessings economic progress has provided, for all the disease and destitution avoided, for all the glories that shine in the best of our civilization, the costs to the natural world, the costs to the glories of nature, have been huge and must be counted in the balance as tragic loss.

Half the world's tropical and temperate forests are now gone.[2] The rate of deforestation in the tropics continues at about an acre a second.[3] About half the wetlands and a third of the mangroves are gone.[4] An estimated 90 percent of the large predator fish are gone, and 75 percent of marine fisheries are now overfished or fished to capacity.[5] Twenty percent of the corals are gone, and another 20 percent severely threatened.[6] Species are disappearing at rates about a thousand times faster than normal.[7] The planet has not seen such a spasm of extinction in sixty-five million years, since the dinosaurs disappeared.[8] Over half the agricultural land in drier regions suffers from some degree of deterioration and desertification.[9] Persistent toxic chemicals can now be found by the dozens in essentially each and every one of us.[10]

Human impacts are now large relative to natural systems. The earth's stratospheric ozone layer was severely depleted before the change was discovered. Human activities have pushed atmospheric carbon dioxide up by more than a third and have started in earnest the dangerous process of warming the planet and disrupting climate. Everywhere earth's ice fields are melting.[11] Industrial processes are fixing nitrogen, making it biologically active, at a rate equal to nature's; one result is the development of more than two hundred dead zones in the oceans due to overfertilization.[12] Human actions already consume or destroy each year about 40 percent of nature's photosynthetic output, leaving too little for other species.[13] Freshwater withdrawals doubled globally between 1960 and 2000, and are now over half of accessible runoff.[14] The following rivers no longer reach the oceans in the dry season: the Colorado, Yellow, Ganges, and Nile, among others.[15]

Societies are now traveling together in the midst of this unfolding calamity down a path that links two worlds. Behind is the world we have lost, ahead the world we are making.

It is difficult to appreciate the abundance of wild nature in the world we have lost. In America we can think of the pre-Columbian world of 1491, of Lewis and Clark, and of John James Audubon. It is a world where nature is large and we are not. It is a world of majestic old-growth forests stretching from the Atlantic to the Mississippi, of oceans brimming with fish, of clear skies literally darkened by passing flocks of birds. As William MacLeish notes in *The Day before America,* in 1602 an Englishman wrote in his journal that the fish schooled so thickly he thought their backs were the sea bottom. Bison once roamed east to Florida. There were jaguars in the Southeast, grizzly bear in the Midwest, and wolves, elk and mountain lions in New England.[16]

Audubon described the breathtaking multitudes of the passenger pigeon migration, as well as the rapacity of their wild and human predators: "Few pigeons were to be seen before sunset; but a great number of persons, with horses and wagons, guns and ammunition, had already established encampments. . . . Suddenly, there burst forth a general cry of 'Here they come!' The noise which they made, though yet distant, reminded me of a hard gale at sea. . . . As the birds arrived, and passed over me, I felt a current of air that surprised me. Thousands were soon knocked down by polemen. The current of birds, however, still kept increasing. . . . The pigeons, coming in by thousands, alighted everywhere, one above another, until solid masses . . . were formed on every tree, in all directions. . . . The uproar continues . . . the whole night. . . . Toward the approach of day, the noise rather subsided. . . . The howlings of the wolves now reached our ears; and the foxes, lynxes, cougars, bears, raccoons, opossums, and pole-cats were seen sneaking off from the spot. Whilst eagles and hawks, of different species, accompanied by a crowd of vultures, came to supplant them, and enjoy their share of the spoil. It was then that the authors of all this devastation began their entry amongst the dead, the dying, and the mangled. The pigeons were picked up and piled in heaps, until each had as many as he could possibly dispose of, when the hogs were let loose to feed on the remainder."[17]

The last passenger pigeon on earth expired in a zoo in Cincinnati in 1914. Some decades later, forester and philosopher Aldo Leopold offered these words at a ceremony on this passing: "We grieve because no living man will see again the onrushing phalanx of victorious birds, sweeping a path for spring across the March skies, chasing the defeated winter from all the woods and prairies. . . . Men still live who, in their youth, remember pigeons. Trees still live who, in their youth, were shaken by a living wind. . . . There will always be pigeons in books and in museums, but these are effigies and images, dead to all hardships and to all delights. Book-pigeons cannot dive out of a cloud to make the deer run for cover, or clap their wings in thunderous applause of mast-laden woods. Book-pigeons cannot breakfast on new-mown wheat in Minnesota and dine on blueberries in Canada. They know no urge of seasons; they feel no kiss of sun, no lash of wind and weather."[18]

Human societies are moving, rapidly now, between the two worlds. The movement began slowly, but now we are hurtling toward the world directly ahead. The old world, nature's world, continues, of course, but we are steadily closing it down, roping it off. It flourishes in our art and literature and in our imaginations. But it is disappearing.

Economic historian Angus Maddison reports that in the year 1000 there were only about 270 million people on earth—fewer than today's U.S. population. Global economic output was only about $120 billion. Eight hundred years later, the man-made world was still small. By 1820, populations had risen to about a billion people with an output of only $690 billion. Over this eight hundred years, per capita income increased by only a couple of hundred dollars a year. But shortly thereafter the take-off began. By 2000, populations had swelled by an additional five billion, and, astoundingly, economic output had grown to exceed forty trillion dollars.[19] The acceleration continues. The size of the world economy doubled since 1960, and then doubled again. World economic activity is projected to quadruple again by midcentury.

Historian J. R. McNeill has stressed the phenomenal expansion of the human enterprise in the twentieth century. It was in the twentieth century, and especially since World War II, that human society truly left the moorings of its past and launched itself on the planet with unprecedented force. McNeill observes that this exponential century "shattered the constraints and rough stability of old economic, demographic, and energy regimes." "In environmental history," he writes, "the twentieth century qualifies as a peculiar century because of the screeching acceleration of so many of the processes that bring ecological change."[20] We live now in a full world, dramatically unlike the world of 1900, or even that of 1950.

Physicists have a precise concept of momentum. To them momentum is mass times velocity, and velocity is not just speed but also direction.

Today the world economy has gathered tremendous momentum—it is both huge in size and growing fast. But what is its direction?

I am seated in my study as I write this, looking at a stack of books about two feet high. They share a common theme, and it is not a happy one to contemplate. We can see this theme immediately in their titles.[21]

By a conservative jurist: Richard A. Posner, *Catastrophe: Risk and Response*

By the president of the Royal Society in the United Kingdom: Martin Rees, *Our Final Hour: How Terror, Error and Environmental Disaster Threaten Humankind's Future*

By a leading American scholar: Jared Diamond, *Collapse: How Societies Choose to Fail or Succeed*

By a British scientist: James Lovelock, *The Revenge of Gaia: Why the Earth Is Fighting Back and How We Can Still Save Humanity*

By an American expert: James Howard Kunstler, *The Long Emergency: Surviving the End of Oil, Climate Change, and Other Converging Catastrophes of the Twenty-first Century*

By a U.S. expert on conflict: Michael T. Klare, *Resource Wars: The New Landscape of Global Conflict*

By an Australian diplomat and historian: Colin Mason, *The 2030 Spike: The Countdown to Global Catastrophe*

That is but a sample of the "collapse" books now on the market. Each of these authors sees the world on a path to some type of collapse, catastrophe, or breakdown, and they each see climate change and other environmental crises as leading ingredients of a devil's brew that also includes such stresses as population pressures, peak oil and other energy supply problems, economic and political instabilities, terrorism, nuclear proliferation, the risks of various twenty-first-century technologies, and similar threats. Some think a bright future is still possible if we change our ways in time; others see a new dark ages as the likely outcome. For Sir Martin Rees, "the odds are no better than fifty-fifty that our present civilization on earth will survive to the end of the present century."[22] Personally, I cannot imagine that the risks are so great, but Rees is a thoughtful individual. In any case, it would be foolish to dismiss these authors. They provide a stark warning of what could happen.

The escalating processes of climate disruption, biotic impoverishment, and toxification that continue despite decades of warnings and earnest effort constitute a severe indictment, but an indictment of what exactly? If we want to reverse today's destructive trends, forestall further and greater losses, and leave a bountiful world for our children and grandchildren, we must return to fundamentals and seek to understand both the underlying forces driving such destructive trends and the economic and political system that gives these forces free rein. Then we can ask what can be done to change the system.

The underlying drivers of today's environmental deterioration have been clearly identified. They range from immediate forces like the enormous growth in human population and the dominant technologies deployed in the economy to deeper ones like the values that shape our behavior and determine what we consider important in life. Most basically, we know that environmental deterioration is driven by the economic activity of human beings. About half of today's world population lives in abject poverty or close to it, with per capita incomes of less than two dollars a day. The struggle of the poor to survive creates a range of environmental impacts where the poor themselves are often the primary victims—for example, the deterioration of arid and semiarid lands due to the press of increasing numbers of people who have no other option.

But the much larger and more threatening impacts stem from the economic activity of those of us participating in the modern, increasingly prosperous world economy. This activity is consuming vast quantities of resources from the environment and returning to the environment vast quantities of waste products. The damages are already huge and are on a path to be ruinous in the future. So, a fundamental question facing societies today—perhaps *the* fundamental question—is how can the operating instructions for the modern world economy be changed so that economic activity both protects and restores the natural world?

With increasingly few exceptions, modern capitalism is the operating system of the world economy. I use "modern capitalism" here in a broad sense as an actual, existing system of political economy, not as an idealized model. Capitalism as we know it today encompasses the core economic concept of private employers hiring workers to produce products and services that the employers own and then sell with the intention of making a profit. But it also includes competitive markets, the price mechanism, the modern corporation as its principal institution, the consumer society and the materialistic values that sustain it, and the administrative state actively promoting economic strength and growth for a variety of reasons.

Inherent in the dynamics of capitalism is a powerful drive to earn profits, invest them, innovate, and thus grow the economy, typically at exponential rates, with the result that the capitalist era has in fact been characterized by a remarkable exponential expansion of the world economy. The capitalist operating system, whatever its shortcomings, is very good at generating growth.

These features of capitalism, as they are constituted today, work together to produce an economic and political reality that is highly destructive of the environment. An unquestioning society-wide commitment to economic growth at almost any cost; enormous investment in technologies designed with little regard for the environment; powerful corporate interests whose overriding objective is to grow by generating profit, including profit from avoiding the environmental costs they create; markets that systematically fail to recognize environmental costs unless corrected by government; government that is subservient to corporate interests and the growth imperative; rampant consumerism spurred by a worshipping of novelty and by sophisticated advertising; economic activity so large in scale that its impacts alter the fundamental biophysical operations of the planet—all combine to deliver an ever-growing world economy that is undermining the planet's ability to sustain life.

The fundamental question thus becomes one of transforming capitalism as we know it: Can it be done? If so, how? And if not, what then? It is to these questions that this book is addressed. The larger part of the book proposes a variety of prescriptions to take economy and environment off collision course. Many of these prescriptions range beyond the traditional environmental agenda.

In Part I of the book, Chapters 1–3, I lay the foundation by elaborating the fundamental challenge just described. Among the key conclusions, summarized here with some oversimplification, are:

- The vast expansion of economic activity that occurred in the twentieth century and continues today is the predominant (but not sole) cause of the environmental decline that has occurred to date. Yet the world economy, now increasingly integrated and globalized, is poised for unprecedented growth. The engine of this growth is modern capitalism or, better, a variety of capitalisms.

- A mutually reinforcing set of forces associated with today's capitalism combines to yield economic activity inimical to environmental sustainability. This result is partly the consequence of an ongoing political default—a failed politics—that not only perpetuates widespread market failure—all the nonmarket environmental costs that no one is paying—but exacerbates this market failure with deep and environmentally perverse subsidies. The result is that our market economy is operating on wildly wrong market signals, lacks other correcting mechanisms, and is thus out of control environmentally.

- The upshot is that societies now face environmental threats of unprecedented scope and severity, with the possibility of various catastrophes, breakdowns, and collapses looming as distinct possibilities, especially as environmental issues link with social inequities and tensions, resource scarcity, and other issues.

- Today's mainstream environmentalism—aptly characterized as incremental and pragmatic "problem solving"—has proven insufficient to deal with current challenges and is not up to coping with the larger challenges ahead. Yet the approaches of modern-day environmentalism, despite their limitations, remain essential: right now, they are the tools at hand with which to address many very pressing problems.

- The momentum of the current system—fifty-five trillion dollars in output in 2004, growing fast, and headed toward environmental disaster—is so great that only powerful forces will alter the trajectory. Potent measures are needed that address the root causes of today's destructive growth and transform economic activity into something environmentally benign and restorative.

In short, my conclusion, after much searching and considerable reluctance, is that most environmental deterioration is a result of systemic failures of the capitalism that we have today and that long-term solutions must seek transformative change in the key features of this contemporary capitalism. In Part II, I address these basic features of modern capitalism, in each case seeking to identify the transformative changes needed.

The market. In Chapter 4, I focus on the need to transform the market to make it work for the environment, reversing the historical pattern. I examine the urgent need to take seriously neoclassical environmental economics with its emphasis on achieving environmentally honest prices and correcting other market signals, and look at the need to restrain "market imperialism" and excessive commodification.

Growth. In Chapter 5, I focus on what has been called the "growth fetish" and on taking seriously the field of ecological economics, including its critique of endless economic growth and its concern that advanced industrial economies may have already exceeded their optimal or sustainable scale. I explore the dimensions of a "post-growth society," where neither nature nor community is sacrificed to the priority of economic growth. In Chapter 6, I develop the idea that today's economic growth in affluent societies is not materially improving human happiness and satisfaction with life and is a poor way to generate solutions to pressing social needs and problems. I call for alternative measures that directly address these social challenges, which now desperately need attention.

Consumption. In Chapter 7, I focus on materialism and consumerism in today's affluent societies—what has been called our affluenza—and suggest ways to encourage both green consumption and living more simply.

The corporation. In Chapter 8, I take up the challenge to the dominance and power of the modern corporation, including that offered by what is often referred to as the antiglobalization movement, and set out a program to transform corporate dynamics.

Capitalism's core. Chapter 9 is more speculative. Is there something beyond both capitalism and socialism? If so, what might be the dimensions of a nonsocialist system beyond today's capitalism?

In Part III, I consider two potential drivers of transformative change:

A new consciousness. In Chapter 10, I focus on the prospect for profound change in social values, culture, and worldviews. I explore how today's dominant values contribute abundantly to social and environmental alienation and what might lead to a new consciousness that gives priority to nonmaterialistic lives and to our relationships with one another and the natural world.

A new politics. In Chapter 11, I address the search for a new and vital democratic politics—one premised on addressing America's growing political inequality and capable of embracing neglected environmental and social needs and sustaining the difficult actions needed. I examine the vital longer-term goal of strong democracy as well as the immediate steps needed to forge a new environmental politics. An important question in this regard is whether a popular movement that can drive real change is being born.

Taken together, the proposals presented in the chapters that follow would, if implemented, take us beyond capitalism as we know it today.

The question whether we would then have an operating system other than capitalism or a reinvented capitalism is largely definitional. In the end, the answer is probably not important. I myself have no interest in socialism or centralized economic planning or other paradigms of the past. As Robert Dahl has quipped, "Socialist programs for replacing market capitalism [have] fallen into the dustbin of history."[23] The question for the future, on the economic side, is how do we harness economic forces for sustainability and sufficiency? The creativity, innovation, and entrepreneurship of businesses operating in a vibrant private sector are essential to designing and building the future. We will not meet our environmental and social challenges without them. Growth and investment are needed across a wide front: growth in the developing world—sustainable, people-centered growth; growth in the incomes of those in America who have far too little; growth in human well-being along many dimensions; growth in new solution-oriented industries, products, and processes; growth in meaningful, well-paying jobs, including green-collar ones; growth in natural resource and energy productivity and in investment in the regeneration of natural assets; growth in social and public services and in investment in public infrastructures, to mention a few. These are the things we should be growing, and it makes good sense to harness market forces to such ends. As I discuss in Chapter 5, even in a "post-growth society," many things still need to grow.

I believe Paul Hawken, Amory Lovins, and Hunter Lovins have it right when they propose these strategies for the new economy in their book *Natural Capitalism:*

- Radically increased resource productivity in order to slow resource depletion at one end of the value chain and to lower pollution at the other end.
- Redesigned industrial systems that mimic biological ones so that even the concept of wastes is progressively eliminated. (This is what the new field of industrial ecology is all about.)

- An economy based on the provision of services rather than the purchase of goods.
- Reversal of worldwide resource deterioration and declines in ecosystem services through major new investments in regenerating natural capital.[24]

The good news is that impressive thinking and some exemplary action have occurred on the issues at hand. Proposals abound, many of them very promising, and new movements for change, often driven by young people, are emerging.[25] These developments offer genuine hope and begin to outline a bridge to the future. The market can be transformed into an instrument for environmental restoration; humanity's ecological footprint can be reduced to what can be sustained environmentally; the incentives that govern corporate behavior can be rewritten; growth can be focused on things that truly need to grow and consumption on having enough, not always more; the rights of future generations and other species can be respected.

America faces huge social problems and needs in addition to its environmental challenges. But priming the economic pump for ever-greater aggregate growth is a poor, sometimes even counterproductive, way to generate solutions on the social front. We need instead to address these problems directly and thoughtfully, with compassion and generosity. A whole world of new and stronger policies is needed—measures that strengthen our families and our communities and address the breakdown of social connectedness; measures that guarantee good, well-paying jobs and minimize layoffs and job insecurity; measures that introduce more family-friendly policies at work; measures that provide more time for leisure activities; measures that provide for universal health care and alleviate the devastating effects of mental illness; measures that provide everyone with a good education; measures to eliminate poverty in America, sharply improve income distribution, and address growing economic and political inequality; measures that recognize responsibilities to the half of humanity who live in poverty.

If you raise these social issues in the councils of our major environmental organizations, you might be told that "these are not environmental issues." But they are. As I explain in the chapters that follow, they are a big part of the alternative to the destructive path we are on. My hope is that the environmental community will come to embrace these measures, these hallmarks of a caring community and a good society.

In the end, then, despite the large volume of bad news, we can conclude with an affirmation. We can say with Wallace Stevens that "after the final no there comes a yes." Yes, we can save what is left. Yes, we can repair and make amends. We can reclaim nature and restore ourselves. There is a bridge at the edge of the world. But for many challenges, like the threat of climate change, there is not much time. A great American once said: "We are now faced with the fact that tomorrow is today. We are confronted with the fierce urgency of now. In this unfolding conundrum of life and history there is such a thing as being too late. Procrastination is still the thief of time. Life often leaves us standing bare, naked and dejected with a lost opportunity. The 'tide in the affairs of men' does not remain at the flood; it ebbs. We may cry out desperately for time to pause in her passage, but time is deaf to every plea and rushes on. Over the bleached bones and jumbled residue of numerous civilizations are written the pathetic words: 'Too late.'" Martin Luther King, 4 April 1967, Riverside Church, New York City.

Let us turn, then, to the costs of being too late.

Part One   System Failure

I Looking into the Abyss

If you take an honest look at today's destructive environmental trends, it is impossible not to conclude that they profoundly threaten human prospects and life as we know it on the planet. That is the abyss ahead. Robert Jay Lifton has said, "If one does not look into the abyss, one is being wishful by simply not confronting the truth. . . . On the other hand, it is imperative that one not get stuck in the abyss."[1] Confronting the truth about environmental conditions and trends is the first step.

I remember looking into another abyss, when I was a sophomore at Yale in 1961, one closer to Lifton's main subjects. It was the prospect of thermonuclear war. My guide was a wonderful professor, Brad Westerfield, who taught Yale's principal course on the Cold War at the time. He took it upon himself to inform us that we had to take seriously the possibility of nuclear war with the Soviet Union. I tried to absorb that, but it was in some way unimaginable. And then one day in 1962, there was President Kennedy on television informing us of the Cuban missile crisis. And at that moment it became all too easy to imagine nuclear war.

I feel now a little like Westerfield must have felt at that moment. I have been sounding off, Dr. Doom-like, about the risks of climate change and other large-scale environmental threats since 1980, when I was in President Carter's White House and we released the *Global 2000 Report*.[2] And, now, sad to say, *Global 2000*'s forecasts are coming true. Those forecasts were issued as warnings, but like many others, they went largely unheeded.

It was not always this bleak. Both in the final days of the Carter administration and in the years that immediately followed, many of us undertook to do the policy analysis that could be the springboard to tackling global-scale environmental challenges. The hopefulness of that era is reflected, for example, in Robert Repetto's volume *The Global Possible* (1985). In my foreword to Repetto's book, I wrote: "This book gives grounds for informed optimism about how the world's governments, businesses and citizens can make headway against an array of difficult environmental challenges. . . . [The book's recommendations] have taken an important step in proposing initiatives for public and private action, thus allaying the restive pessimism that stands between the world we have and the world we want."[3] Now one can see, more than two decades later, that the road to sustainability was the road not taken. The disturbing trends set out in *Global 2000* continued, and we find ourselves where we are today.

The World We Live In

To assess environmental performance to date, it is useful to distinguish two sets of environmental challenges. A set of predominantly local and regional concerns drove the first Earth Day in 1970. The insults then were acute and obvious: air pollution; water pollution; strip mining; clearcutting; dam building and river channelization; nuclear power; loss of wetlands, farmland, and natural areas; massive highway building programs; urban sprawl; destructive mining and grazing practices; toxic dumps and pesticides; and so on. On a portion of these first-generation Earth Day issues, the United States has made progress. Some see the part of the glass that is filled. Others, including our leading environmental groups, point to the continuation of these problems, the still unmet promises of the far-reaching legislation of the 1970s, and the emergence of serious new threats. Environmental deterioration in the United States remains surprisingly severe (see Chapter 3).

A different agenda emerged a decade later in the *Global 2000 Report* of 1980 and elsewhere. The issues on this newer agenda are more global, more insidious, and more threatening (see table 1).

On these "global change" issues, as they are sometimes called, progress has been dismal. As I noted in *Red Sky at Morning*, my generation is a generation of great talkers, overly fond of conferences. We have analyzed, debated, discussed, and negotiated these global issues almost endlessly. But on action, we have fallen far short.

As a result—with the notable exception of international efforts to protect the stratospheric ozone layer and the partial exception of progress on acid rain—the threatening global trends highlighted a quarter century ago continue to this day and have become more serious and more intractable. It is now an understatement to say we are running out of time. For such crucial issues as climate change, deforestation, and loss of biodiversity, we ran out of time quite a while ago. Appropriate action is long overdue.

Let us review where we stand with the eight major global-scale challenges where progress has been seriously lacking.[4] The presentation of conditions and trends in these eight areas does not always make for easy reading, but understanding what's happening to the planet is the backdrop to concern and action.

Climate Disruption

Of all the issues, global warming is the most threatening. The possibilities here are so disturbing that some—like Sir David King, the chief

Global Environmental Threats

Trend	Overuse of renewable resources	Pollution		
Effects of trend	Biotic impoverishment and resource scarcity	Toxification and threats to public health	Atmospheric change	Chemical imbalances in ecosystems
Issues	Marine losses Desertification Deforestation Freshwater system decline Biodiversity loss	Persistent toxic chemicals	Ozone depletion Climate change	Acid rain Nitrogen excess

Source: From James Gustave Speth and Peter M. Haas, *Global Environmental Governance* (2006), 19

scientist in the British government—believe that climate change is the most severe problem the world faces, bar none.[5]

Scientists know that the "greenhouse effect" is a reality: without the naturally occurring heat-trapping gases in the earth's atmosphere, the planet would be about 30°C cooler on average—an ice ball rather than a life-support system. The problem arises because human activities have now sharply increased the presence of greenhouse gases in the atmosphere. These gases prevent the escape of earth's infrared radiation into space. In general, the more gases that accumulate, the more heat the atmosphere traps.

The atmospheric concentration of carbon dioxide, the principal greenhouse gas contributed by human actions, has increased by more than a third over the preindustrial level due mainly to the use of fossil fuels (coal, oil, natural gas) and to large-scale deforestation. Carbon dioxide in the atmosphere is now at its highest level in at least 650,000 years. The concentration of methane, another greenhouse gas, is about 150 percent above preindustrial levels. Methane accumulates from the use of fossil fuels, cattle raising, rice growing, and landfill emissions. Atmospheric concentrations of still another gas, nitrous oxide, are also up due to fertilizer use, cattle feedlots, and the chemical industry, and it is also an infrared trapping gas. A number of specialty chemicals in the halocarbon family, including the chlorofluorocarbons (CFCs) of ozone-depletion notoriety, are also potent greenhouse gases.

The major international scientific effort to understand climate change and what can be done about it is the Intergovernmental Panel on Climate Change (IPCC). The fourth of its periodic reports, released in 2007, underscores the reality that human activities are already changing the planet in major ways:

- "Warming of the climate system is unequivocal, as is now evident from observations of increases in global average air and ocean temperatures, widespread melting of snow and ice, and rising global average sea level."

- "Eleven of the last twelve years (1995–2006) rank among the 12 warmest years in the instrumental record of global surface temperature (since 1850)."
- "Most of the observed increase in global average temperatures since the mid-twentieth century is very likely due to the observed increase in anthropogenic greenhouse gas concentrations. Discernible human influences now extend to other aspects of climate, including ocean warming, continental-average temperatures, temperature extremes and wind patterns."
- "Mountain glaciers and snow cover have declined on average in both hemispheres. Widespread decreases in glaciers and ice caps have contributed to sea level rise. New data . . . now show that losses from the ice sheets of Greenland and Antarctica have very likely contributed to sea level rise over 1993 to 2003."
- "More intense and longer droughts have been observed over wider areas since the 1970s, particularly in the tropics and subtropics. Increased drying linked with higher temperatures and decreased precipitation has contributed to changes in drought."
- "The frequency of heavy precipitation events has increased over most land areas, consistent with warming and observed increases of atmospheric water vapor."[6]

The IPCC's Fourth Assessment also identifies the likely *future* impacts of climate change in a variety of contexts—the larger the buildup of greenhouse gases, the more severe these impacts will become. Here are some of the IPCC's projections:[7]

The availability of fresh water will shift. Some areas will get much wetter, others much dryer. Both drought and flooding will likely increase. Water stored in glaciers and snowpack will decline, reducing water supplies to more than a billion people.

The health of ecosystems will be damaged by an unprecedented combination of climate change and other drivers of global change such as land use change, pollution, and overexploitation of resources. About

20 to 30 percent of the plant and animal species studied so far will be at increased risk of extinction. As the oceans take up more carbon dioxide from the atmosphere, shellfish and corals will be harmed. The oceans absorb a large portion of all carbon dioxide emitted, and as the resulting carbonic acid increases in the seawater, the extra acidity hurts the ability of marine organisms to form shells. The impacts could eventually be devastating. On top of that, ocean warming will lead to more frequent coral bleaching and mortality.

Coastal and low-lying areas are expected to be hard-hit. Rising sea levels will increase coastal erosion, flooding, and wetland loss. The IPCC report concludes that "many millions more people are projected to be flooded every year due to sea-level rise by the 2080s. Those densely-populated and low-lying areas where adaptive capacity is relatively low, and which already face other challenges such as tropical storms or local coastal subsidence, are especially at risk. The numbers affected will be largest in the mega-deltas of Asia and Africa while small islands are especially vulnerable."[8] The IPCC ominously notes that "the last time the polar regions were significantly warmer than present for an extended period (about 125,000 years ago), reductions in polar ice volume led to 4 to 6 meters of sea level rise."[9]

Human health will also suffer in various ways. As the IPCC concludes: "Projected climate change-related exposures are likely to affect the health status of millions of people, particularly those with low adaptive capacity, through:

- increases in malnutrition and consequent disorders, with implications for child growth and development;
- increased deaths, disease and injury due to heat waves, floods, storms, fires and droughts;
- the increased burden of diarrheal disease;
- the increased frequency of cardio-respiratory diseases due to higher concentrations of ground level ozone related to climate change; and,
- the altered spatial distribution of some infectious disease vectors."[10]

Other reports besides that of the IPCC have drawn special attention to particular risks. The *Arctic* is warming at nearly twice the rate as the rest of the globe. Projections see the Arctic icecap continuing to diminish and eventually disappearing altogether in the summer, perhaps as early as 2020.[11] Governments of the circumpolar north have begun positioning themselves strategically to claim sovereign control over new shipping lanes opened up by the disappearing ice. In an ironic twist, they all seek also to exploit the region's large fossil fuel resources. The loss of ice on Greenland more than doubled in the last decade of the twentieth century and may have doubled again by 2005.[12]

On *human health*, the World Health Organization estimated in 2004 the loss of 150,000 lives each year due to climate change. Its most recent report projects that loss of life caused by climate change could double by 2030 due largely to diarrhea-related disease, malaria, and malnutrition. Most of the casualties would fall in the developing world.[13]

A major area of ongoing climate change impact is in the North American West, where *tens of millions of acres of forest* are being devastated by bark beetles and other infestations. The pests—which have attacked pine, fir, and spruce trees in the western United States, British Columbia, and Alaska—are normally contained by severe winters. The milder winters in the region have increased their reproduction, abundance, and geographic range.[14]

Natural areas in the United States could be hit hard. Assuming business as usual in greenhouse gas emissions throughout this century, the maple-beech-birch forests in New England could simply disappear, while much of the Southeast could become a vast grassland savanna, too hot and dry to support trees.[15] Meanwhile, other studies project that human-caused climate change is likely to lead to extreme drought throughout the Southwest, starting soon.[16] The Great Lakes also appear to be undergoing disruptive changes due to climate change. Not only are the lakes warming, but water levels are declining and fish disease is increasing.[17]

A major concern is *sea level rise*, and the greatest fear is a catastrophic rise caused by movement into the oceans of landed ice on Greenland and Antarctica. Disturbing and unpredicted movements of ice have occurred in both places. Ten thousand years ago, when the continental ice sheets melted, sea levels rose more than twenty yards in five hundred years. While the IPCC is projecting somewhat less than a three-foot sea level rise in this century, some scientists believe that a continuation of greenhouse gas emission growth could lead to yards of sea level rise per century.[18]

Even with "modest" sea level rise, we could see the displacement of large numbers of people from small island nations and the low-lying delta areas of Egypt, Bangladesh, Louisiana, and elsewhere. Today, as Alaskan permafrost melts, Inuit villages are being moved inland. Beaches, coastal marshes, and near-coast development in the United States and elsewhere could also be severely affected. Related to this, evidence is accumulating that ocean warming and increased evaporation are contributing to stronger hurricanes.[19]

Sea level rise is only one of the consequences of climate change that could contribute to the *forced migrations of large numbers of people*. Depletion of water in regions supplied by glacial melt, changes in monsoon patterns, and spreading drought could combine to cause many refugees from climate change. One study has estimated that as many as 850 million people could be displaced in these ways later in this century.[20] Prospects such as these are a reminder that climate change is not only an environmental and economic issue. It is also a profoundly moral and human issue with major implications for social justice and international peace and security.[21]

Although many people assume that the impacts of climate change will unfold gradually, as the earth's temperature slowly rises, the buildup of greenhouse gases may in fact lead to abrupt and sudden, not gradual, changes. A National Academy of Sciences report in 2002 concluded that global climate change could have rapid impacts: "Recent scientific evidence shows that major and widespread climate changes have occurred with startling speed. . . . [G]reenhouse warming and other human alterations of the earth system may increase the possibility of large, abrupt, and unwelcome regional or global climatic events."[22]

The possibility of abrupt climate change is linked to what may be the most problematic possibility of all—"positive" feedback effects where the initial warming has effects that generate more warming. Several of these feedbacks are possible. First, the land's ability to store carbon could weaken. Soils and forests can dry out or burn and release carbon; less plant growth can occur, thus reducing nature's ability to remove carbon from the air. Second, carbon sinks in the oceans could also be reduced due to ocean warming and other factors. Third, the potent greenhouse gas methane could be released from peat bogs, wetlands, and thawing permafrost, and even from the methane hydrates in the oceans, as the planet warms and changes. Finally, the earth's albedo, the reflectivity of the earth's surface, is slated to be reduced as large areas now covered by ice and snow diminish or are covered by meltwater. All these effects would tend to make warming self-reinforcing, possibly leading to a greatly amplified greenhouse effect.

The real possibility of these amplifying feedbacks has alarmed some of our top scientists. James Hansen, the courageous NASA climate scientist, is becoming increasingly outspoken as his investigations lead him to more and more disturbing conclusions. He offered the following assessment in 2007: "Our home planet is now dangerously near a 'tipping point.' Human-made greenhouse gases are near a level such that important climate changes may proceed mostly under the climate system's own momentum. Impacts would include extermination of a large fraction of species on the planet, shifting of climatic zones due to an intensified hydrologic cycle with effects on freshwater availability and human health, and repeated worldwide coastal tragedies associated with storms and a continuously rising sea level. . . .

"Civilization developed during the Holocene, a period of relatively tranquil climate now almost 12,000 years in duration. The planet has been warm enough to keep ice sheets off North America and Europe, but cool enough for ice sheets on Greenland and Antarctica to be stable. Now, with rapid warming of 0.6°C in the past 30 years, global temperature is at its warmest level in the Holocene.

"This warming has brought us to the precipice of a great 'tipping point.' If we go over the edge, it will be a transition to 'a different planet,' an environment far outside the range that has been experienced by humanity. There will be no return within the lifetime of any generation that can be imagined, and the trip will exterminate a large fraction of species on the planet.

"The crystallizing scientific story reveals an imminent planetary emergency. We are at a planetary tipping point. We must move onto a new energy direction within a decade to have a good chance to avoid setting in motion unstoppable climate change with irreversible effects.

"We live in a democracy and policies represent our collective will. We cannot blame others. If we allow the planet to pass tipping points . . . it will be hard to explain our role to our children. We cannot claim . . . that 'we did not know.'"[23]

In short, there is little doubt that the process of human-induced global warming has begun in earnest, that the consequences are already serious, and that they could be devastating if the buildup of greenhouse gases is not halted.[24] Yet the process of halting their buildup has hardly started. Global carbon dioxide emissions climbed by 22 percent between 1980 and 2000. Since 2000, the growth rate of emissions has tripled over the average for 1990–1999.[25] The International Energy Agency projects that if societies continue on a business-as-usual path between 2004 and 2030, the result will be a rise in carbon dioxide emissions of 55 percent globally. Even in its most optimistic scenario, where environmental actions are taken, global emissions climb by 31 percent.[26] Congress is finally waking up, but it is terribly late.

To date, industrial nations have contributed far more to the buildup of greenhouse gases than developing countries. The developed countries with 20 percent of the world's people have contributed more than 75 percent of the cumulative carbon dioxide emissions and are responsible for about 60 percent of today's emissions. The United States emits roughly the same amount of greenhouse gases as 2.6 billion people living in 150 developing nations. The rich countries have reaped huge economic benefits in the process. That said, developing country emissions of greenhouse gases are increasing rapidly, especially in China and India. The developing world was the source of the majority of carbon dioxide emissions growth in 2004. It is doubtful that the developing nations will act to curb their emissions unless the industrial nations help provide powerful incentives, technology, and other assistance, as well as a good example.

At the same time, the developing world is more vulnerable to climate change. Its people are more directly dependent on the natural resource base, more exposed to extreme weather events, and less capable economically and technologically to make needed adaptations. The disruption of water supplies or agriculture, the loss of glacial meltwater in spring and summer, as well as rising sea levels, declining ecosystem services, and other impacts, could easily contribute to social tensions, violent conflicts, humanitarian emergencies, and the creation of ecological refugees. If these north-south differences are not addressed with care, they will emerge as an increasing source of international tension.

Governments must now address the urgent need for a major, concerted international response, one that is effective but also both equitable and economically efficient. Many climate scientists such as NASA's Hansen believe that a global average temperature increase of 2°C or more over the preindustrial level would run risks too great to accept.[27] The European Union has set a goal of holding warming to no more than +2°C. Yet current estimates are that we have already committed to 1.5°C warming (or even more if we clean up traditional pollution), due to past emissions.[28] Given that societies seem unlikely to halt the rise of greenhouse gas concentration at today's levels, these estimates suggest that the warming could easily continue until it enters dangerous territory. The news, in short, underscores the case for urgency.

The Stern Review, *The Economics of Climate Change,* concluded that the risks of climate change could be substantially reduced if greenhouse gas levels in the atmosphere can be stabilized between 450 and 550ppm carbon dioxide equivalent (CO_2e).[29] (CO_2e measures the presence of all greenhouse gases in the atmosphere.) Today's level, Stern reported, is 430ppm carbon dioxide equivalent, and it is rising at more than 2ppm each year. Many scientists would favor the lower portion of the Stern range, and that is why they believe we have only a short period to see greenhouse gas emissions globally peak and then begin to decline.

In sum, it is likely that societies are already too late to head off very serious climate change impacts. The worst impacts can still be averted, but action must be taken with swiftness and determination or a ruined planet is the likely outcome, based on the best science we have. Yet right now, we are on a path to more than double the preindustrial level of greenhouse gases in the atmosphere and reap a calamitous 4–5°C warming of the planet.

What types of cuts in emissions are needed to cap the buildup at tolerable levels? The Stern Review's conclusion is that "stabilization . . . requires that annual emissions be brought down to more than 80% below current levels. . . . Even if the rich world takes on responsibility for absolute cuts in emissions of 60–80% by 2050, developing countries must take significant action too."[30] Chinese greenhouse emissions recently passed those of the United States, making China the leader in this dubious achievement.

It is notable that this goal—an 80 percent cut in greenhouse gas emissions by 2050—is the target that California and New Jersey have set. Many analyses have identified measures, particularly changes in the U.S. energy system, needed to reach a goal of this extraordinary magnitude. In a nutshell, the United States could reduce its emissions by 80 percent by 2050 through a combination of steps: (1) energy efficiency gains, both in electricity generation and use and in transportation, including more fuel-efficient vehicles; (2) renewable energy development, especially wind and solar energy; (3) other energy efficiency gains including improvements in residential and commercial buildings; (4) shifting to low-carbon fuels; (5) geologic disposal (sequestration) of carbon dioxide; (6) reducing emissions of greenhouse gases other than carbon dioxide; and (7) enhanced forest and soil management practices. Eventually, if some of the more serious fears come to pass, it may become necessary to explore ways to remove carbon dioxide directly from the atmosphere. There are several means of doing this involving enhanced vegetative growth, human engineering, or both together, but some of these entail their own significant risks.[31]

Losing the Forests

About half of the world's temperate and tropical forests have already been lost, mostly to clear land for agriculture. Deforestation contributes to species loss, climate change, loss of economic value, landslides, flooding, and soil depletion. Forest loss has been particularly serious in the tropics, home to about two-thirds of our planet's plant and animal species. In recent decades, the rate of deforestation in the tropics has been about an acre each second, a pattern that continued unabated between 2000 and 2005.[32] Meanwhile, the industry-oriented International Tropical Timber Organization reported that only 3 percent of tropical forests were being sustainably managed even though two-thirds have been designated as under some type of management regime.[33]

The causes of deforestation in the developing world are many, including cutting for tropical timber, fuelwood use, expansion of export-oriented plantations and agriculture, and other pressures such as mineral development. The tropical forests are also the victims of chronic corruption, cronyism, and illegal logging.

Deforestation is widespread, but it is especially prevalent in Brazil, Indonesia, and the Congo River basin. Indonesia has lost about 40 percent of its forest in the past fifty years. About nine thousand square miles of rain forest are cleared there each year, and at current rates of loss, almost all lowland forests on Sumatra and Borneo will be gone in a matter of years, not decades.[34] Indonesia's deforestation, forest fires, and peat land degradation have made it the world's number three greenhouse gas emitter, after the United States and China.[35] Similarly, it is estimated that two-thirds of the Congo basin forests could disappear in fifty years if logging and mining continue at current rates.[36] Forest loss in the Amazon, the highest in the world, may have been severely underestimated according to new results indicating that as much of the Amazon has been lost to selective logging as to clear-cut type deforestation typically measured.[37] Altogether, between 2000 and 2005, the world lost forest acreage the size of Germany.[38]

Losing the Land

Desertification involves more than spreading deserts. It includes all the processes that degrade productive land, eventually turning it into wasteland. Soil erosion, salinization, devegetation, and soil compaction can all be involved. The process is most prevalent in arid and semiarid areas, which cover about 40 percent of the planet's land surface. These lands account for about a fifth of the world's food production. About a fourth of the developing world's people—some 1.3 billion in all—live on these dry and other fragile lands.

The United Nations estimates that an area larger than Canada or China suffers from some degree of desertification and that each year fifty million acres become too degraded for crop production or are lost to urban sprawl. That's an area the size of Nebraska.[39] Africa is particularly affected by desertification, but so are large areas in Asia and the Western Hemisphere, including the southwestern United States and northern Mexico. Among the many consequences of desertification are large losses in food production, greater vulnerability to drought and famine, loss of biodiversity, the creation of ecological refuges, and social unrest.

Desertification is typically caused by overcultivation, overgrazing, and poor irrigation practices. But behind these immediate pressures are deeper factors such as population growth, poverty and lack of alternative livelihoods, and concentrated patterns of land ownership in the developing regions.

Losing Freshwater

It has been said that there are alternative sources of energy, but there are no alternatives to water. There are several dimensions to what has correctly been called the world water crisis.[40]

First, there is the crisis of natural watercourses and their attendant wetlands. No natural areas have been as degraded by human activities as freshwater systems. Natural water courses and the vibrant life associated with them have been extensively affected by dams, dikes, diversions, stream channelization, wetland filling and other modifications, and, of course, pollution. Sixty percent of the world's major river basins have been severely or moderately fragmented by dams or other construction. Since 1950 the number of large dams has increased from 5,700 worldwide to more than 41,000. Much of this activity is done to secure access to the water, but power production, flood control, navigation, and land reclamation have also been important factors. As freshwater is diverted from natural sources, ecosystems dependent on that water suffer, including aquatic systems, wetlands, and forests. About half the world's wetlands have been lost, and more than a fifth of known freshwater species have already been driven to extinction.[41]

The second crisis is the crisis of freshwater supply. Human demand for water climbed sixfold in the twentieth century, and the trend continues today. Humanity now withdraws slightly over half of accessible freshwater, and water withdrawals could climb to 70 percent by 2025.[42] Meeting the world's demands for freshwater is proving problematic. About 40 percent of the world's people already live in countries that are classified as "water stressed," meaning that already 20 to 40 percent of the available freshwater is being used by human societies. Projections indicate that the percentage of people living in water-stressed countries could rise to 65 percent by 2025.[43]

A large portion of freshwater withdrawals, about 70 percent, goes to agriculture. Since 1960, acreage under irrigation has more than doubled. A special problem is occurring in India, China, and elsewhere in Asia where tens of millions of tubewells are depleting "fossil" groundwaters. The *New Scientist* reports that "hundreds of millions of Indians may see their land turned to desert."[44] Overall, according to a study by top water specialists from around the world, world demand for water could double by 2050.[45] "At the worst," the *New York Times* reported, "a deepening water crisis would fuel violent conflicts, dry up rivers and increase groundwater pollution. . . . It would also force the rural poor to clear ever-more grasslands and forests to grow food and leave many more people hungry."[46]

Last, there is the crisis of pollution. Pollutants of all types are discharged into the world's waters in enormous quantities, reducing the capacities of bodies of water to support life in the water and to support human communities. Contamination denies a large portion of the world's population access to clean water supplies. About a billion people, a fifth of the world's population, lack clean drinking water; 40 percent lack sanitary services. The World Health Organization calculates that each year about 1.6 million children die from diseases caused by unsafe drinking water and lack of water for sanitation and hygiene.[47]

Water supply issues will become increasingly prevalent in the United States. Freshwater withdrawals per capita from surface and groundwaters in the United States are twice that of the OECD (Organisation for Economic Co-operation and Development) as a whole. The Environmental Protection Agency estimates that if current American water use remains constant at a hundred gallons per person per day, thirty-six states will face water shortages by 2013. As a result, humanity's "first need" will soon be privatized. Investors are moving into a water-related market that is estimated to be worth at least $150 billion in the United States by 2010. "Water is a growth driver for as long and as far as the eye can see," a Goldman Sachs water analyst told the *New York Times* in 2006.[48]

Losing Marine Fisheries

The negative impact that human societies are having on the health of marine fisheries and on the world's oceans and estuaries generally is difficult to exaggerate. In 1960, 5 percent of marine fisheries were fished to capacity or overfished. Today that number is 75 percent. The global catch of fish has gone down steadily since 1988 (taking the highly volatile Peruvian anchoveta catch, the chief supply of fishmeal, out of the calculation).[49] In 2003, scientists reported that populations of large predator fish—including such popularly consumed varieties as swordfish, marlin, and tuna—are down 90 percent over original stocks; only 10 percent remain.[50] And in 2006, fisheries scientists projected that essentially all ocean commercial fisheries would collapse by 2050 if current patterns persist. This projection is controversial, but it at least suggests the magnitude of the problem.[51]

The core problem here is overfishing. It is driven by powerful fishing-industry interests and the deep subsidies they have secured from governments. But the marine environment is also being affected by destruction of mangroves and coastal wetlands, by pollution and silt from runoff, and other factors. About 80 percent of marine pollution originates on the land, and the marine environment is increasingly polluted by sewage, agricultural waste, and other discharges.[52] Particularly hard-hit have been the coral reefs. About 20 percent of coral reefs worldwide have been lost, and a further 20 percent are severely threatened.[53]

Like forest loss, overfishing is exacerbated by illegal harvesting and wasteful and destructive practices (large portions of many catches are unwanted by-catch that are thrown back, typically dead or dying, and deep-sea trawling is destroying underwater habitats) compounded by weak or nonexistent regulation. In the United States, of sixty-seven depleted fish stocks identified in the mid-1990s for special care, sixty-four remain scarce today, and probably half are still being overfished.[54] Aquaculture (fish farming) is soaring, but much of it depends critically on wild-caught fish made into fishmeal.[55]

Toxic Pollutants

There are many serious environmental threats to human health, including numerous persistent organic pollutants, or POPs. Certain pesticides and other POPs can cause cancer and birth defects as well as interfere with hormonal and immune system functioning. Child health experts at Mount Sinai School of Medicine in New York report that today virtually every person on earth can be shown to harbor detectible levels of dozens of POPs and other toxic substances.[56] Samples of Canadians were tested for the presence of eighty-eight harmful chemicals; on average forty-four were found in each person. Blood and urine samples from a Toronto mother were found to contain thirty-eight reproductive and respiratory toxins, nineteen chemicals that disrupt hormones, and twenty-seven carcinogens. A First Nation volunteer living remotely on Hudson Bay had fifty-one of the eighty-eight chemicals.[57] Researchers do not know the long-term health effects of living with this chemical cocktail, but it is known that chemicals like phthalates, bisphenol A, polybrominated diphenyl ethers, formaldehyde, carbofuran, atrazine, polycyclic aromatic hydrocarbons, and many others are dangerous in experimental studies, particularly in prenatal and neonatal contexts.[58]

One important subcategory of these chemicals is the endocrine disrupting substances (EDSs)—the so-called gender benders. Many can disrupt natural hormone functioning in humans, leading to feminization, low sperm count, and hermaphroditism. Although they acknowledge that large uncertainties remain in our knowledge of these EDSs, the Mount Sinai researchers believe that "enough evidence has accumulated to justify moving aggressively to limit environmental dispersion of endocrine disruptors."[59]

Inorganic chemicals, notably heavy metals like mercury, can also cause serious problems. Mercury is a potent neurotoxin; much of it comes from coal-fired power plants. Beyond mercury, a wide range of toxic substances continues to pose environmental threats, including hazardous and radioactive wastes and other heavy metals, lead and arsenic among them. Some three hundred to five hundred million tons of hazardous waste were generated annually in the 1990s; the United States was the largest producer by far.[60]

Losing Biodiversity

Biological diversity, or biodiversity, has three dimensions: the genetic variety within a given species; the millions of individual species of plants, animals, and microorganisms; and the diversity of different types of ecosystems such as alpine tundra, southern hardwood bottomlands, or tropical rain forests. An alarming global homogenization and simplification of biodiversity is occurring at all three levels. Massachusetts Institute of Technology professor Stephen Meyer has offered this particularly bleak assessment: "Over the next 100 years or so as many as half of the earth's species, representing a quarter of the planet's genetic stock, will functionally if not completely disappear. The land and the oceans will continue to teem with life, but it will be a peculiarly homogenized assemblage of organisms unnaturally selected for their compatibility with one fundamental force: us. Nothing—not national or international laws, global bioreserves, local sustainability schemes, or even 'wildlands' fantasies—can change the current course. The broad path for biological evolution is now set for the next several million years. And in this sense the extinction crisis—the race to save the composition, structure, and organization of biodiversity as it exists today—is over, and we have lost."[61]

Unfortunately, certain trends point in the direction Meyer has outlined. A major United Nations survey of available information reached these conclusions: "Trends of some 3,000 wild populations of species show a consistent decline in average species abundance of about 40% between 1970 and 2000; inland water species declined by 50%, while marine and terrestrial species both declined by around 30%. Studies of amphibians globally, African mammals, birds in agricultural lands, British butterflies, Caribbean and Indo-Pacific corals, and commonly harvested fish species show declines in the majority of species assessed.

"More species are becoming threatened with extinction. The status of bird species show a continuing deterioration across all biomes over the last two decades, and preliminary findings for other major groups, such as amphibians and mammals, indicate that the situation is likely worse than for birds. Between 12% and 52% of species within well-studied higher taxa are threatened with extinction."[62]

Habitat loss through land conversion and other human activities is now the principal source of the problem. Scientists estimate that the past loss of about half the tropical forests, home to a majority of the planet's species, may have cost us 15 percent of species in these forests.[63] Destruction of aquatic and wetland habitats has also contributed to serious biodiversity declines. Nonnative invasive species have emerged as a huge threat to biodiversity, second only to habitat loss. About 40 percent of the species listed in the United States as endangered or threatened are on the list because of threats from invasives. But overharvesting of particular plant and animal species is also a major cause of biodiversity loss, whether we look at codfish, mahogany, or tropical birds. Toxic chemicals, extra ultraviolet radiation from ozone layer depletion, and acidification from acid rain can also contribute to ecosystem impoverishment. Climate change is not yet a major source of biodiversity loss, but many scientists believe it could rival habitat loss as the key culprit before long.[64]

The cumulative effect of all the factors is that species loss today is estimated to be about a thousand times the natural or normal rate that species go extinct.[65] Many scientists believe we are on the brink of the sixth great wave of species loss on earth, the only one caused by humans. The World Conservation Union, which keeps the books on species, estimates that two of every five recognized species on the planet risk extinction, including one in eight birds, one in four mammals, and one in three amphibians.[66] Almost 95 percent of the leatherback turtles in the Pacific have disappeared in the past twenty years;[67] at least nine and perhaps 122 amphibian species have gone extinct since 1980;[68] tigers are on the verge of extinction in the wild;[69] populations of nearly half the world's waterbird species are in decline, and populations of twenty common American meadow birds like the bobwhite and the meadowlark have lost more than half their populations in forty years.[70]

Overfertilizing with Nitrogen

Earth's atmosphere is mostly nitrogen, but it is not biologically active. Bacteria such as those associated with legumes "fix" nitrogen, changing it to a biologically active form, which plants can use. But we humans have started fixing nitrogen also. Today, the man-made nitrogen comes primarily from two sources: about 75 percent from fertilizers and 25 percent from fossil fuel combustion. At present humans are fixing as much nitrogen as nature does. Once fixed, nitrogen remains active for a long time, cascading through the biosphere.

Nitrogen in waterways leads to overfertilization and, when heavy, to algal blooms and eutrophication—aquatic life simply dies from lack of oxygen. There are now more than two hundred dead zones in the oceans, mostly due to excess fertilization, some of them huge, like the one at the mouth of the Mississippi. Not all of the effects of extra nitrogen are negative: the extra nitrogen is contributing to forest growth and carbon sequestration.[71]

Implications

These eight global-scale environmental problems, as well as acid deposition and ozone layer depletion, do not exist in isolation—they are constantly interacting with one another, typically worsening the situation. The loss of forests, for example, contributes to biodiversity loss, climate change, and desertification. Climate change, acid rain, ozone depletion, and water reductions can in turn adversely affect world forests. Changing climate will affect everything. Among other things, it is likely to worsen desertification, lead to both additional flooding and increased droughts, reduce freshwater supplies, adversely affect biodiversity and forests, and further degrade aquatic ecosystems.

What is one to make of all this? A number of prominent scientists have taken a hand at describing what all these trends mean. In 1998, ecologist Jane Lubchenco, in her address as president of the American Association for the Advancement of Science, drew the following conclusions: "The conclusions . . . are inescapable: during the last few decades, humans have emerged as a new force of nature. We are modifying physical, chemical, and biological systems in new ways, at faster rates, and over larger spatial scales than ever recorded on earth. Humans have unwittingly embarked upon a grand experiment with our planet. The outcome of this experiment is unknown, but has profound implications for all of life on Earth."[72]

In 1994, fifteen hundred of the world's top scientists, including a majority of living Nobel Prize–winners, issued a plea for more attention to environmental problems: "The earth is finite," they stated. "Its ability to absorb wastes and destructive effluents is finite. Its ability to provide food and energy is finite. Its ability to provide for growing numbers of people is finite. Moreover, we are fast approaching many of the earth's limits. Current economic practices that damage the environment, in both developed and underdeveloped nations, cannot be continued with the risk that vital global systems will be damaged beyond repair."[73]

The Millennium Ecosystem Assessment was a massive four-year effort involving 1,360 scientists and other experts worldwide to assess conditions and trends regarding the world's ecosystems. At the conclusion of this unprecedented effort in 2005, the board governing the assessment issued the following statement: "Nearly two thirds of the services provided by nature to humankind are found to be in decline worldwide. In effect, the benefits reaped from our engineering of the planet have been achieved by running down natural capital assets.

"In many cases, it is literally a matter of living on borrowed time. By using up supplies of fresh groundwater faster than they can be recharged, for example, we are depleting assets at the expense of our children. . . .

"Unless we acknowledge the debt and prevent it from growing, we place in jeopardy the dreams of citizens everywhere to rid the world of hunger, extreme poverty, and avoidable disease—as well as increasing the risk of sudden changes to the planet's life-support systems from which even the wealthiest may not be shielded.

"We also move into a world in which the variety of life becomes ever-more limited. The simpler, more uniform landscapes created by human activity have put thousands of species under threat of extinction, affecting both the resilience of natural service and less tangible spiritual or cultural values."[74]

In 2007, the *Bulletin of the Atomic Scientists* moved its Doomsday Clock closer to midnight, citing environmental threats.[75] The Doomsday Clock reminds us that today's alarming environmental trends have consequences far beyond the environment. They can also contribute to conflicts over human access to water, food, land, and energy; ecological refugees and humanitarian emergencies; failed states; and armed movements spurred by declining circumstances. They are profound affronts to fundamental fairness and justice in the world and discriminate against both those too poor and powerless to hold their own against these tides and voiceless future generations. And they bring large economic costs. The Stern Review estimated that the total cost of a business-as-usual approach to climate change could be "around a 20% reduction in current per capita consumption, now and forever." And that's just from climate change.[76]

An interesting and important question is whether measures can be devised to "sum up" the various human impacts on the planet's environment. The most sustained efforts in this regard have been made by the Global Footprint Network, which has developed the Ecological Footprint for each nation. It seeks to measure a country's demand on the biosphere in terms of the area of biologically productive land and sea required to provide the resources consumed in each country and absorb the wastes generated. The footprint of a country includes all the cropland, grazing land, forest, and fishing grounds required to produce the food, fiber, and timber it consumes, to absorb the wastes emitted in generating the energy it uses, and to provide space for its infrastructure. Since the late 1980s, the Global Ecological Footprint has exceeded the earth's biocapacity, as of 2003 by about 25 percent—a measure of the degree we are not living off nature's interest but instead are drawing down its capital. "For how long will this be possible?" they ask. "A moderate business-as-usual scenario, based on United Nations projections showing slow, steady growth of economies and populations, suggests that by mid-century, humanity's demand on nature will be twice the biosphere's productive capacity. At this level of ecological deficit, exhaustion of ecological assets and large-scale ecosystem collapse become increasingly likely."[77]

The Ecological Footprint analysis also provides one way to estimate the responsibility of each region for these enormous pressures on the planet's environment. The billion people in the high-income countries, about 15 percent of the world's people, are responsible for about 45 percent of the Global Ecological Footprint, and the United States is responsible for almost half of that total.[78]

Another way to measure responsibility for ecological pressures on the planet is to examine international resource consumption patterns. An analysis prepared for the *1998 Human Development Report* found that the 20 percent of the world's people in the highest-income countries account for 86 percent of total private consumption expenditures, 45 percent of meat and fish consumption, 58 percent of energy consumption, 84 percent of paper consumption, and 87 percent of the world's vehicle fleet.[79] This list could be extended.

How Do We Respond?

The challenges are daunting; the reality they reflect is frightening. How do people respond? It is possible to assume any number of attitudes. Here are some I've encountered:

Resignation. All is lost.
Divine providence. It's in God's hands.
Denial. What problem?
Paralysis. It's too overwhelming.
Muddling through. It's going to be all right, somehow.
Deflection. It's not my problem.
Solutionist. Answers can and must be found.

Most of us are solutionists; certainly this book is. We have not denied the problems nor assumed they will be solved merely because we've solved other problems. We are not resigned to their great force, nor are we paralyzed by them. Nor have we left them to God or somebody else.

Solutionists can take refuge from time to time in one last predisposition, the existentialist one. "The struggle itself toward the heights is enough to fill a man's heart. One must imagine Sisyphus happy," Albert Camus says in *The Myth of Sisyphus.* Here, it is the struggle itself that matters and provides meaning. As the angels said as they carried Faust to heaven, "Whoever strives with all his power, we are allowed to save."

Solutionist thinking may be the most hopeful, but there are many varieties of solutionist thinking. Not all solutions are the same, nor are all equally promising. Paul Raskin and his coauthors in *Great Transition* and others have sketched a range of alternative scenarios of the future.[80] These scenarios each reflect different solutions; they embody different worldviews; they seek to bracket the possible ways of dealing with these challenges, with options ranging from breakdown to true solutions.

1. *Fortress World.* This is a solution but a highly unattractive one. It evolves as a result of social breakdown and disintegration as the well-to-do escape to protected enclaves and wall out the global underclass. Varieties of Fortress World are the backdrop to countless science fiction stories, but unfortunately, one can see signs of Fortress World today in gated communities, armed civilians, private security protection and mercenary armies, the size of prison populations, the emergence of large gaps between the rich minority and the poor majority, and countless natural and other amenities that only the rich can afford. A related possibility is the slow growth of authoritarianism; if conditions deteriorate and the public is increasingly fearful, draconian measures could seem more and more acceptable.

2. *Market World.* This solution is Promethean and cornucopian. Market cornucopians have faith in free markets and competition to resolve problems. They tend to see nature as boundless and thus unlikely to exercise significant constraints over human action. They are optimistic about the economy's ability to innovate and develop ever-more efficient and cleaner technologies, thus keeping environmental problems under control. In their view, economic growth is wholly positive. It facilitates technological innovation and solutions to natural resource scarcity.

3. *Policy Reform World.* Reformists or institutionalists believe in policy fixes. They emphasize that skillful policy guidance relying on close connections among governments, scientists, nongovernmental organizations (NGOs), and indigenous communities is capable of recognizing emerging scarcities and threats and devising responses. Strong and effective institutions, laws, and policies at the national and

international levels can make this possible. Economic growth can be consistent with environmental preservation, but only if appropriately guided by regulations, market corrections, and other measures.

4. *New Sustainability World.* This just-emerging worldview seeks to protect and reclaim natural and human communities and, to that end, envisions major changes in values, lifestyles, and human behavior. It involves a deep change in social values—away from ever-increasing material consumption and toward close community and personal relationships, social solidarity, and a strong connection to nature. It sees this new consciousness as essential to resolving today's environmental and social dilemmas. The natural environment is seen as having a "carrying capacity" that must limit the scale of resource consumption and pollution. It recognizes that ecosystems and the services they provide are being lost due to harvesting above regeneration rates or pollution beyond assimilative capacities. Growth is not viewed as a high priority. Market forces are seen as useful but as only one of many tools at society's disposal.

5. *Social Greens World.* Social greens argue that the true questions have to do with power within society and with inequitable resource access and distribution. They look at the social and political contexts in which resource decisions are taken and focus on redistributive policies—including power redistribution—to address environmental questions. Many favor a thoroughgoing decentralization and strong protection of local economies and communities. They question both the political impartiality of expertise and the ability of governments as commonly constituted to guide sensible behavior.

In recent decades, Market World advocates have very much controlled the actual levers of power and decision-making. As necessary, they have made concessions to the reformers, and today's laws and institutions are the result. This pattern continues to be the dominant one in national and international environmental affairs.[81] As I discuss in Chapter 3, today's environmentalism operates largely in Policy Reform World, and it has offered an abundance of reform proposals addressing global-scale as well as national and local environmental challenges. But the system for selecting and implementing proposals for action both limits their effectiveness and puts off-limits more far-reaching ideas for change.

Since this pattern is not yielding the desired results, something new clearly is needed. The solutions of the New Sustainability World and the Social Greens World point positively beyond today's situation to the new vision and new worldview that are needed. Cultural historian Thomas Berry has written that "history is governed by those over-arching moments that give shape and meaning to life by relating the human venture to the larger destinies of the universe. Creating such a movement might be called the Great Work of a people." He goes on to describe the Great Work of Greek civilization and others in Europe and Asia. "The Great Work now," he writes, "is to carry out the transition from a period of human devastation of the Earth to a period when humans would be present to the planet in a mutually beneficial manner. . . . Perhaps the most valuable heritage we can provide for future generations is some sense of the Great Work that is before them of moving the human project from its devastating exploitation to a benign presence."[82]

We must now begin this work in earnest.

2 Modern Capitalism: Out of Control

Is anything in our society more faithfully followed than economic growth? Its movements are constantly watched, measured to the decimal place, deplored or praised, diagnosed as weak or judged healthy and vigorous. Newspapers, magazines, and cable channels report endlessly on it. It is examined at all levels—global, national, and corporate. In just a tiny sample of business news stories appearing in the summer of 2006, the *Financial Times* reported, "The world is set to enjoy a fifth record year of high growth next year"; *Business Week* noted, "If oil keeps flowing, [U.S.] growth will, too"; and the *Wall Street Journal* headlined, "Google sees content deal as key to long-term growth."[1] And, indeed, the world in the middle of the first decade of the twenty-first century has been growing—the global economy at about 5 percent a year, the United States at about 3.5 percent, the OECD as a whole at about 3 percent. At 5 percent a year, the world economy would double in size in fourteen years.

The Growth Imperative

Promoting growth—achieving ever-greater economic wealth and prosperity—may be the most widely shared and robust cause in the world today. Economic growth has been called "the secular religion of the advancing industrial societies."[2] Leading macroeconomists declare it the summum bonum of their craft.

Consumption spurs growth, and to keep consumers motivated, advertising expenditures globally have expanded even faster than the world economy. The *Economist* editorialized in 2006 "in praise of America's fearless consumers of new ideas and products."[3] And when Americans' zeal to consume slackens, U.S. consumers are implored to go shopping, even by the president, as George W. Bush did after 9/11 and again just before Christmas in 2006. Looking ahead to 2007, *Business Week* assured its readers that they could "count on [American] consumers to keep spending."[4] That proved a good prediction. By June 2007, the *Financial Times* could write that a "sharp rise in consumer spending heralds [a] strong rebound in U.S. growth."[5]

When one wants to kill a proposal for government action, the most effective argument is that it will hurt the economy, exactly what President Bush said when he rejected the international climate treaty's Kyoto Protocol early in his administration.

It is not enough just to grow. Economies are judged by how rapidly they grow. To read the harsh criticism in the business press, one would think that Japan had recently experienced a prolonged depression or at least recession. In fact, between 1990 and 2005 Japan grew at 1.3 percent a year—not the 2.5 percent to 3.5 percent expected in the United States and Europe, but still not a downturn. Japan is, in fact, an interesting case of prolonged slow growth, suggesting that such a thing is possible.[6]

Understanding growth and how to keep it up is what modern-day macroeconomics is all about. Paul Samuelson and William Nordhaus are explicit about this in their justly famous text *Macroeconomics*.

"Above all," they write, "macroeconomics is concerned with economic growth.... The major macroeconomic goals are a high level and rapid growth of output, low unemployment, and stable prices.... Two issues have dominated macroeconomics since its birth: the need to reduce the instability of the market economy ... and the desire to increase a nation's rate of growth of output and consumption."[7]

In a remarkable passage of his environmental history of the twentieth century, *Something New under the Sun,* historian J. R. McNeill writes that the "growth fetish" solidified its hold on imaginations and institutions in the twentieth century: "Communism aspired to become the universal creed of the twentieth century, but a more flexible and seductive religion succeeded where communism failed: the quest for economic growth. Capitalists, nationalists—indeed almost everyone, communists included—worshiped at this same altar because economic growth disguised a multitude of sins. Indonesians and Japanese tolerated endless corruption as long as economic growth lasted. Russians and eastern Europeans put up with clumsy surveillance states. Americans and Brazilians accepted vast social inequalities. Social, moral, and ecological ills were sustained in the interest of economic growth; indeed, adherents to the faith proposed that only more growth could resolve such ills. Economic growth became the indispensable ideology of the state nearly everywhere.

"The growth fetish, while on balance quite useful in a world with empty land, shoals of undisturbed fish, vast forests, and a robust ozone shield, helped create a more crowded and stressed one. Despite the disappearance of ecological buffers and mounting real costs, ideological lock-in reigned in both capitalist and communist circles.... *The overarching priority of economic growth was easily the most important idea of the twentieth century.*"[8]

There is more debate over the relative priority of economic growth in Europe than in the United States. Frequent targets of Europe's pro-growth economic reformers are the Continent's shorter workweeks, its longer vacations, and the job security and social welfare policies of

European governments. The "reform" battle presses on in France and elsewhere; the *New York Times* reports that there are "large European populations ready to explode in furious opposition when changes [in these policies] are presented to them."[9]

In the United States, it is growth at any cost. "Ours is the Ruthless Economy," Samuelson and Nordhaus write in *Macroeconomics*. "People are increasingly judged on their current productivities rather than past contributions. Old-fashioned loyalty to firm or community counts for little. Suppose a firm finds it profitable to lay off 1000 workers, or moves from New England to the Sunbelt, or moves from the Sunbelt to Mexico. It is likely to move in the relentless pursuit of profits . . . and as a protection against another firm gaining a competitive advantage. Market-oriented economists will tell you that inequality is the price we pay for invention—that you can't make an omelet without breaking eggs. This hardheaded focus on efficiency pays no mind to the incomes of laid-off workers, of bankrupt firms, of crumbling cities, or of nations or regions which lose their comparative advantage.

"A closer look finds a silver lining behind this ruthlessness of the marketplace. With increased foreign competition, deregulation of many industries, and labor unions at their weakest since the Great Depression, labor and product markets have nowadays become increasingly competitive. With more vigorous competition, America's macroeconomic performance has perceptibly improved."[10]

One final point on growth is its geography. Although it is certainly true that the highest growth rates and much of the recent expansion of the world economy has been in Asia, the advanced OECD economies still loom large in the picture. Between 1980 and 2005, 70 percent of the growth in the world economy occurred in the nations of the OECD.

Growth versus Environment

The relation between economic gains and environmental losses is close, as McNeill notes. The economy consumes natural resources (both renewable and nonrenewable resources), occupies the land, and releases pollutants. As the economy has grown, so have resource use and pollutants of great variety. As Paul Ekins says in *Economic Growth and Environmental Sustainability,* "the sacrifice of the environment to economic growth . . . has unquestionably been a feature of economic development at least since the birth of industrialism."[11] We saw in detail in Chapter 1 that this sacrifice has been and remains enormous.

Growth is traditionally measured as an increase in Gross Domestic Product, and GDP growth is what is meant here by growth. It has given much of the world remarkable material progress—progress in the things that economies can produce and money can buy—but this prosperity has been and is being purchased at a huge environmental cost. McNeill reports the following increases over the century from the 1890s to the 1990s:[12]

World economy	up	14 fold
World population	up	4 fold
Water use	up	9 fold
Sulfur dioxide emissions	up	13 fold
Energy use	up	16 fold
Carbon dioxide emissions	up	17 fold
Marine fish catch	up	35 fold

Such trends continue into the present. Over the past quarter century—a period during which major environmental programs were in place and operational in many countries—the following increases occurred globally on average each decade from 1980 to 2005:[13]

Gross world product	46 percent
Paper and paper products	41 percent
Fish harvest	41 percent
Meat consumption	37 percent
Passenger cars	30 percent
Energy use	23 percent

Fossil fuel use	20 percent
World population	18 percent
Grain harvest	18 percent
Nitrogen oxide emissions	18 percent
Water withdrawals	16 percent
Carbon dioxide emissions	16 percent
Fertilizer use	10 percent
Sulfur dioxide emissions	9 percent

Each of these indicators measures environmental impact in some way, and each shows that impacts are increasing, not declining. It is significant that these growth rates of resource consumption and pollution are lower than the growth of the world economy. The eco-efficiency of the economy is improving through "dematerialization," the increased productivity of resource inputs, and the reduction of wastes discharged per unit of output. However, eco-efficiency is not improving fast enough to prevent impacts from rising. Donella Meadows summed it up nicely: things are getting worse at a slower rate.[14]

What the environment cares about, moreover, is not the rate of growth but the total loading. These loadings—for example, the amount of fish harvested—were already huge in 1980, so that even modest growth per decade produces large increases in environmental impacts—impacts that were already too large. By 2004, the world was consuming annually 369 million tons of paper products, 275 million tons of meat, and 9 trillion tons of fossil fuels (in oil equivalent). Freshwater for human use was being withdrawn from natural supplies at a rate of about a thousand cubic miles a year.

Behind these numbers is the phenomenon of exponential expansion. A dominant feature of modern economic activity is its exponential growth. A thing grows linearly when it increases by the same quantity over a given time. If college tuition goes up three thousand dollars a year, the increase is linear. A thing grows exponentially when it increases in proportion to what is already there. If college tuition goes up 5 percent a year, the increase is exponential. The modern economy tends to grow exponentially because a portion of each year's output is invested to produce even more output. The amount invested is related to the amount of the economic activity. Food production, resource consumption, and waste generation also increase because they are linked to population and output growth.

Or so it has been thus far. But what of the future? The world economy is poised for explosive exponential economic growth. It could double in size in a mere fifteen to twenty years. So the potential is certainly present for large and perhaps catastrophic increases in environmental impacts in a period when they should be decreasing rapidly.

There are many good reasons for concern that future growth could easily continue its environmentally destructive ways. First, economic activity and its enormous forward momentum can be accurately characterized as "out of control" environmentally, and this is true in even the advanced industrial economies that have modern environmental programs in place. Basically, the economic system does not work when it comes to protecting environmental resources, and the political system does not work when it comes to correcting the economic system.

Economist Wallace Oates has provided a clear description of "market failure," one reason the market does not work for the environment: "Markets generate and make use of a set of prices that serve as signals to indicate the value (or cost) of resources to potential users. Any activity that imposes a cost on society by using up some of its scarce resources must come with a price, where that price equals the social cost. For most goods and services ('private goods' as economists call them), the market forces of supply and demand generate a market price that directs the use of resources into their most highly valued employment.

"There are, however, circumstances where a market price may not emerge to guide individual decisions. This is often the case for various forms of environmentally damaging activities. . . . The basic idea is straightforward and compelling: the absence of an appropriate price for certain scarce resources (such as clean air and water) leads to their excessive use and results in what is called 'market failure.'

"The source of this failure is what economists term an externality. A good example is the classic case of the producer whose factory spreads smoke over an adjacent neighborhood. The producer imposes a real cost in the form of dirty air, but this cost is 'external' to the firm. The producer does not bear the cost of the pollution it creates as it does for the labor, capital, and raw materials that it employs. The price of labor and such materials induces the firm to economize on their use, but there is no such incentive to control smoke emissions and thereby conserve clean air. The point is simply that whenever a scarce resource comes free of charge (as is typically the case with our limited stocks of clean air and water), it is virtually certain to be used to excess.

"Many of our environmental resources are unprotected by the appropriate prices that would constrain their use. From this perspective, it is hardly surprising to find that the environment is overused and abused. A market system simply doesn't allocate the use of these resources properly."[15]

Political failure perpetuates, indeed magnifies, this market failure. Government policies could be implemented to correct market failure and make the market work for the environment rather than against it. But powerful economic and political interests typically stand to gain by not making those corrections, so they are not made or the correction is only partial. Water could be conserved and used more efficiently if it were sold at its full cost, including the estimated cost of the environmental damage of overusing it, but both politicians and farmers have a stake in keeping water prices low. Polluters could be made to pay the full costs of their actions, in terms of both damages and cleanup, but typically they do not. Natural ecosystems give societies economic services of tremendous value. A developer's actions can reduce these services to society, but rarely does the developer pay fully for those lost services.

Governments not only tend to shy away from correcting market failure but exacerbate the problem by creating subsidies and other practices that make a bad situation worse. In *Perverse Subsidies*, Norman Myers and Jennifer Kent estimate that governments worldwide have established environmentally damaging subsidies that amount to about $850 billion annually. They conclude that the impact of these subsidies on the environment is "widespread and profound." They note: "Subsidies for agriculture can foster overloading of croplands, leading to erosion and compaction of topsoil, pollution from synthetic fertilizers and pesticides, denitrification of soils, and release of greenhouse gases, among other adverse effects. Subsidies for fossil fuels aggravate pollution effects such as acid rain, urban smog, and global warming, while subsidies for nuclear energy generate exceptionally toxic waste with an exceptionally long half-life. Subsidies for road transportation lead to overloading of road networks, a problem that is aggravated as much as relieved by the building of new roads when further subsidies promote overuse of cars; the sector also generates severe pollution of several sorts. Subsidies for water encourage misuse and overuse of water supplies that are increasingly scarce. Subsidies for fisheries foster overharvesting of already depleted fish stocks. Subsidies for forestry encourage overexploitation at a time when many forests have been reduced by excessive logging, acid rain, and agricultural encroachment."[16]

We live in a market economy where prices are a principal signal for guiding economic activity. When prices reflect environmental values as poorly as today's prices do, the system is running without essential controls. And there are other problems too, discussed shortly. Today's market is a strange place indeed. At the core of the economy is a mechanism that does not recognize the most fundamental thing of all, the living, evolving, sustaining natural world in which the economy is operating. Unaided, the market lacks the sensory organs that would allow it to understand and adjust to this natural world. It's flying blind.

This problem of political failure is exacerbated in our era of globalization and international competition. One of globalization's foremost analysts, Thomas Friedman, has described what he calls "the golden straitjacket." "When your country . . . recognizes the rules of the free market in today's global economy, and decides to abide by them, it puts on what I call 'the Golden Straitjacket.' . . . As your country puts on the Golden Straitjacket, two things tend to happen: your economy grows and your politics shrinks. That is, on the economic front the Golden Straitjacket usually fosters more growth and higher average incomes—through more trade, foreign investment, privatization and more efficient use of resources under the pressure of global competition. But on the political front, the Golden Straitjacket narrows the political and economic policy choices of those in power to relatively tight parameters."[17] *Business Week* struck a similar theme in a cover story in 2006, "Can Anyone Steer This Economy?" Its conclusion? "Global forces have taken control of the economy. And government, regardless of party, will have less influence than ever. . . . Globalization has overwhelmed Washington's ability to control the economy."[18] If Washington has trouble controlling the economy for economic ends like job creation and wage growth, imagine the difficulty of controlling it to benefit the environment.

An Automatic Correction?

Another reason for concern about the growth coming our way is the absence of adequate natural self-correcting forces within the economy. One area of hope in this regard has been the natural evolution of technology. The economy of the future will not be identical to that of the past because technology is changing. It is creating opportunities to reduce materials consumed and wastes produced per unit of output; it is opening up new areas and new products that are lighter, smaller, more efficient. Clearly these things are happening. Resource productivity is increasing.

There is a large literature on these trends. The principal finding is reflected in the conclusion of a 2000 report of five major European and U.S. research centers: "Industrial economies are becoming more efficient in their use of materials, but waste generation continues to increase. . . . Even as decoupling between economic growth and resource throughput occurred on a per capita and per unit GDP basis, overall resource use and waste flows into the environment continued to grow. We found no evidence of an absolute reduction in resource throughput. One half to three quarters of annual resource inputs to industrial economies are returned to the environment as wastes within a year."[19]

Tellingly, one review of a large number of countries found that "with the exception of one specific case, no absolute decline of direct material input of industrial economics took place as those economies grew. . . . [T]he trend of material use in industrial countries is relatively steady." It also found that, as economies grow, pressures on domestic resources are reduced by shifting the burden abroad to developing economies.[20] More resource-intensive goods are imported.

Another major review of studies of "dematerialization" found that "there is no compelling macroeconomic evidence that the U.S. economy is 'decoupled' from material inputs, and we know even less about the net environmental effects of many changes in materials use. We caution against gross generalizations about materials use, particularly the 'gut' feeling that technical change, substitution, and a shift to the information age inexorably lead to decreased materials intensity and reduced environmental impact."[21]

Technology expert Arnulf Grubler has noted, "At best, dematerialization has led to a stabilization of absolute material use at high levels. . . . Improved materials and increased environmental productivity have substantially lessened the environmental impacts of output growth, even if, to date, output growth has generally outstripped improvements."[22]

A related area of inquiry has been the so-called environmental Kuznets curve—the hypothesis that environmental pollution initially increases with development and growth but then declines at higher per capita incomes. This argument has been offered repeatedly by growth advocates, and it does seem intuitively plausible. Public demand for environmental amenities does increase with rising incomes.

The view that economic growth is a panacea for improving environmental quality got a boost from studies showing that some local air pollutants do seem to follow the Kuznets curve pattern, the inverted "U." But it is problematic to make too much of these data. We know, for example, that it is usually much cheaper to prevent environmental decline than to cure it. And some environmental and human losses can never be repaired, even with money. The Kuznets pattern has now been found in only a few cases. In some instances pollutants first rise, then decline, then rise again. Other pollutants, like carbon dioxide, just keep rising. Indeed, many negative environmental trends remain positively correlated with increasing incomes even at high levels. One thorough review of the Kuznets curve hypothesis found that the hypothesis is "not unequivocally supported for *any* environmental indicator and is rejected by . . . studies of environmental quality as a whole. . . . Overall impact . . . rises throughout the relevant income range."[23]

The Root Causes

To sum up, we live in a world where economic growth is generally seen as both beneficent and necessary—the more, the better; where past growth has brought us to a perilous state environmentally; where we are poised for unprecedented increments in growth; where this growth is proceeding with wildly wrong market signals, including prices that do not incorporate environmental costs or reflect the needs of future generations; where a failed politics has not meaningfully corrected the market's obliviousness to environmental needs; where economies are routinely deploying technology that was created in an environmentally unaware era; where there is no hidden hand or inherent mechanism adequate to correct the destructive tendencies. So, right now, one can only conclude that growth is the enemy of environment. Economy and environment remain in collision.

Under these circumstances, it is imperative that we dig deeper to understand better the underlying forces driving these results. Only if we understand the driving forces will we be able to correct the situation.

What, then, is the operating system at work here? It is a complex of political, economic, and social arrangements that can be accurately described as features of modern-day capitalism. Immediately one says: but communism was worse for the environment, and that's true. Its authoritarian political system and highly centralized economic planning produced one environmental disaster after another. But this argument is largely irrelevant since communism is largely irrelevant. We live in a world dominated by a variety of capitalisms. In the end, no form of economy does well on the environment unless forced to by vigorously enforced rules and powerful incentives and penalties created by government and consumers.

What are the elements of this operating system? Several are captured in the definition of capitalism as an *economic* system. In *Understanding Capitalism*, Samuel Bowles and his colleagues define capitalism as an "economic system in which employers hire workers to produce goods and services that will be marketed with the intention of making a profit."[24] The employers own the capital goods used by the employees, and they own the goods and services, the commodities, that are produced and marketed. The markets are more or less free and competitive, and the goods and services are typically sold at market-determined prices. The markets also include labor markets, where wages and salaries of employees are determined.

The key to Bowles's analysis is a concept that goes back to Adam Smith, surplus product. Surplus product is that part of economic output that exceeds what is needed to pay for labor, materials, and other inputs used in production. In capitalism, the surplus product takes the form of profits. Profit provides the basis of the capitalist's income, whether interest, dividends, rent, or capital gains. When profits are spent on buying new machinery for a factory or on other goods and services intended to raise productivity in the future, the spending is investment.

Bowles and his colleagues point out, "Competition for profits arises because the only way a firm can stay in business is to make profits. Each business owner has no choice but to engage in a never-ending race to avoid falling behind. The surest way to stay ahead is to produce better goods or services at lower cost. To keep up each firm must not only replace the capital goods and materials that are used up in the production process, it must also expand and improve its own product line, break into new markets, introduce new technology, and find lower-cost ways of getting the necessary work done.

"Competition thus compels the owners of each business to *invest* (rather than consume) most of the profits they make. . . . The process of investment as part of competition for profits is called *accumulation*. . . .

"Thus, if a firm is not making a profit, it cannot grow: zero profit means zero growth. And if a firm does not grow, others that do grow will soon outpace it. In a capitalist economy, survival requires growth, and growth requires profits. This is capitalism's law of the survival of the fittest, analogous to Charles Darwin's notion of the evolution of species through natural selection. In the capitalist version, Darwin's idea of fitness—success in producing offspring—becomes success in making profits.

"Capitalism is differentiated from other economic systems by its drive to accumulate, its predisposition toward change, and its built-in tendency to expand."[25]

Bowles's analysis makes it easy to see why economy and environment are constantly colliding. First, the capitalist economy, to the degree that it is successful, is inherently an exponential growth economy. A leading economist, William Baumol, summed up the relationship nicely: "Under capitalism, innovative activity—which in other types of economy is fortuitous and optional—becomes mandatory, a life-and-death matter for the firm. And the spread of new technology, which in other economies has proceeded at a stately pace, often requiring decades or even centuries, under capitalism is speeded up remarkably because, quite simply, time is money. That, in short, is the . . . explanation of the incredible growth of the free-market economies. The capitalist economy can usefully be viewed as a machine whose primary product is economic growth. Indeed, its effectiveness in this role is unparalleled."[26]

Second, the profit motive powerfully affects the capitalist's behavior. Surplus product—profit—can be increased by preserving and perpetuating the market failures Oates described. Surplus product can also be increased through environmentally perverse subsidies and other advantages. Today's corporations have been called "externalizing machines," so committed are they to keeping the real costs of their activities external to (that is, off) their books. They might also be called "rent-seeking" machines, so committed are they to finding subsidies, tax breaks, and regulatory loopholes from government. The environment, of course, suffers as a result.

Third, as Karl Polanyi described long ago in *The Great Transformation*, the spread of the market into new areas, with its emphasis on efficiency and ever-expanding commodification, can be very costly environmentally and socially. It is a pleasure to read Polanyi. He saw so clearly in 1944 the costs of unbridled capitalism, yet he believed this "19th century system," as he called it, was collapsing. He saw the self-adjusting market as a "stark utopia." "Such an institution could not exist for any length of time without annihilating the human and natural substance of society; it would have physically destroyed man and transformed his surroundings into a wilderness. . . .

"To allow the market mechanism to be sole director of the fate of human beings and their natural environment, indeed, even of the amount and use of purchasing power, would result in the demolition of society. . . . Nature would be reduced to its elements, neighborhoods and landscapes defiled, rivers polluted, military safety jeopardized, the power to produce food and raw materials destroyed. . . .

"[T]he commodity fiction disregarded the fact that leaving the fate of soil and people to the market would be tantamount to annihilating them."[27]

Of course, the ever-expanding, self-adjusting market that Polanyi feared did not collapse. It took off again after World War II, became more fearsome and expansive, and the consequences that Polanyi warned against came to pass. Landscapes are defiled, rivers polluted. Polanyi would, I suspect, be both surprised and appalled by the ascendancy of the ruthless capitalism of the Anglo-American variety and by the erosion of social democracy of the European variety.

The dynamics of today's financial marketplace enhance the pressure on corporate managers to achieve high profit growth. The prime measure of corporate success to investors is growth in market capitalization and stock price. Market value responds to a number of factors, but one of the most influential is the expected rate of profit growth. When earnings growth fails to meet expectations, even for one quarter, stock prices can plummet. Differences of pennies per share can drive financial analysts' recommendations to buy or sell. The message to managers is clear: expand markets, contain costs, and increase profitability. Grow.

Last, there are fundamental biases in capitalism that favor the present over the future and the private over the public. Future generations cannot participate in capitalism's markets. From an environmental perspective, that is a huge flaw because the essence of sustainable development is equity toward future generations. Regarding the bias toward the private over the public (private spending versus public spending, private property versus public property, and so on), economists have even had to invent theories of government spending and public goods to justify the public sector's existence. Greater emphasis on the public side would serve our environment better. In America, for example, large public investments are overdue in land conservation; in environmental education, research, and development; and in incentives to spur new ecologically sophisticated technologies.

But the system that drives today's unsustainable growth includes other powerful elements beyond these. First, there is what the modern corporation has become. The corporation, the most important institution and agent of modern capitalism, has become both huge and hugely powerful. There are today more than sixty-three thousand multinational corporations. As recently as 1990, there were fewer than half that. Of the one hundred largest economies in the world, fifty-three are corporations. Exxon Mobil is larger than 180 nations.[28] Corporations are required by law and driven by self-interest to increase their monetary value for the benefit of their owners, the shareholders, and pressures to show quick results in this regard have grown steadily. The corporate sector wields great political and economic power and has routinely used that power to restrain ameliorative governmental action.[29] And it has driven the rise of transnational capital as the basis for economic globalization. The international system of investing, buying, and selling is becoming a single global economy. Unfortunately, what we have today is the globalization of market failure.

Second, there is what society has become. Values today are strongly materialistic, anthropocentric, and contempocentric. Today's consumerism places high priority on meeting human needs through ever-increasing purchase of material goods and services. We may say "the best things in life are free," but not many of us act that way. The anthropocentric view that nature belongs to us rather than we to nature eases the exploitation of the natural world. The habit of focusing on the present and discounting the future leads away from a thoughtful appraisal of long-term consequences and the world we are making.[30]

And third, there is what government and politics have become. Growth serves the interests of governments by boosting approval ratings, keeping difficult social justice and other issues on the back burner, and generating larger revenues without raising tax rates. Capitalist governments do not own the economy, even if some own a sizable state sector. So they must feed their growth habit by providing what corporations need to keep growing. In the United States today, the government in Washington is hobbled, corrupted by money, and typically at the service of economic interests, focused on the short-time horizons of election cycles, and poorly guided by an anemic environmental politics, a poorly informed public, and a pathetic level of public discourse on the environment. Finally, today's nation-states are motivated to varying degrees by an economic nationalism. The state seeks to enhance and project its power, both hard and soft, in part through economic strength and growth.[31]

These features, presented starkly without caveats and qualifications that could be added, aptly characterize key dimensions of today's world operating system. They are all features of contemporary capitalism. They are linked, mutually supportive, indeed mutually reinforcing. Taken together, they have given rise to an economic reality that is both enormously large and, from an environment perspective, largely out of control and therefore very destructive. Capitalism as we know it today is incapable of sustaining the environment.

There are some who have faced this complex of powerful institutions and ideas, and what it is doing to us and to the planet, and asked fundamental questions. Globalization scholar Jan Scholte has put it this way: "This is the crucial question facing contemporary globalization studies: technical tinkering or radical overhaul? Opting for the former is intellectually less taxing and painful, but the promises of reformist liberalism have been heard before. Students of globalization must surely take seriously the possibility that underlying structures of the modern (now globalized) world order—capitalism, the state, industrialism, nationality, rationalism—as well as the orthodox discourses that sustain them, may be in important respects irreparably destructive."[32]

Political scientist John Dryzek is even more pointed: "Here I will focus on currently dominant arrangements in the Western world and on what might replace them. These arrangements can be characterized in terms of a nexus of capitalism, liberal democracy, and the administrative state. The initial question is: To what extent can these institutions—in isolation or in combination—cope with the ecological challenge?" Dryzek goes on to indicate that by "liberal democracy" he means representational, interest group politics dominated by financial interests and addicted to economic growth. He concludes that these three institutions "are each thoroughly inept when it comes to ecology, that any combination of them can only compound error, and also that any redeeming features are to be found only in the possibilities that they open up for their own transformation."[33]

Political philosopher Richard Falk in his *Explorations at the Edge of Time* distinguishes between today's "modernist" politics and a postmodern politics that reflects "the human capacity to transcend the violence, poverty, ecological decay, oppression, injustice, and secularism of the modern world." He believes that the transition to a postmodern politics requires, above all, confidence in the future. "Such confidence involves both a vision of something desirable and a willingness to risk a great deal to attain it. Without sacrifice, commitment, and risk, it is impossible to confront successfully a well-entrenched system of beliefs, institutions, and practices. In this regard, it is important to appreciate the resilience and continuing success of the state as a focus for political loyalty, of nationalism as a mobilizing ideology, of the market as a basis for allocating resources, [and] of war potential as the fulcrum of international stability. . . . We cannot achieve a postmodern reality without transforming the essential nature of these main pillars of modernism."[34]

Falk characterizes today's preliminary challenges to modernism as "mainly an expression of oppositional imagery active only at the margins of modernism, a kind of critical reflection, little more than a snapping at the heels of modernism: initiatives contra violence, bureaucracy, centralizing technology, hierarchy, patriarchy, ecological carelessness. But it is also beginning to nourish some new modes of action: nonviolent practices, participatory organizations, soft energy paths and gentle technology, democratizing politics, feminizing leadership and tactics, spiritualized nature, green consciousness. The mixing of these axial elements in a variety of concrete embodiments as innovative forms of social action provides inspiration and heralds the possible approach of an axial moment."[35]

Appraisals such as these are challenging. But they open the door, inviting an exploration of what can be done. That is the search pursued in the remainder of the book. One thing that will become clear in this search is that many of the solutions will be found outside the environmental sector—in alliance with communities of concern that are not in the first instance environmental. And the question will arise: Is the operating system just described delivering the goods for these other communities? If today's growth and capitalism are delivering high levels of life satisfaction, genuine well-being, and true happiness to societies broadly, then there may be scant chance for real change. But if what we actually have is "spiritual hunger in an age of plenty," there is a large space for hope.[36] A system that cannot deliver the well-being of people and nature is in deep trouble. It invites ideas and actions that are transformative.

Whenever I think of the place of far-reaching ideas in American history, I am reminded of what Richard Hofstadter wrote in his wonderful book, *The American Political Tradition*. "Although it has been said repeatedly that we need a new conception of the world to replace the ideology of self-help, free enterprise, competition, and beneficent cupidity upon which Americans have been nourished since the foundation of the Republic, no new conceptions of comparable strength have taken root and no statesman with a great mass following has arisen to propound them. . . .

"Almost the entire span of American history under the present Constitution has coincided with the rise and spread of modern industrial capitalism. In material power and productivity the United States has been a flourishing success. Societies that are in such good working order have a kind of mute organic consistency. They do not foster ideas that are hostile to their fundamental working arrangements. Such ideas may appear, but they are slowly and persistently insulated, as an oyster deposits nacre around an irritant. They are confined to small groups of dissenters and alienated intellectuals, and except in revolutionary times they do not circulate among practical politicians."[37]

Today, in the United States and no doubt elsewhere, material power and productivity to which Hofstadter refers are no longer sufficient for "flourishing success," and our society is not in "good working order." Proposals are needed to change the fundamental working arrangements.

3 The Limits of Today's Environmentalism

There are a hundred shades of green. There are the insiders lobbying and litigating for environmental causes in Washington and grassroots organizers fighting for environmental justice in their communities. There are corporate greens and antiglobalization activists, *Vanity Fair* greens and consumption-avoiding downshifters, crunchy cons and ecosocialists (at least in Europe). There are environmentalists who work for government and those who wouldn't think of it.

One shudders to think what the world would look like today without this "environmental community" and all their efforts and hard-won victories in recent decades. However serious the environmental challenges, they would be even more critical had not these people taken a stand in countless ways. And society needs environmental proponents of all stripes now more than ever.

Here I will focus on what can be thought of as the main body of environmental thought and action as practiced in the United States. This is the environmentalism reflected in the work of many leading American environmentalists in and out of government, in many (but not all) of the activities of national environmental organizations, and in the major federal environmental laws and programs, including the more recent projection of these approaches into the international arena.[1]

Modus Operandi

The world of today's environmentalism is a world many will know well. It is a world of environmental impact statements and environmental regulations of many types; of good subsidies (wind energy) enacted by Congress to balance bad ones (fossil fuels); of cost-benefit analysis and analysis of risks; of environmental disclosure requirements such as the Toxics Release Inventory; of citizen suits and government enforcement actions in court; of international cooperation, conventions, and protocols; of parks and protected areas and species; of ecolabeling and product certification; of green consumer campaigns like those that have affected the policies of great banks; of corporate greening and social responsibility; of sustainable development and the triple bottom line of economy, society, environment. Increasingly, it is a world of using market incentives as a means to achieve environmental ends. Many Americans know this world. It's as nearby as today's newspaper at the doorstep.

It is a world awash in good proposals for sensible environmental action. In 1989, almost two decades ago, we at the World Resources Institute greeted the incoming administration of George H. W. Bush and the new Congress with a report setting out an agenda to address climate change, energy security, acid rain, and biodiversity loss. We urged the president and Congress to declare protection of the global atmosphere a priority national objective, and we called for a new national energy policy "that gives balanced attention to adequate and affordable energy supply, national security, and environmental protection, including the need to reduce emissions of carbon dioxide and other greenhouse gases." We called for a carbon tax, and we called on the administration to launch an international process leading to a climate treaty.[2] Then in 1991, we called for international negotiation of a global partnership to save tropical forests.[3] Two years later, in 1993, when the Clinton administration arrived, we presented it with a ten-point agenda of initiatives, including a call for the transformation of the United Nations Environment Programme (UNEP) into something akin to a world environment agency.[4] And most impressively, in 1996, WRI led the President's Council on Sustainable Development, a group that included many top business executives and senior administration officials as well as environmental leaders, in generating an agreed set of major recommendations for government and private sector action that brought innovative environmental and social thinking together.[5]

These stories do more than just underscore that the landscape is littered with worthy but badly neglected proposals for government action on the environment. They also point out that when today's environmentalism recognizes problems, it believes they can be solved within the system, typically with new policies and, more recently, by engaging the corporate sector. It believes in the efficacy of government action, the usefulness of legislation and regulation, the effectiveness of environmental groups and of environmental advocacy within the system. It believes that good-faith compliance with the law will be the norm and that corporations can be made to behave and are increasingly weaving environmental objectives into business strategy. Today's environmentalism is forever hopeful on all this. And it is persistent, dogged, and determined.

The second notable feature of today's environmentalism is that it tends to be pragmatic and incrementalist. Its actions are aimed at solving problems, often one at a time. It is more comfortable proposing innovative policy solutions than framing inspirational messages. These characteristics are closely allied to a third: the tendency to deal with effects rather than underlying causes. Most of our major environmental laws and treaties, for example, address the resulting environmental ills much more than what causes them. In the end, environmentalism accepts compromises. It takes what it can get.

Fourth, today's environmentalism believes that problems can be solved at acceptable economic costs—and often with net economic benefit—without significant lifestyle changes or threats to economic growth. It will not hesitate to strike out at an environmentally damaging facility or development, but it sees itself, on balance, as a positive economic force.

Fifth, it sees solutions coming largely from within the environmental sector. Environmentalists may worry about the flaws in and corruption of our politics, for example, but that is not their professional concern. That's what Common Cause or other groups do.

Sixth, today's environmentalism is not focused strongly on political activity or organizing a grassroots movement. Electoral politics and mobilizing of a green political movement have played second fiddle to lobbying, litigating, and working with government agencies and corporations. The civil rights movement was an in-the-streets movement. The women's movement campaigned politically for the Equal Rights Amendment. The environmental movement has been politically tamer from the start.

And last, today's environmentalism entrusts major action to expert bureaucracies—the regulators at the Environmental Protection Agency, the land managers at the Interior Department, the experts at UNEP. There is a belief in the good intention of these agencies as the norm; wayward tendencies can be dealt with through public exposure, public participation in their proceedings, and citizen suits, which in turn presume a fair and impartial judiciary.[6]

A central precept, in short, is that the system can be made to work for the environment. Identify the problem; mobilize support for action, mostly through the media and now increasingly through networks of activists; craft reasonable, responsible corrective measures; advocate them; hope in the end to get much of what is sought.

Of course, not everything fits within these patterns. There have always been exceptions, and recent trends reflect broadening approaches. Greenpeace has certainly worked outside the system, the League of

Conservation Voters and the Sierra Club have had a sustained political presence, groups like the Natural Resources Defense Council and Environmental Defense have developed effective networks of activists around the country and are doing more grassroots work, the World Resources Institute has augmented its policy work with on-the-ground sustainable development projects, and environmental justice concerns and the emerging climate crisis have spurred the proliferation of grassroots efforts and student organizing.

The Results

Mainstream environmentalism has moved forward in the swirling, swift currents of American politics for almost four decades. How has the environment fared? There are two big stories to tell here. I relate one in *Red Sky at Morning*. It is the story of the international community's record in addressing the most serious environmental issues—global-scale environmental concerns—and America's role in the process.[7]

Although there has been strong progress in protecting the ozone layer and some improvement on acid rain, most of the threatening environmental trends highlighted a quarter century ago have worsened. As we saw in Chapter 1, global-scale problems are now deeper and more urgent than ever. It would be nice to think that the international treaties and action plans, the main focus of efforts to date, have given us the policies and programs we need, so that we could at last get on with it. But that is not the case. Despite all the conferences and negotiations, the international community has not laid the foundation for rapid and effective action.

The results of two decades of international environmental negotiations are deeply disappointing. The bottom line is that today's treaties and their associated agreements and protocols cannot drive the changes needed. In general, the issue with the major treaties is not weak enforcement or weak compliance; the issue is weak treaties. Typically, these agreements are easy for governments to slight because the treaties' impressive—but nonbinding—goals are not followed by clear requirements, targets, and timetables. And even when there are targets and timetables, the targets are often inadequate and means of enforcement are lacking. As a result, the climate convention is not protecting climate, the biodiversity convention is not protecting biodiversity, the desertification convention is not preventing desertification, and even the older and stronger Convention on the Law of the Sea is not protecting fisheries. The same can be said for the extensive international discussions on world forests, which never have reached the point of a convention.

In sum, global environmental problems have gone from bad to worse, governments are not yet prepared to deal with them, and at present, many governments, including some of the most important, lack the leadership to get prepared.

How can one explain this failure of green governance at the international level? Powerful underlying forces drive deterioration—including the forces examined in Chapter 2. In response, complex and far-reaching multilateral action is required, yet the political base, the constituency, for international action is inherently weak. It can be easily overrun by economic opposition and claims of sovereignty, and typically is. The United States has stymied effective action on climate, tropical timber countries on forests, major fishing nations on fisheries. In all these cases and many others, governments have been far more effective representatives of their countries' business interests than of their citizens' environmental interests. Here and more broadly, the findings of political analysts David Levy and Peter Newell are pertinent: "Government negotiating positions in Europe and the United States have tended to track the stances of major industries active on key issues, such that the achievement of global environmental accords is impossible if important economic sectors are unified in opposition."[8]

In response, the international community has mounted a flawed effort: the root causes of deterioration have not been addressed seriously; intentionally weak multilateral institutions have been created, none, for example, rivaling the clout of the World Trade Organization; debilitating, consensus-based negotiating procedures have been left in place; and the economic and political context in which treaties must be prepared and implemented has been largely ignored. Legislating effectively at the international level in a world of almost two hundred sovereign nations is fiercely difficult, but little has been done to make it easier.

These unsatisfactory results can be attributed in part to miscalculations, but as I describe in *Red Sky at Morning*, the lion's share of the blame must go to the wealthy, industrial countries and especially to the United States, the principal footdragger. If the United States and other major governments had wanted a strong, effective international process, they could have created one. If they had wanted treaties with real teeth, they could have shepherded them into being. That a tougher approach has not been used to protect the global environment reflects conscious decisions by the United States and others to stick with a weak and largely ineffectual approach, decisions made primarily at the behest of economic interests. Undoubtedly, an ideological opposition has been present, too: those who want to shrink national government to the point that it can be "drowned in a bathtub" are even more against international action. But the example of the powerful World Trade Organization and U.S. support for it certainly prove that economic interests drive the process.

If that's the unfortunate track record at the global level, what can we say about our domestic issues? First, it must be said that the vigorous U.S. air and water pollution laws of the early 1970s have had a major impact. The air is better; the water is cleaner. Since 1980, U.S. carbon monoxide emissions are down 74 percent, nitrogen oxide emissions are down 41 percent, and sulfur dioxide emissions are down 66 percent.[9] These gains have been made in the teeth of great economic expansion, and the negative health consequences avoided have been huge.[10]

What is distressing, though, is that serious air and water quality problems have persisted even in the face of some of the toughest pollution control laws in the world. In 1972, the Clean Water Act set the goal of returning U.S. waters to fishable and swimmable quality by 1983. Yet in 2002, after thirty years of effort, the Environmental Protection Agency (EPA) announced that more than a third of the rivers surveyed and half the lakes were still too polluted to meet this standard.[11] Another EPA study in 2007 surveyed the quality of the nation's estuaries and found that 37 percent were in "poor" condition (measured by presence of pollution, contaminated fish tissue, and other factors). Only 32 percent were found to be in "good" health.[12] Analyzing EPA data, the Natural Resources Defense Council reported in 2007 that U.S. beach closings in 2006 were the highest in the seventeen years it has been tracking them.[13] The Great Lakes were once cited as a case study in recovery, but experts studying the lakes reported to Congress in 2006 that parts of the Great Lakes were nearing a tipping point beyond which their ecosystems would move to a new degraded state from which it would be very difficult, if not impossible, to recover.[14]

On the air quality front, EPA reported in 2007 that a third of all Americans live in counties with air pollution levels that fall short of EPA standards.[15] The thorough 2006 report of the American Lung Association, which analyzed EPA data, noted that while air quality had improved, nearly one in five Americans lives in areas with unhealthful year-round levels of particulate pollution, one of the most dangerous pollutants. The air pollutants that EPA normally regulates and others such as polycyclic aromatic hydrocarbons can contribute to asthma, chronic bronchitis, cardiovascular disease, and in utero developmental disorders. The report concluded that both smog and particulates "remain a persistent threat across large parts of the United States."[16]

Another study noted in 2004 that "despite overall trends of decreasing emissions for the major pollutants in North America, regional disparities still exist that are often obscured by national averages. Fine particulate matter and ground-level ozone levels [smog] have shown no appreciable decrease, with many counties along the northeastern seaboard and in California having levels of these pollutants consistently exceeding EPA standards."[17]

Although acid rain does not make the news as it did when the issue was new, scientists tracking it remain concerned. A recent study concluded that acid rain's damage to forests in the United States might be more serious than previously believed. Also, despite reductions in emissions of sulfur dioxide and nitrogen oxides, the sources of the acidity, little actual recovery of the thousands of acid-damaged lakes has actually occurred. Scientists are calling for deeper cuts in emissions.[18]

One comprehensive effort to assess our pollution laws was carried out by Terry Davies and colleagues at Resources for the Future. Here are its main conclusions: "First, the fragmented system is seriously broken. Its effectiveness in dealing with current problems is questionable, it is inefficient, and it is excessively intrusive. These are fundamental problems.

"Second, the problems cannot be fixed by administrative remedies, pilot programs, or other efforts to tinker at the margins. They are problems that are built into the system of laws and institutions that Congress has erected over thirty years. We recognize the difficulty of ever achieving fundamental, nonincremental change in the American government, but nothing short of such change will remedy the problems we have identified."[19]

Air and water pollution control are areas where the United States started well in the early 1970s with tough laws, yet the goals set then remain unrealized. In many other areas, America's environmental efforts have been dramatically less successful. American energy consumption has climbed by 50 percent since 1970, accompanied by major growth in carbon dioxide emissions. The United States in 2007 consumed about twenty-one million barrels of oil a day, about the same as Japan, Germany, Russia, China, and India combined. The inability to move U.S. energy development on to a green path has been a major failure.

Another important area of failure has been the loss of the American land, including precious wetlands. In recent decades, Americans have protected an area the size of California as "forever wild" wilderness, an extraordinary accomplishment, but since 1982 the country has also paved, built on, and otherwise developed thirty-five million once-rural acres, an area the size of New York State. Each year, the United States is losing about two million acres of open space—six thousand acres a day—and about 1.2 million acres of farmland, with prime farmland disappearing 30 percent faster than average. Total forest acreage in the United States has held steady or increased a bit, but this figure disguises the loss of some of the best and most accessible forests. An area of wildlife habitat the size of West Virginia in or adjoining thirty-five metropolitan areas is projected to be lost to development in the next twenty-five years.[20] And despite a federal policy of no net loss of wetlands, tidal marshes, swamps, and other wetlands continue to disappear at a rate of about a hundred thousand acres a year.[21]

The United States has a rich wildlife heritage, but much of it is now threatened despite decades of effort to protect it. Current estimates are that about 40 percent of U.S. fish species are vulnerable to extinction or imperiled, about 35 percent of amphibians and flowering plants, and between 15 and 20 percent for birds, mammals, and reptiles.[22]

Between 1970 and 2003, the miles of paved roads in the United States went up 53 percent. Vehicle miles traveled increased 177 percent. The size of the average new single family home went up about 50 percent. Municipal solid waste *per person* rose 33 percent.[23] Huge trash dumps now rise like mountains around our cities.

This destruction of the American land can be reported in statistics such as these, but that does not tell the human story of loss of place and home. The personal tragedy is recounted faithfully in books like Melissa Holbrook Pierson's *The Place You Love Is Gone*, Bettina Drew's *Crossing the Expendable Landscape*, and James Howard Kunstler's *Geography of Nowhere*.

Americans' exposure to the chemical cocktail discussed in Chapter 1 remains a serious concern three decades after the Toxic Substances Control Act.[24] Pesticides, a major product of the modern chemical industry, are released into the environment precisely because they are toxic. Political scientist John Wargo has described the scale of the pesticide challenge: "As we [enter] the twenty-first century, an additional 5 to 6 billion pounds of insecticides, herbicides, fungicides, rodenticides, and other biocides are added to the world's environment each year, with roughly one-quarter of this amount released or sold in the United States."[25] It has been estimated that far less than 1 percent of this material may actually reach a pest.[26] Also, releases of hazardous chemicals from industrial facilities remain high. EPA's Toxics Release Inventory reports that in 2005, 4.34 billion pounds of some 650 chemicals (for which reporting is mandated by law) were disposed of in the environment, as opposed to being treated or recycled. Forty percent of this huge amount was released to the surrounding air or waterways.[27]

Among the numerous toxic threats are the endocrine-disrupting substances, the gender-bending pollutants. Congress seems finally to have come alive to their risks. A recent news report suggests why: "Smallmouth and largemouth bass possessing both male and female characteristics are present in the Potomac River and its tributaries across the Maryland and Virginia region, U.S. Geological Survey officials said this week. Male fish with the capability to develop immature eggs inside their sex organs were first found in a West Virginia stream in 2003, raising fears that there were endocrine disruptors polluting the water that scientists were not finding in repeated water quality tests. . . . U.S. Geological Survey fish pathologist Vicki Blazer said that tests carried out by her agency on smallmouth bass in the Shenandoah River in Virginia and in the Monocacy River in Maryland—both of which feed the Potomac—concluded that more than 80 percent of all the male bass were growing eggs." Since members of Congress read that, they have been urging EPA to act.[28]

Another dimension of failure on the environmental front is U.S. population growth. The United States is the third most populous country in the world after India and China. The nation is now at three hundred million and slated to grow to 420 million by 2050. That's a huge increase. Natural increase will account for 60 percent of this growth; immigration, 40 percent. The problem, of course, is that each

American has a huge environmental impact, the largest in the world.[29] By any objective standard, U.S. population growth is a legitimate and serious environmental issue. But the subject is hardly on the environmental agenda, and the country has not learned how to discuss the problem even in progressive circles. For a while back in the 1970s there was a "stop at two" boomlet. I was part of it—until we had our third child. Environmentalists and others have got to learn how to reengage with this issue without seeming to join the vigilantes patrolling our southern border.

Political scientist Richard Andrews has provided an overall assessment of U.S. environmental programs: "Even after more than three decades of the modern 'environmental era,' [U.S. environmental policies] have only selectively, modestly, and temporarily held back the larger national and global forces of human population growth, landscape transformation, natural resource use, and waste generation. . . . Nor were [they] designed to manage more pervasive causal factors in human behavior patterns and economic activity, such as the continuing urbanization of the landscape and its ecosystems and the increasing use of energy and materials per capita. Not surprisingly, therefore, by and large they failed to do so."[30]

Those of us in the American environmental community certainly tried hard over several decades to address these issues, both domestically and internationally. But in far too many ways our efforts have not succeeded. Unfortunately, there is now proof that today's environmentalism doesn't work well enough. A great experiment has been conducted. The evidence is in. Current approaches have been tried for almost four decades. And look what has happened. We have won many victories, but we are losing the planet. It is important to ask why.

Limiting Success

To begin, there are those answers that link failure to particular circumstances in America's recent history. For example, journalist Ross

Gelbspan and others have pointed to the shortcomings of the media, which have not kept critical issues on the front burner.[31] In the 1970s, environmental issues were fresh, we environmentalists were constantly sought out by reporters, and the beat was covered by top journalists like Gelbspan, and the *New York Times* reporters Ned Kenworthy, David Burnham, and Phil Shabecoff. And there was always Walter Cronkite with his ongoing in-depth CBS News series, "Can the World Be Saved?" But the novelty faded, and so did editors' interest. The beat did not always get the top reporters. Fortunately, this situation is changing today, at least on the climate issue. Indeed, one can appreciate how influential the media actually are as we see one cover story, television special, and film after another on the climate issue. It is easy to see what has been missing.

Gelbspan also notes two other important and related patterns. One, the desire of American journalists to seek "balance" by presenting two sides to even one-sided issues, can actually introduce bias. Gelbspan notes that "the formulaic use of journalist balance has put the United States years behind the rest of the world in beginning to act on the climate crisis."[32]

The other pattern Gelbspan sees stems from the acquisition of most news outlets by a small group of conglomerates. With this change, Gelbspan believes that "the direction of the business has been determined by the profit-driven demands of Wall Street. One result is that marketing strategy is replacing news judgment. Another result is that most newspapers have been cutting staff and failing to provide reporters with the time they need for thorough reporting of complex stories. At the same time, they have sacrificed real news coverage to increase readership and advertising through more celebrity coverage, more self-help articles, and more trivial medical news."[33]

A second target in the blame game has been the environmental organizations themselves. In his book, *Losing Ground*, Mark Dowie notes that the national environmental organizations crafted an agenda and pursued a strategy based on the civil authority and good faith of the federal government. "Therein," he believes, "lies the inherent weakness and vulnerability of the environmental movement. Civil authority and good faith regarding the environment have proven to be chimeras in Washington." Dowie also argues that the national environmental groups "misread and underestimate[d] the fury of their antagonists."[34]

The mainstream environmental organizations were challenged again in 2004 in the now-famous *Death of Environmentalism*. In it, Michael Shellenberger and Ted Nordhaus write that America's mainstream environmentalists are not "articulating a vision of the future commensurate with the magnitude of the crisis. Instead they are promoting technical policy fixes like pollution controls and higher vehicle mileage standards—proposals that provide neither the popular inspiration nor the political alliances the community needs to deal with the problem. . . .

"The entire landscape in which politics plays out has changed radically in the last 30 years, yet the environmental movement acts as though proposals based on 'sound science' will be sufficient to overcome ideological and industry opposition. Environmentalists are in a culture war whether we like it or not. It's a war over our core values as Americans and over our vision for the future, and it won't be won by appealing to the rational consideration of our collective self-interest."[35]

I worry that when the critics focus on the environmentalists as part of the problem, they come close to blaming the victim. I believe the critics have made some excellent points and have identified a number of things that should be happening but are not. However, organizations that were built to litigate and lobby for environmental causes or to do sophisticated policy studies are not necessarily the best ones to mobilize a grassroots movement or build a force for electoral politics or motivate the public with social marketing campaigns. These things need to be done, and to get them done it may be necessary to launch new organizations and initiatives with special strengths in these areas.

We must ask, too, whether it was really a mistake for the national environmental groups to "trust Washington" and work within the system. In fact, this approach has accomplished much. The methods and style of today's environmentalism are not wrongheaded, just far too restricted as an overall approach.[36] The problem has been the absence of a huge, complementary investment of time and energy in *other* approaches to change, such as those mentioned in the preceding paragraph and in several of the chapters that follow. And here, the leading environmental organizations must indeed be faulted for not doing more to ensure that these investments were made.

More important than the shortcomings of the media and the mainstream environmental groups has been the rise of the modern right in recent American politics. Today's environmentalism had roots in the activism of the 1960s and early 1970s. It sought major regulatory intervention in the economy. It sometimes even talked about limits to growth. And just as it was getting started, so were the Olin Foundation and other funders of the "New Right," to whom these ideas were anathema. As the environmental organizations were gaining traction, the American Enterprise Institute, the Heritage Foundation, the Cato Institute, the Pacific Legal Foundation, and other right-leaning groups were, too.[37] Market fundamentalism gained strength in parallel with today's environmentalism.

Frederick Buell in his valuable and undernoticed book, *From Apocalypse to Way of Life*, has chronicled what happened: "Something happened to strip the environmental [cause] of what seemed in the 1970s to be its self-evident inevitability. Something happened to allow environmentalism's antagonists to stigmatize its erstwhile stewards as unstable alarmists and bad-faith prophets—and to call their warnings at best hysterical, at worst crafted lies. Indeed, something happened to allow some even to question (without appearing ridiculous) the apparently commonsensical assumption that environmentalists were the environment's best stewards.

"The most important explanation for these events isn't hard to find.

In reaction to the decade of crisis, a strong and enormously successful anti-environmental disinformation industry sprang up. It was so successful that it helped midwife a new phase in the history of the U.S. environmental politics, one in which an abundance of environmental concern was nearly blocked by an equal abundance of anti-environmental contestation. . . . [T]he public drive for environmental change had been 'neutralized' by the 1980s, blocked by an increasingly organized and elaborate corporate and conservative opposition.

"There have been few areas in which right-wing abuse was so fecund as with anti-environmentalism. How did the right revile environmentalists? Let us count the ways . . . In its magazine, Policy Review, the Heritage Foundation, a leading conservative think tank, called the environmental movement 'the greatest single threat to the American economy.'"

Buell notes another development: "Once the first round of [environmental] improvements had been carried out . . . controlling environmental decay in the face of growth meant stepping still more heavily on still more toes. . . . [A]s time passed, people forgot that the conditions they enjoyed were the result of earlier gains won by the environmental movement. People became ripe for disinformation."[38]

Fundamentals

These patterns could change. The right could lose its grip on things, as it may be doing. The media could wake up, as it is doing at least on climate change. The environmental groups could engage more with their critics and with politics, as they are beginning to do. But there are other limits on today's environmentalism that are more permanent and more severe. Here are the major ones.

First, today's capitalist world serves up an ever-increasing volume of environmental insults. That is its nature, born of powerful technology in the hands of powerful corporations with little transparency, weak oversight, and overriding commitments to profits and growth.

As a result, established concerns persist and new issues proliferate, such as genetic engineering and nanotech.[39] America had just begun to address the local and national Earth Day agenda when the global agenda became visible. And once-dead issues come back, such as nuclear power and strip-mining, now called mountaintop removal, and mineral developments in pristine areas. The list of concerns is now dauntingly long. Meanwhile, the world also serves up a steady stream of competing threats—most recently the war on terrorism and the war in Iraq. These seemingly more urgent threats can and do frequently occupy the available political space, eclipsing the environment and much else.

The drive for profits and growth keeps the environmental problem spigot fully open. Mark Hertsgaard in *Earth Odyssey* addresses this issue well: "The profit motive is what makes capitalism go, but it is so basic to the working of the system that it tends to override other social goals. . . . In theory, governments are supposed to police corporate greed, channeling it . . . away from the corner-cutting that threatens public health and safety. But regulation is an iffy thing. Corporations are constantly pressuring governments to relax environmental regulations if not eliminate them altogether. This pressure is often supplemented by bribery—most commonly, the legal bribery known as campaign contributions, which has turned so many politicians in the United States into spineless corporate supplicants unwilling to bite the hands that feed them. . . . Capitalism needs and promotes ceaseless expansion, yet the evidence that human activity is already overwhelming the earth's ecosystems is all around us."[40] Also overwhelmed is the capacity of environmental efforts to cope.

Second, environmental issues are increasingly complex and scientifically difficult, and they are increasingly chronic and often subtle, slow to unfold. The public has a harder time with these newer issues than the more obvious issues of the 1970s. There are other dimensions to increasing complexity. Environmental protection efforts have spawned a huge and impenetrable regulatory and management apparatus.

Environmental regulations today are quite literally beyond comprehension. Who among us knows what's going on with the "prevention of significant deterioration" regulations that are to protect western vistas or the "total maximum daily load" regulations under the Clean Water Act or the "new source review" of power plants or the implementation of the Supreme Court's decision on wetlands protection? All these are significant issues with relatively high profiles, but they are hard to follow, and even environmental professionals have difficulty keeping up when they move out of their specialties. At the international level, the complexities of the Kyoto Protocol rules also call for death-defying skill and determination. The problem of technical complexity is matched only by political complexity when one moves—as one must—into the international arena, where efforts to frame accords must cope with the north-south divide, development versus environment, northern consumption growth versus southern population growth, and the exclusion of citizens' groups from meaningful roles, all in a world of about two hundred nations claiming sovereignty, demanding to be heard, and pursuing their national interests. This increasing complexity weakens an already weak environmental politics.

Third, there is the regulatory slippage problem—the problem of the slip twixt cup and lip—inherent in today's policy reform approaches. What if a regulation covered 80 percent of the problem, and 80 percent of those regulated tried to comply, and 80 percent of that effort was successful? Oops, $0.8 \times 0.8 \times 0.8$: EPA just missed 50 percent of the problem. And the problem is growing, driven as we have seen by economic expansion. If a regulation controls 50 percent of an effluent but the sources producing effluents double in size, pollution is right where it was before the regulation. And there are more and more problems. Steve Pacala and his coauthors writing in *Science* in 2003 point out another reason much of the problem can be missed: "Problems of detecting warning signals and overcoming vested interests inevitably lead to delay in regulation, often incurring damages that could have been prevented with higher sensitivity" to environmental alarms.[41]

Fourth, there are the limits that stem from the pragmatic, compromising, deal-with-the-effects approach of modern environmentalism. That approach often leads to quick fixes and to picking the low-hanging fruit. Quick fixes address symptoms, not the underlying causes.[42] They don't get at the problem and can thus mask what needs to be done. Building codes can make homes more efficient, but what if consumers and builders want ever-larger homes? Auto efficiency standards can be tightened, but what if consumers drive more and more miles in part because good rapid transit options do not exist?

Picking the low-hanging fruit can yield gains that are politically easy and economically attractive, but as the situation looks improved and becomes more tolerable—like the U.S. environment today—and as the costs of further improvement mount, support can melt away, and environmental leaders can find themselves trapped and unable to move forward with the job half done. And given the tendency of environmentalists—and almost all other communities of interest—to work mainly with themselves, when one does get trapped, there are few friends to help out.

Modern environmentalism endeavors to make the system work for the environment, but many observers, like longtime *Washington Post* reporter William Greider, are deeply skeptical. "The regulatory state has become a deeply flawed governing mess," he writes in *The Soul of Capitalism*. "Many of the enforcement agencies are securely captured by the industries they regulate, others are blocked from effective action by industry's endless litigation and political counterattacks. Stronger laws are tortuously difficult to enact and invariably studded with purposeful loopholes designed to delay effective enforcement for years, even decades."[43]

In sum, the full burden of managing accumulating environmental threats, and the powerful forces of modern capitalism driving those threats, have fallen to the environmental community, both those in government and those outside. But the burden is too great. The system of modern capitalism as it operates today will generate ever-larger environmental consequences, outstripping efforts to manage them. Indeed, the system will seek to undermine those efforts and constrain them within narrow limits. The main body of environmental action is carried out within the system as currently designed, but working within the system puts off-limits major efforts to correct many underlying drivers of deterioration, including most of the avenues of change discussed in the pages that follow. Working only within the system will, in the end, not succeed when what is needed is transformative change in the system itself.

Part Two   The Great Transformation

4

The Market: Making It Work for the Environment

We live in Market World—in supermarkets, stock markets, labor markets, housing markets, to mention a few. Competitive markets are central to capitalism. They are the arena where buyers and sellers exchange goods and services at a price determined by supply and demand. For many, many purposes the market and the price mechanism work well, for example, in manufacturing, retail sales, and other areas. No better system of allocating scarce resources has yet been invented, nor is it likely to be in the foreseeable future.

Democratic government has been and remains the principal counterbalance to the market. All but the most ideological advocates of laissez-faire recognize the necessity of government intervention in the market on many fronts for many purposes. In Washington today, business and finance are protected by the Securities and Exchange Commission and the Justice Department; consumers are protected by the Food and Drug Administration and the Consumer Products Safety Commission; the environment by the Environmental Protection Agency and the Department of the Interior; and on and on through the capital's alphabet soup.

Market forces are enormously powerful today, prices are potent signals, and businesses are constantly seeking to expand markets to new products and new geographic areas. It follows that if the market does not work for the environment, the stage is set for huge and hugely negative environmental consequences, and that is what the world has seen. It is vital to understand why this has happened and what can be done about it. The goal in this regard should be twofold: first, to transform the market into a powerful instrument for environmental protection and restoration, and second, to limit what Robert Kuttner has called the imperialism of the market. "Even in a capitalist economy," he reminds us in *Everything for Sale*, "the marketplace is only one of several means by which society makes decisions, determines worth, allocates resources, maintains a social fabric, and conducts human relations."[1] As economist Arthur Okun has noted, "The market needs a place, but the market needs to be kept in its place."[2] Paul Hawken, Amory Lovins, and Hunter Lovins put it well in *Natural Capitalism* when they write, "Markets are only tools. They make a good servant but a bad master and a worse religion."[3]

Environmental economics is the modern-day economist's answer to the failure of the market to care for the environment. Primarily, it is today's neoclassical microeconomics applied to environment. It has a strong foothold in academia. Of all the avenues explored in this book, it is the most taught and the most theoretically rigorous. And it is the most consistent with our market-based economy.

Wallace Oates and other environmental economists contend that environmental economics makes three major contributions.[4] First, it makes a compelling, persuasive case for public intervention in the free market in order to correct market failure.

Second, it provides guidance on how far this government intervention should go in prescribing environmental goals and standards. Typically, as one moves from lax to tough controls, the first steps are the cheapest, and the costs of compliance rise as the proposed controls get tighter. Meanwhile, the extra social benefits of tougher intervention will decline, for example, as pollution is reduced to more tolerable levels. Environmental economics teaches that government should mandate investment in environmental protection up to the point that the (rising) cost of compliance equals the (declining) social benefits. To invest more would be wasteful because the marginal costs would exceed the marginal benefits.

And third, Oates and others point out that once one sets a goal or standard, by whatever means, environmental economics can guide us to the least-cost, most efficient way of achieving that goal.

Let's take up each of these three contributions.

The Case for Public Intervention

Economists make a compelling case for the right kind of government intervention. I phrase the matter this way because governments often intervene in the wrong way, creating perverse subsidies that further distort prices that are already environmentally misleading. They are misleading because they fail to reflect the true, full costs of production, namely, the environmental costs that are external to the firm—the so-called negative externalities. And subsidies created by governments can make this situation worse.

Economist Theo Panayotou has provided an excellent and succinct summary of the resulting situation: "A combination of institutional, market and policy failures results in underpricing of scarce natural resources and environmental assets, which is then translated into underpricing of resource-based and environment-intensive goods and services. Institutional failures such as absence of secure property rights, market failures such as environmental externalities and policy failures such as distortionary subsidies, drive a wedge between the private costs and the social costs of production and consumption. As a direct result producers and consumers do not receive correct signals about the true scarcity of resources they use up or the cost of environmental damage they cause. This leads to the socially wrong mix of economic output: overproduction and overconsumption of commodities that are resource-depleting and environment-polluting, and underproduction and underconsumption of commodities that are resource-saving and environment-friendly. Thus, the emerging pattern of economic growth and structure of the economy is one that undermines its own resource base, and is ultimately unsustainable, since relative scarcities are not respected."[5]

In *Markets and the Environment*, environmental economists Nathaniel Keohane and Sheila Olmstead call attention to three distinct types of market failure where the environment is concerned. First, there are the negative externalities noted above, for example, all the indirect costs of the environmental damage imposed on those downstream of polluters and on the public at large, costs that the unaided market does not require the polluter to pay. The other two categories of market failure are public goods and the tragedy of the commons: "Some environmental amenities, such as biodiversity, are enjoyed by lots of people, whether or not those people help pay for them. Economists call such goods *public goods*. A market failure arises because some individuals will end up being free riders: Rather than helping to provide the public good themselves, they merely enjoy what others provide for them.

"A third class of environmental problems is known as the *tragedy of the commons*. When a natural resource—such as a fishery or an underground aquifer—is made available to all, individuals will tend to exploit the resource far beyond the optimal level. This problem arises because the incentives of individuals diverge from the common good. We call it a tragedy because everyone would be better off if they could all commit themselves to act less selfishly. Thus individually rational actions add up to a socially undesirable outcome."[6]

Environmental economists have indeed made a powerful case for government intervention to correct market failure and perverse subsidies. But unfortunately, that is not to say that environmental economists are powerful. Market failures and pro-business subsidies persist in abundance.

Market Incentives

Below, I take up the environmental economists' second contribution, which addresses how standards should be set. At this point we will consider the third contribution—using market incentives and market mechanisms to achieve efficient, least-cost results, regardless of how the standard of protection is set. Here is where environmental economics has truly taken off and come into its own.

It was not always thus. As I write, I am looking at a short book, *Environmental Improvement Through Economic Incentives,* written thirty years ago by my friend Fred Anderson and economists at Resources for the Future, a Washington think tank.[7] The book is inscribed to me by Anderson, but, truth be told, I and most other environmentalists three decades ago did not like the approach it advocated. Throughout the 1970s, when our major antipollution laws were being written, an intellectual war of sorts was under way. On one side were we lawyers and our allies in the scientific community, and we had the upper hand. We favored what are now somewhat pejoratively called "command and control" regulations. These regulations were often based on the best available antipollution technology. The idea was to set mandatory emission and effluent standards—performance standards—that would compel companies to adopt the best pollution control technology that was available and affordable. Because new sources of pollution had more flexibility—for example, they could easily make changes in their production processes—higher technology-based standards were applied to them. EPA elaborated discharge and emission limits based on available technology for each industry, and these limits were written into permits enforced against individual polluters. Occasionally, as under key provisions of the Clean Air Act, standard-setting was based not on best technology but on what was required to protect health and the environment.

On the other side of this little war were the economists, arguing instead for using market-based mechanisms and economic incentives.

They were the voices in the wilderness in that era. We paid scant attention to them because we saw pollution charges, for example, as allowing companies to buy the right to pollute, and we worried greatly about the uncertainty one would have if emission and discharge limits were not prescribed carefully in permits.

In retrospect, I now think we were wrong not to have listened to the economists back then. The performance standards approach made a big difference, but I do wish we had started earlier with market mechanisms. That would have led to earlier and better integration of environmental objectives into business planning and would have forged a stronger alliance between environmentalists and economists.

Neglect of market-based approaches began to be corrected in the 1980s, to the point that today market mechanisms have become commonplace, embraced by both environmentalists and industry. Environmental Defense and the World Resources Institute, for example, have been leading advocates for these approaches. Economist Paul Portney says that market approaches are now the default position in environmental policy.[8] In 2001, the OECD noted that "over the last decade, economic instruments have been playing a growing role in environmental policies of OECD countries. In this context, a distinctive feature is the increasing role of environmentally related taxes. All countries have introduced environmental taxes to a varying extent. . . . The revenue from environmentally related taxes averages roughly 2% of GDP in member countries."[9] One of the most hopeful developments is the tax shift idea adopted in Germany and other European nations. Moving in four stages starting in 1999, Germany is shifting the tax burden from something one wants to encourage—work and the wages that result—to something one wants to discourage—energy consumption and the resulting pollution.

Effluent charges and other environmental charges have been furthest developed in Europe. In the United States, we have seen the rise of "cap and trade" schemes under which an overall ceiling is placed, say, on sulfur emissions in a particular region, and polluters in the region are allowed to trade emission rights or allowances among themselves in order to achieve the overall least-cost response to the cap. The caps are quantitative limits on the volume of pollutants that can be released.

The grand experiment with cap and trade in the United States was launched in the 1990 amendments to the Clean Air Act with the cap on sulfur emissions from power plants, designed to address the acid rain threat. Documented economic savings from cap and trade approaches, including in the U.S. acid rain program, have been real and substantial. The source of these savings is the ability of economic instruments to take advantage of the wide variation across firms in compliance costs. Deeper cuts are made where it is cheaper to do so. Virtually all of the climate protection bills before the Congress in 2007 seek to regulate carbon dioxide emissions with cap and trade. It seems likely that tradable permits and other market-based mechanisms for addressing environmental ills will continue to make inroads. So score another one for the economists.

The push to introduce economic incentives and market mechanisms has come about primarily to improve the efficiency and effectiveness of environmental programs. Environmental economists have been highly inventive in identifying a variety of market instruments to achieve these goals: establishing property rights to overcome the tragedy of the commons, creating markets where emission and effluent quantities can be traded, imposing pollution taxes and charges, designing "feebate" and rebate systems where charges are imposed on environmental harms but returned for good behavior, and so on. A "feebate" scheme, for example, might charge polluters a fee depending on the volume of pollution and then rebate the proceeds to the polluters in proportion to their output. Good performers therefore get their money back and more.

The Right Prices

Environmental economists have thus been successful in making the intellectual case for government intervention and the practical case for using economic incentives. But there has been much less progress on the second contribution in Oates's framework, setting the environmental standard by equating marginal costs and benefits. Recall that the idea here is to move to a system whereby the marginal environmental cost of an activity is incorporated into the price of the product being produced. These environmental costs are normally external to the company—externalities, not paid by the company—and thus not incorporated in price. One way to overcome this market failure is to impose a tax or fee on the damaging activity, with the tax set equal to the value of the damage. For air pollutants, for example, the charge would be set equal to the value of the damages from an additional unit of emissions. Economists call this "getting the prices right," and it can be done equally well by capping emissions at the optimum level and allowing emissions trading rather than taxes to determine the price.[10]

If there does not seem to be a groundswell of U.S. support for the key idea of environmental economics on how to set environmental standards, we should ask why. One reason, certainly, has been the lack of an informed political constituency for it. But political difficulties are not the only problem. Bigger and more fundamental is what is called the valuation problem. "Getting the prices right" involves putting a dollar value on environmental damages, and here there are many problems.

At the top of this list has got to be the sheer technical and analytical difficulty of applying this approach. Tom Tietenberg, in his leading environmental economics text, first explains how the pollution tax should be set to equalize marginal costs and benefits, and then has this to say: "Although the efficient levels of these policy instruments can be easily defined in principle, they are very difficult to implement in practice. To implement [them], it is necessary to know the level of pollution at which the two marginal cost curves cross for every emitter. That is a tall order, one that imposes an unrealistically high information burden on control authorities. Control authorities typically have very poor information on [the polluter's] control costs and little reliable information on [environmental] damage functions.

"How can environmental authorities allocate pollution control responsibility in a reasonable manner when the information burdens are apparently so unrealistically large? One approach, the approach now chosen by a number of countries (including the United States) is to select specific legal levels of pollution based upon some other criterion, such as providing adequate margins of safety for human or ecological health. Once these thresholds have been established, by whatever means, half of the problem has been resolved. The other half deals with deciding how to allocate the responsibility for meeting predetermined pollution levels among the large numbers of emitters."[11]

In short, "getting the prices right" involves knowing the extra environmental damages caused by each increment of pollution from each polluter. Imagine trying to calculate that for sulfur and nitrogen emitters where there are complex health effects, as well as all the terrestrial and aquatic effects associated with acid rain.

Conclusions similar to Tietenberg's can be found in other overviews of environmental economics. David Pearce and Edward Barbier, two environmental economists who are staunch defenders of "getting the prices right," nevertheless state in *Blueprint for a Sustainable Economy:* "[Our earlier book] did place emphasis on the importance of placing money values on environmental assets and services. It proved to be probably the most controversial issue in terms of the popular discussion of the book in the media and in public forums. This perhaps diverted attention from the fact, also made clear in [our earlier book], that the case for market-based approaches to solving environmental problems can be justified quite independently of whether valuation takes place."[12] In short, what even environmental economists are saying is this: set the environmental goal or standard on the basis of what is needed to protect the environment sufficiently or at the level the political traffic will bear, not on the basis of internalizing all the difficult-to-monetize marginal costs of the pollution. Then, use market-based instruments and economic incentives to achieve that goal in the most efficient, least-cost way. This, of course, is tantamount to abandoning the environmental economists' "second contribution."

Some of the difficulties inherent in putting a dollar value on environmental assets and human life and health can be seen in the growing field of cost-benefit analysis, where economists have been more determined and inventive, and more controversial. Cost-benefit analysis can be applied to assess projects such as new dams or to evaluate policies and programs, such as the Clean Air Act. It requires that both costs and benefits be expressed in comparable terms, that is, dollars. That is, cost-benefit analysis requires valuation.

In *Priceless*, Frank Ackerman and Lisa Heinzerling are severely critical of the cost-benefit approach: "The basic problem with narrow economic analysis of health and environmental protection is that human life, health, and nature cannot be described meaningfully in monetary terms; they are priceless. When the question is whether to allow one person to hurt another, or to destroy a natural resource; when a life or a landscape cannot be replaced; when harms stretch out over decades or even generations; when outcomes are uncertain; when risks are shared or resources are used in common; when the people 'buying' harms have no relationship with the people actually harmed—then we are in the realm of the priceless, where market values tell us little about the social values at stake.

"There is no reason to think that the right answers will emerge from the strange process of assigning dollar values to human life, human health, and nature itself, and then crunching the numbers. Indeed, in pursuing this approach, formal cost-benefit analysis often hurts more than it helps. . . .

"In essence, the economists' position is that everything has a price. . . . But for most people, there are matters of rights and principles that are beyond economic calculation. Setting the boundaries of the market helps to define who we are, how we want to live, and what we believe in. There are many activities that are not allowed at any price. . . .

"Assigning monetary values to everything we care about is not a practical plan for government. [That] would bury us in a blizzard of hypothetical valuations, obscuring rather than clarifying our collective priorities. It would also raise the impossible problem of numerically 'valuing' things about which people disagree. Is the 'existence value' of abortion clinics a positive or negative number? It depends who you ask. It is likely that no one would be happy about making a decision based on society's average monetary valuation of the right to choose abortion."[13]

The Ackerman-Heinzerling critique goes beyond the issue of how difficult the valuation issue is to the ethical and political issues it raises. Developmental disorders in pregnancy, the loss of Adirondack lakes, the extinction of a species, the drying out of the American Southwest or the Amazon—it is easy to see why many people find it ethically offensive to place a dollar value on these things for the purpose of weighing whether losing them is acceptable. That said, environmental economists are quick to point out that environmental regulations, willy-nilly, do place a price on even the value of a statistical life, as long as we are willing to figure out how much the regulation costs and how many lives are saved.

The valuation controversy is only one of several that swirl about in the effort to bring the reigning paradigm of neoclassical economics into sync with environmental realities and needs.[14] Is a model based at its core on egoistic, anthropocentric, rationalistic calculation appropriate for making environmental choices? How should one set the discount rate used in evaluating costs and benefits that can stretch far into the future? And will "getting the prices right" in the economist's sense guarantee that the natural patrimony passes undiminished to future generations? These are all important issues, but my goal here is not to catalog the challenges faced by environmental economics. Rather, it is to describe some core concepts that if implemented could transform the market into a benign and restorative force.

A New Market

What are those key concepts? First, we live in a market economy where prices guide decisions and where environmental assets are increasingly scarce and threatened. We are not running out of economically relevant natural resources; we are running out of environment. In such a world it should be very expensive to do environmental harm and relatively inexpensive to do things that are environmentally harmless or restorative. It has been noted that the planned Soviet economy failed because prices did not reflect economic realities. Today we live in a market economy that risks failing because prices do not reflect environmental realities. Two initial steps are needed to move prices in this direction: governments must undo the damage they have done in creating environmentally perverse subsidies, and they must intervene in the economy to implement the "polluter pays" principle, broadly conceived.

As an initial platform for the move to sustainability, there must be a serious attack on that very juicy target, subsidies. In their 2001 book *Perverse Subsidies*, Norman Myers and Jennifer Kent analyzed the hundreds of studies that quantify subsidies in agriculture, energy, transportation, water, fisheries, and forestry. They classified as "perverse" those subsidies that had demonstrable negative effects both economically and environmentally. Their conclusion was that, at the behest of powerful interests, the world's governments have intervened in the marketplace to create perverse subsidies that now total about $850 billion annually. Admittedly a rough estimate, these subsidies come to about 2.5 percent of the global economy, creating a huge economic incentive for environmental destruction.[15] The Congressional Research Service estimates that U.S. energy subsidies alone were between thirty-seven billion and sixty-four billion dollars in 2003 and were increased by two to three billion dollars annually by the provisions of the Energy Policy Act of 2005.[16]

The polluter pays principle, writ large, says that polluters—indeed, any environmental consumer or despoiler—should be required to bear the full costs of all environmental damage caused to humans or nature, of all cleanup and remediation, and of all expenses required to reduce impacts to sustainable levels. Basically, there are three philosophies of environmental regulation. Each has a place, and each moves the polluter pays principle forward.

Getting the technology right. Regulatory standards can be based on what can be achieved with available technology or management practices. Here the gold standard is what can be done by applying the very best technology available.

Getting the prices right. Standards can be based on requiring despoilers to pay for their damages. Victim compensation schemes do this, as do requirements for environmental cleanup and restoration. Using taxes, charges, or tradable allowances to require despoilers to internalize their external costs also falls into this category. Here the gold standard is "getting the prices right" by internalizing all environmental costs.

Getting the environment right. Standards can also be based on what is needed to achieve a prescribed quality of the ambient environment. Here the gold standard is full protection of human health, no harvesting of resources beyond long-term sustainable yields, no release of waste products beyond assimilative capacities, and full protection of ecosystem structure and function.

Economic incentives and market mechanisms can be used in each of these three approaches to make them more cost-effective, and each approach has the result of driving up the market prices of environmentally destructive goods and services. In each case, the gold standard may mean no discharge or no impact or no product, for example where a particularly impressive technology is available or where phasing out a particularly harmful product is involved (for example, lead in gasoline, CFCs, or DDT).

Of the three approaches to regulation, the last, "getting the public health and ecological quantities right," should now be the preferred approach for most cases. It will likely drive prices further in the right directions than other approaches, will best engage the talents of both scientists and economists, will force more technological innovation, and will be most protective of the environment and best understood by the public.

Environmental economists have developed an extensive literature on matching problems with the right "choice of instrument" to achieve an efficient and effective result.[17] Under a cap and trade system, for example, the amount of the pollutant is fixed, and that is sometimes very important, but there is uncertainty about where the emissions will occur. For pollutants where there is little concern about location (sulfur dioxide, CFCs, carbon dioxide), cap and trade can be a good choice. Pollution fees and other economic incentive programs are not desirable, though, where metering of releases is difficult, where changes in ambient conditions can shift quickly (for example, stream flows can decline or atmospheric inversions can occur), where particularly hazardous substances or activities are involved, or where cap and trade or emission taxes can result in "hot spots" of concentrated pollutants. In such cases direct regulation is best.[18]

Whatever philosophy of standard setting is used, and whatever economic instrument or other approach is chosen, the goal in all cases must be to ensure that the price on destruction of the environment of all types is discouragingly, forbiddingly high. One place to begin this project would be to identify those goods and services, both intermediate and final, that have the greatest environmental impacts. Industrial ecologists in Europe have made an excellent start at this.[19] One could then work back through the production chain, imposing emission and effluent taxes, user fees, and other requirements on the most damaging activities. These charges could be steadily increased in an effort to close the gap between the private and public costs of production.

A second set of core concepts for market transformation is those put forward by Paul Hawken, Amory Lovins, and Hunter Lovins in

Natural Capitalism. As I described in the Introduction, they advocate a national investment strategy promoted by businesses and government that stresses radically increased resource productivity and large-scale regeneration of natural capital. Changes in the federal tax code could spur action in these areas, as could virgin materials extraction charges, appropriate governmental and private research and development programs, and major government support for environmental restoration initiatives.

A third area for market transformation stems from the work of economists Richard Norgaard and Richard Howarth.[20] They show that "getting the prices right" for the current generation will not ensure sustainability, which is a matter of intergenerational equity. Sustainability requires that each generation consciously decide to redistribute sufficient resources to future generations, a process akin to redistributing resources within the current generations. To that end, they urge consideration of such measures as applying resource use taxes, building futures markets, holding mineral and other resources in public trust for future use, and subsidizing resource owners to slow the rate of extraction and depletion. A further measure in this context would be to require that a portion of the earnings from nonrenewable resource development (the portion above normal profits) be reinvested in developing renewable substitutes.

A fourth area for government action in market transformation stems from the fact that prices do not always work as well in practice as they do in theory. At one level, some factors mute price signals—a phenomenon of which economists are well aware. For example a 2006 study of energy markets by McKinsey and Company found that the global potential for energy productivity gains was huge, but realizing them would require more than high energy prices.[21] The reasons? Some sectors have low price elasticity, so that higher prices do not generate big responses. Consumers lack the information and capital to improve energy productivity, and their price response is further muted by the priority given to convenience, comfort, style, or safety. Businesses also forego valuable energy productivity investments because of small or fragmented energy costs. Government measures that reduce transaction costs, provide information and capital, and reduce risks can aid in overcoming these behavioral and institutional barriers.

A final area for government action to promote market transformation is the need to fix another misleading or, at least, misused and overused economic signal—Gross Domestic Product, or GDP. As currently constructed, GDP is widely recognized as a poor measure of national economic welfare, whatever its value as a measure of national output. Societies need a true measure of economic welfare to gauge how successfully market economies are providing for their populations. The limits of GDP and proposals for alternative indicators are discussed in Chapter 6.

These changes and others should make the market work for the environment, reversing the historical pattern. But there is also the complementary need to recognize limits to and boundaries on market penetration. Commodification occurs when a nonmarketed good or service moves onto the market and is sold for a price. As natural assets become commodified, the human perspective on nature as something subservient to humans, existing for our use and benefit, to be bought and sold, intensifies.

Advocates for the poor are seeking to have access to drinking water declared a fundamental human right that must be recognized by governments and others. But water has in fact become a huge international commodity, with major business lines in wastewater services, drinking water supply, and bottled water. It is perfectly appropriate to demand that water be priced at its full costs to large consumers but inappropriate not to provide a drinking water lifeline affordable by and available to all.

A related trend is privatization. The shift of once-public responsibilities and functions into private hands for market-based management is far advanced. In 2007, *Business Week* reported that investors are clamoring to take over America's highways, bridges, and airports:

"With state and local leaders scrambling for cash to solve short-term fiscal problems, the conditions are ripe for an unprecedented burst of buying and selling. All told, some $100 billion worth of public property could change hands in the next two years, up from less than $7 billion over the past two years."[22] Meanwhile, the outsourcing of the federal government continues apace. The amount spent by Washington on private contractors has doubled in the past six years, and Uncle Sam now has more contract workers than federal employees.[23] It has even been seriously proposed that our national parks be privatized. There will undoubtedly be some environmental benefits from these trends, as resources and services are priced more accurately, but there are large downsides for the environment and the public as well.

Robert Kuttner notes that many encroachments of the market are signs "not of the market's virtue but of its tendency to invade realms where it doesn't belong."[24] There are indeed places the market should not go; there are activities and resources that should not be commodified; there are things that are priceless. We need to protect autonomous spaces, in our lives, in our communities, in nature, just as Karl Polanyi said.[25]

In his *Economy of the Earth*, Mark Sagoff has noted that while markets can and do fail, society does not intervene to correct market failure. "Social regulation of safety in consumer products, the workplace, and the environment historically responds to a need to make markets more humane, not necessarily to make them more efficient. . . . [S]ocial regulation expresses what we believe, what we are, what we stand for as a nation. . . . And there is no methodology for making 'hard decisions' and 'trade-offs.' We have to rely on the virtues of deliberation—open-mindedness, attention to detail, humor, and good sense."[26] Sagoff expresses well the reality that transforming the market is about politics, not economics. It will require extremely difficult political decisions—uprooting subsidies, pushing up prices of gasoline and food flown in from halfway around the world, setting aside resources for future generations, restricting the reach of the market itself. Yet bringing about the transformation of the market is bedrock: in a market economy, there is simply no substitute for environmentally honest prices and other initiatives that can make the market as a whole work for the environment rather than against it. A serious if partial effort has begun in this direction. The further and faster market transformation is pursued, the better off our children and grandchildren will be.

Economic Growth:
Moving to a Post-Growth Society

Economic growth is modern capitalism's principal and most prized product. The idea that there are or should be limits to growth is typically met with derision. Yet not all economists have been dismissive. John Maynard Keynes writing eighty years ago looked forward to the day when the "economic problem" would be a thing of the past. His writing is itself priceless: "Suppose that a hundred years hence we are eight times better off than today. Assuming no important wars and no important increase in population, the *economic problem* may be solved. This means that the economic problem is not—if we look into the future—*the permanent problem of the human race.*

"Why, you may ask, is this so startling? It is startling because the economic problem, the struggle for subsistence, always has been hitherto the primary, most pressing problem of the human race. . . . Thus for the first time since his creation man will be faced with his real, his permanent problem—how to use his freedom from pressing economic cares, how to occupy the leisure . . . how to live wisely and agreeably and well.

"There are changes in other spheres too which we must expect to come. When the accumulation of wealth is no longer of high social importance, there will be great changes in the code of morals. The love of money as a possession—as distinguished from the love of money as a means to the enjoyments and realities of life—will be recognized for what it is, a somewhat disgusting morbidity, one of those semi-criminal, semi-pathological propensities which one hands over with a shudder to the specialists in mental disease. . . .

"I see us free, therefore, to return to some of the most sure and certain principles of religion and traditional virtue—that avarice is a vice, that the exaction of usury is a misdemeanour, and the love of money is detestable, that those walk most truly in the paths of virtue and sane wisdom who take least thought for the morrow. We shall once more value ends above means and prefer the good to the useful. We shall honour those who can teach us how to pluck the hour and the day virtuously and well, the delightful people who are capable of taking direct enjoyment in things, the lilies of the field who toil not, neither do they spin.

"But beware! The time for all this is not yet. For at least another hundred years we must pretend to ourselves and to every one that fair is foul and foul is fair; for foul is useful and fair is not. Avarice and usury and precaution must be our gods for a little longer still. For only they can lead us out of the tunnel of economic necessity into daylight. . . .

"Meanwhile there will be no harm in making mild preparations for our destiny, in encouraging, and experimenting in, the arts of life as well as the activities of purpose.

"But, chiefly, do not let us overestimate the importance of the economic problem, or sacrifice to its supposed necessities other matters of greater and more permanent significance. It should be a matter for specialists—like dentistry. If economists could manage to get themselves thought of as humble, competent people, on a level with dentists, that would be splendid!"[1]

Keynes foresaw a world in which society had outgrown the need for growth and where the principal costs of that growth lie not with the environment but with how its pursuit distorted human virtue and morality. Since we are approaching Keynes's "100 years hence" and "eight times better off," perhaps it is time to question the priority of endless, limitless economic growth. Indeed, long before arriving at the point where the economic problem is solved, there are good reasons to question the fixation on aggregate economic expansion as an unalloyed good and panacea.

For example, UNDP's *1996 Human Development Report* scanned the economic performance of nations and found many examples of:

- *Jobless growth*—where the overall economy grows but does not expand the opportunities for employment.
- *Ruthless growth*—where the fruits of economic growth mostly benefit the rich.
- *Voiceless growth*—where growth in the economy has not been accompanied by an extension of democracy or empowerment.
- *Rootless growth*—where growth causes people's cultural identity to wither.
- *Futureless growth*—where the present generation squanders resources needed by future generations.[2]

Those of us at UNDP at the time saw many varieties of growth other than good growth, which we defined as growth with equity, employment, environment, and empowerment. We also found that the association between economic growth and poverty reduction was far from perfect, and that the association was even less close if one uses measures of poverty other than conventional income, typically a dollar a day per individual for "absolute poverty."[3] We documented that a successful national anti-poverty strategy will have much more in it than simply a commitment to economic growth.[4] But, that said, we also stressed that economic growth *is* urgently needed in the developing world. The alleviation of poverty will not get very far without it.

Although achieving good growth in developing countries remains one of the world's greatest challenges, my focus here is on those societies at or nearing the end of Keynes's journey: the well-to-do countries of North America, Europe, Japan, Australia, New Zealand, Singapore, and some of the Gulf States, where the challenges are more those of affluence than those of poverty.

In considering the future of growth among the rich, we should keep in mind three distinct concepts:

- *Growth of production.* Growth in production or output is what is commonly described as economic growth. It includes growth in both monetary and nonmonetary production. The system of national accounts computes the dollar value of a subset of this production, mainly marketed goods and services and government expenditure, and calls the aggregate Gross Domestic Product.
- *Growth in the economy's biophysical throughput.* "Throughput" includes all the material taken from the natural world that passes through the economy and emerges in some form sooner or later as wastes. Recycling and expanding capital stocks can slow but not stop most throughput from becoming wastes, eventually. As such, throughput is a collection of quantities, not dollars. One cannot simply add up these quantities since the environmental impacts of various activities and residuals are very different. Throughput can be thought of as measuring, or at least symbolizing, the physical size or scale of the economy. So throughput and its growth are the origin of much of the economy's burden on the environment. A key point is that throughput growth is highly correlated with growth in economic production, given the nature of today's economy and the way GDP is measured. Note also that resource-saving technological change can and does get more production out of a given throughput.
- *Growth in human welfare.* Human well-being or welfare involves much more than growth in economic production and the consumption derived from it. Numerous measures of welfare now exist—including the Index of Sustainable Economic Welfare and the Human

Development Index.[5] These indicators are taken up subsequently, in the next chapter.

Gross Domestic Product is frequently used as a proxy for throughput, just as GDP per capita is frequently used as a proxy for welfare. They are imperfect measures for these purposes. Using GDP and GDP per capita as measures of throughput and welfare creates the impression that environment and well-being are strongly at odds—as GDP rises, welfare increases but so does throughput and, hence, environmental loss. If we had good overall measures for environmental well-being and human well-being, we might find the opposite.

With this background, let us take up four questions in turn:

1. Does it make sense to challenge economic growth directly?
2. What would be the basis for such a challenge?
3. What policies or prescriptions are available to implement or act on such a challenge?
4. What are the political and practical prospects for a challenge to growth?

To Grow or Not To Grow

Does it make sense to challenge economic growth directly? Most people would say no, and they fall generally into two camps. First, there are those who see economic growth as an unalloyed good. Recall from Chapter 1 the worldview of Market World. Those with this Promethean and cornucopian perspective have faith in free markets and competition to resolve problems. They tend to see nature as boundless and thus unlikely to exercise significant constraints over human action. Economic growth, in their view, is wholly positive; it facilitates technological innovation and solutions to natural resource scarcity.

I hope that the discussion of growth and modern capitalism in Chapter 2 demonstrated the unreality of this perspective. In the recent past and in the present, the economic growth actually experienced has been and remains the principal source of our major environmental problems. As J. R. McNeill wrote in his environmental history of the twentieth century, growth was useful "in a world with empty land, shoals of undisturbed fish, vast forests, and a robust ozone shield," but now is the source of "acute ecological disruption."[6]

Another group shying away from challenging growth per se are those who share the worldview of the Policy Reform World, and this group includes many mainstream environmentalists. Here, the view is that growth can be consistent with environmental preservation, but only if appropriately guided by regulations, market corrections, and other government action.

Those in the Policy Reform World are undoubtedly correct that growth can be much greener than it is today; both traditional and innovative environmental policies have much to offer as pathways to greener growth. Indeed, policies already in place have made growth more environmentally friendly than it would otherwise have been. But as reviewed in previous chapters, there are many limits to these approaches.

A core belief of those who hold that we need not worry about growth per se, because we can green growth to acceptable levels, is that technological change of an environment-saving sort can be driven so rapidly that it more than compensates for the additional environmental stresses growth produces. The well-known "IPAT equation" helps in examining this proposition.[7]

$$I = PAT$$

Environmental Impact $=$ Population $\times$ Affluence $\times$ Technology

This equation is actually an identity:

$$Impact = Population \times \frac{GDP}{Population} \times \frac{Impact}{GDP}$$

or

$$Impact = GDP \times \frac{Impact}{GDP}$$

where GDP per capita is a measure of affluence and where environmental impact per dollar of GDP (or unit of output) is a reflection of the technology deployed in the economy.

If GDP is going up at 3 percent a year, and if one wants to reduce environmental impacts greatly, then the environmental impacts of each dollar of GDP and each unit of economic output must decline at rates substantially in excess of 3 percent a year. To reduce environmental impacts faster than the economy is growing requires rapid technological change. That is why I and many others have called for policies that promote an environmental revolution in technology—an urgent ecological modernization of the economy that would include both the transformation of existing capital stocks and, through innovation and entrepreneurship, the creation of new environmentally friendly industries, products, and services.[8] A major way to reduce pollution and consumption of natural resources while experiencing economic growth is to bring about a wholesale transformation in the technologies that today dominate manufacturing, energy, construction, transportation, and agriculture. The twentieth-century technologies that have contributed so abundantly to today's problems should be phased out and replaced with twenty-first-century technologies designed with environmental sustainability and restoration in mind. The economy should be "dematerialized" to the fullest possible extent through a new generation of technologies that sharply reduce the consumption of natural resources and the generation of residual wastes per unit of economic output.

As an example, consider what this means in the context of global warming and fossil fuel use. Assume that in order to stabilize greenhouse gas concentrations in the atmosphere at "safe" levels, it will be necessary to reduce U.S. carbon dioxide releases from fossil fuel use by 80 percent over the next forty years. Assume also that the U.S. economy will grow 3 percent a year during this period. The "carbon dioxide intensity of production" can be described as follows:

$$\frac{CO_2}{GDP} = \frac{CO_2}{\begin{array}{c}\text{Total Btu}\\\text{from}\\\text{fossil fuels}\end{array}} \times \frac{\begin{array}{c}\text{Total Btu}\\\text{from}\\\text{fossil fuels}\end{array}}{\text{Total Btu}} \times \frac{\text{Total Btu}}{GDP}$$

which is a convenient way of noting that the carbon dioxide intensity of the economy (CO_2/GDP) depends on the fossil fuel mix (the percent of energy that comes from coal versus oil versus natural gas), the importance of fossil fuels in overall energy use, and energy efficiency.

These assumptions require the carbon dioxide intensity of the U.S. economy to decline by about 7 percent each year for the next forty years, using exponential rates of change. Is such a goal achievable? Can natural gas be substituted for coal and oil fast enough to reduce carbon dioxide emissions per British thermal unit (Btu) of fossil fuels used by 1 percent each year for forty years? Can a switch to renewable energy drive fossil fuels' share of U.S. energy use down by 2 percent each year between 2010 and 2050? Can U.S. energy efficiency improve by 4 percent a year over this period? A great deal may depend on the plausibility of affirmative answers to questions like these.[9] Energy efficiency in the United States did improve by 3.5 percent a year for a short while in the early 1980s when energy prices were high, but for the three decades from 1970 to 2000 as a whole, the rate has been about 2 percent a year.

The needed rates of technological improvement are thus high, and they must be continuously sustained. And there are many, many areas where such technological changes must occur, beyond those affecting carbon dioxide emissions—in agriculture, construction, manufacturing, transportation, and elsewhere. In the carbon dioxide example, almost half the required rate of change is needed simply to compensate for the effects of economic growth. It is like running up a down escalator—a very fast down escalator. Perhaps it can be done. I am doubtful,[10] but here is a key point: it is not being done today, and no government that I know of is systematically, adequately promoting the universal, rapid, and sustained penetration of green technology, at home and abroad, on the scale required. Governments are, however, profoundly committed to promoting growth.

Real speed is required for technological change to stay well ahead of growth, but the social and political institutions that can create the incentives for rapid technological change can be slow to respond, as can the needed science and technology. The development of international environmental law and regulation is painfully slow, for example. But the world economy and urbanization surge ahead, faster than societies can respond. Chlorofluorocarbons were produced for decades before scientists raised concerns. Then it took a decade to agree on a phaseout, which took another decade. Yet the problem was relatively simple compared to most, and the response was fast by international standards. Our capacity to anticipate and respond effectively today has not greatly improved. Yet by the time today's university students reach leadership positions, the world economy will likely be twice its current size.

Another way to address whether it is necessary to challenge growth is to ask whether adopting all the prescriptions described in Chapter 4 would make growth benign and restorative and thus render such a challenge to growth itself superfluous. In theory, if all those prescriptions were indeed adopted quickly and vigorously and fully enforced, we could say yes, that would suffice. The economy could proceed down the paths that remained open, and although that might give rise to certain social pathologies, the environment would be spared. Throughput growth would halt and then decline. But theory is not reality, and in reality Chapter 4's far-reaching prescriptions will be adopted only slowly and, in all likelihood, partially. And if growth remains an overriding priority, their adoption will remain problematic. The powerful forces driving the clash of economy and environment thus will continue, and that makes it necessary to address those forces—growth, consumerism, corporate behavior among them. So it makes very good sense to question economic growth and the growth imperative. Right now and for the foreseeable future, there's a trade-off: economy versus environment. The planet cannot sustain capitalism as we know it.

Uneconomic Growth

Which brings us to the second question: What would a challenge to growth look like? Here it is best to begin by examining the historical record. Early challenges to growth included John Kenneth Galbraith's. In 1956 he wrote that "sooner rather than later our concern with the quantity of goods produced—the rate of increase in Gross National Product—would have to give way to the larger question of the quality of life that it provided."[11] Kenneth Boulding's "Economics of the Coming Spaceship Earth" followed in 1966,[12] and E. J. Mishan's *Costs of Economic Growth* in 1967.[13] But the publication that created the firestorm was Dennis and Donella Meadows's *The Limits to Growth*.[14] I was never a big fan of *The Limits to Growth*. It emphasized the physical limits of raw materials availability—limits that would lead the economy to overshoot and collapse. The real question is *should* we grow, not *can* we grow. Within a few years of its publication, *The Limits to Growth* had sold four million copies. It became an easy target for economists, some of whom demonstrated that one could change the assumptions of the Meadows's model a bit and show that there were no such hard and fast physical limits to growth.

After the 1970s, the focus on growth faded, and one heard little about it for two decades. Now, however, interest has rekindled. It is coming from two reinforcing quarters. First, social critics are noting that growth is not delivering the social goods—that although incomes are rising, individual and social well-being are not improving and in fact by many indicators are declining. This perspective is discussed in the next chapter. The new interest in challenging growth is also coming from those who see, as argued here, that growth is overwhelming environmental gains and that the more traditional paths to environmental protection are not working well enough.

Much of the latest thinking has been brought together creatively by Australian policy intellectual Clive Hamilton in his 2003 book *Growth Fetish*. Here is Hamilton rising to his subject: "In the face of the fabulous promises of economic growth, at the beginning of the 21st century we are confronted by an awful fact. Despite high and sustained levels of economic growth in the West over a period of 50 years—growth that has seen average real incomes increase several times over—the mass of people are no more satisfied with their lives now than they were then. If growth is intended to give us better lives, and there can be no other purpose, it has failed.... The more we examine the role of growth in modern society, the more our obsession with growth appears to be a fetish—that is, an inanimate object worshipped for its apparent magical powers.

"The fact that neoliberalism remains unchallenged is extraordinary given the events of recent history, for laissez-faire capitalism has been marked by devastating failures.... In addition, the costs of economic growth, which fall largely outside the marketplace and so do not appear in the national accounts, have become inescapably apparent—in the form of disturbing signs of ecological decline, an array of social problems that growth has failed to correct, and epidemics of unemployment, overwork and insecurity....

"For the most part, capitalism itself has answered the demands that inspired 19th century socialism.... But attainment of these goals has only brought deeper sources of social unease—manipulation by marketers, obsessive materialism, environmental degradation, endemic alienation, and loneliness. In short ... in the marketing society, we seek fulfillment but settle for abundance. Prisoners of plenty, we have the freedom to consume instead of the freedom to find our place in the world."[15] Hamilton presents a forceful case. His critique has merit and deserves wide attention.

Many in the new school of "ecological economics" are also challenging growth. Notable among them is Herman Daly, one of the founders of this new school. It must be said that ecological economics has been enjoying rapid growth.

In their 2004 textbook *Ecological Economics,* Herman Daly and Joshua Farley challenge customary thinking about the economy and economic growth: "More contentious (and more important) is the call by ecological economics for an end to growth. We define growth as an increase in throughput, which is the flow of natural resources from the environment, through the economy, and back to the environment as waste. It is a quantitative increase in the physical dimensions of the economy and/or of the waste stream produced by the economy. This kind of growth, of course, cannot continue indefinitely, as the Earth and its resources are not infinite. While growth must end, this in no way implies an end to development, which we define as qualitative change, realization of potential, evolution toward an improved, but not larger, structure or system—an increase in the quality of goods and services (where quality is measured by the ability to increase human well-being) provided by a given throughput. . . .

"Where conventional economics espouses growth forever, ecological economics envisions a steady-state economy at optimal scale. Each is logical within its own preanalytic vision, and each is absurd from the viewpoint of the other. The difference could not be more basic, more elementary, or more irreconcilable."[16]

Daly and Farley believe we are now in a "full world" where "continued physical expansion of the economy threatens to impose unacceptable costs."[17] They note that the most binding constraint on economic growth may be the waste absorption capacity of the environment rather than resource depletion, long thought to be the likely constraint.

Over the past decade ecological economics has become an increasingly sophisticated analytical system. From the perspective of many of its practitioners, environmental challenges are unlikely to be met successfully within the framework of neoclassical economics because this well-established system of economic thought recognizes optimal allocation but not sustainable scale. Ecological economists contend that for any given ecosystem setting, there is an optimum scale of the economy beyond which physical growth in the economy (throughput) starts costing more than it is worth in terms of human welfare. They see diminishing returns to growth as consumers' more basic needs are met; at some point the limit of consumer satiation is reached. Meanwhile, the costs of extra growth increase, environmental costs prominent among them. Eventually a society reaches the point where more growth is not worth it. Practically, Daly and others would maintain we have already reached or passed this point and are now experiencing, in Daly's phrase, "uneconomic growth."

Bridling Growth

If challenging growth makes sense, what policy prescriptions are available? They are of two types. First, there are the environmental policies advocated by ecological economists. And second, there are those prescriptions that fall outside the environmental arena.

Ecological economists stress the "ecologically right quantities" approach to environmental protection, as discussed in the preceding chapter. The basic idea here is first to determine the quantities of a pollutant allowed to be discharged or the quantities of resources allowed to be harvested. For a pollutant, one wants to determine what quantity would exceed the environment's assimilative capacity for that pollutant and then set discharges below that level. For a harvested renewable resource—fish, timber—one wants to determine the quantity that can be taken at a sustainable rate, so that the regenerative capacity of that resource is not exceeded. For ecological economists, sustainability is defined in terms of not exceeding assimilative and regenerative capacities. So the first step in ecological economics is to get the biophysical quantities right. That will cap overall throughput at a sustainable scale.

These quantitative limits can then be implemented by either tax or cap and trade mechanisms, as discussed in Chapter 4. Tradable pollution permits and tradable resource extraction permits can be used, as can pollution taxes and taxes on virgin materials. These market-based mechanisms can be combined. This approach is the same as that advocated by many traditional environmental economists, with one big caveat. Ecological economists tend to insist that the quantitative limits be set so that the environment—and human health—are fully protected. Put otherwise, ecological economists want to see natural capital fully protected and, indeed, regenerated. They thus take a position that is called "strong sustainability." In strong sustainability, the environment is sustained. Natural capital is sustained. In "weak sustainability," it is the prospect for long-term economic growth that is sustained. In weak sustainability, natural capital can be consumed provided there are substitutes for it, like man-made capital. Many traditional economists, including many environmental economists, favor the weak sustainability approach. The strong and weak approaches are very different, but they both march under the banner of sustainability, and therein lies the source of much confusion. Everyone prefers sustainability, but they define it differently.[18]

Perhaps the most important prescriptions challenging unbridled growth come from outside the environmental sector. Explored in more detail in the chapters that follow, they include measures such as more leisure, including a shorter workweek and longer vacations; greater labor protections, job security, and benefits, including retirement and health benefits; restrictions on advertising; new ground rules for corporations; strong social and environmental provisions in trade agreements; rigorous consumer protection; greater income and social equality, including genuinely progressive taxation for the rich and greater income support for the poor; major spending on public sector services and environmental amenities; a huge investment in education, skills, and new technology to promote both ecological modernization and sharply rising labor productivity to offset smaller workforces and shorter hours. People deserve more free time, more security, and more opportunity for companionship and continuing education. They deserve to be free of the growth-at-all-costs paradigm and the ruthless economy described by Samuelson and Nordhaus.

A post-growth society thus should not be a stagnant society. It should include dynamic initiatives that recognize the real sources of human well-being. Clive Hamilton has put the matter well: "A post-growth society will consciously promote the social structures and activities that actually improve individual and community wellbeing. It will aim to provide a social environment in which people can pursue true individuality, rather than the pseudo-individuality that is now obtained through spending on brand names and manufactured lifestyles."[19]

The Outlook

What are the practical and political prospects for a post-growth society? Clearly, abandoning the growth fetish will not come quickly or easily. As Daniel Bell noted, growth is tantamount to a secular religion.[20] Harvard's Benjamin Friedman, in his book *The Moral Consequences of Economic Growth*, sees "tolerance for diversity, social mobility, commitment to fairness, and dedication to democracy" all dependent on the steadfast pursuit of economic growth.[21] I doubt that he is right, but many people today agree with him.

Another constraint comes from the analysis of capitalism itself. We have seen there that the drive to grow is inherent in capitalism. Bowles notes, "In a capitalist economy, survival requires growth. . . . Capitalism is differentiated from other economic systems by its drive to accumulate . . . and its built-in tendency to expand." Or as Baumol says, "The capitalist economy can usefully be viewed as a machine whose primary product is economic growth."[22] So a challenge to growth is close to a challenge to capitalism.

A ray of hope comes from Robert Collins in his book *More: The Politics of Economic Growth in Postwar America*. Collins points out how "the pursuit of economic growth came to become a central and defining feature of U.S. public policy in the half-century after the end of World War II. Commentators in the 1950s coined the term 'growthmanship' to describe the seemingly single-minded pursuit of exuberant economic growth that was then appearing to dominate the political agenda and the public dialogue throughout the Western industrialized world, nowhere more dramatically than in that bastion of materialistic excess, the United States. . . .

"What made the postwar pursuit of growth distinctively modern was the availability of new state powers and means of macroeconomic management dedicated to achieving growth that was more exuberant, more continuous and constant, more aggregately quantifiable, and also more precisely measured than ever before. Perhaps we can best appreciate what made postwar growthmanship distinctive by looking at the context from which it emerged, for it was the ambivalence of New Deal economic policy that made the subsequent emergence of growthmanship seem like a striking departure."[23]

If our current growthmania is indeed an artifact of the postwar world, then there is hope that it is not a permanent or inevitable feature of the economic landscape. But Collins is realistic about the scale of the challenge. He observes that "the acceptance of limits in the pursuit of growth brings its own painful consequences. Growth has often been America's 'out'—the way, many believed, that the nation could somehow square the circle and reconcile its love of liberty with its egalitarian pretensions. Without the promise of particularly rapid growth to resolve this tension at the core of the American enterprise, we are at century's end left with a task fully challenging enough to test, and perhaps again to tap, whatever reserves of national genius and greatness we carry with us into the new millennium."[24] The good news is that there are ways other than rapid growth to "resolve this tension," as the chapter that follows shows.

If challenging growth seems difficult, one should remember Milton Friedman's observation: "Only a crisis—actual or perceived—produces real change. When that crisis occurs, the actions that are taken depend on the ideas that are lying around. That, I believe, is our basic function: to develop alternatives to existing policies, to keep them alive and available until the politically impossible becomes politically inevitable."[25] That is one philosophy—be ready for the coming crisis. Another, taken from Mahatma Gandhi, is more active: "First they laugh at you," he said, "then they ignore you, then they fight you, then you win."

Might economic growth slow of its own accord? In October 2005, the OECD issued a report saying that global economic growth could fall considerably over the next three decades unless older people began to work longer to offset declining birthrates. The report called for curtailing pension and welfare benefits to encourage older workers to stay in the labor force. The OECD recommendations point in exactly the wrong directions—more work and less leisure time. Fortunately, its prescriptions are not likely to be heeded. A story in the same October 11, 2005, issue of the *Financial Times* reported the following: "Much of Belgium was brought to a standstill last Friday as thousands of workers barricaded streets and went on strike over government plans to raise the pension age. The outcry had a resonance well beyond Belgium, however—many countries are seeking to overhaul welfare systems threatened by the need to care for aging populations."[26]

Every world region is experiencing declining fertility rates, including steep declines in Asia and Latin America, and the United Nations reports that by 2050, fifty countries will have lower populations than today. By 2030 even China's population will have started to decline, according to projections.[27] In the United States, population growth and immigration remain higher than in Europe, but the participation rate—the proportions of working-age population in the labor force—seems to have peaked. The trend is unlikely to reverse because the huge surge of women into the U.S. workforce has slowed. Some analysts predict that these trends could dampen growth prospects.

It seems possible that slower labor force growth and greater preferences for leisure could lead to slower growth, initially in the richer countries. Some analysts argue against this conclusion. There are numerous examples of countries with slow or no population growth achieving moderate to high rates of economic growth. And there are rich countries where fertility rates first declined and then "recovered."[28] Also, if labor markets do tighten in economies with aging populations, that could lead to a further shift in investments to regions where labor is plentiful and wages are low, and it could also lead to demands for increased immigration and guest worker programs. How all this will play out is difficult to predict, but it would surely be a leap of misplaced faith to count on slow economic growth in the affluent countries.

In the end, what has to be modified is the open-ended commitment to aggregate economic growth—growth that is consuming environmental and social capital, both now in short supply. At the same time, it is abundantly clear that American society and many others need growth along many dimensions that can increase human welfare, now and in the future: growth in good jobs and in the incomes of the poor; growth in availability and efficiency of health services; growth in education and training; growth in security against the risks of illness, job displacement, old age, and disability; growth in investment in public infrastructure for urban and interurban transport, water, waste management, and other urban services; growth in the deployment of green technologies, as rapidly as possible; growth in the replacement of America's obsolete energy system; growth in the restoration of ecosystems; growth in nonmilitary government spending at the expense of military; and growth in international assistance for sustainable, people-centered development, to mention some prominent needs. We need to be reducing throughput and growing the things that increase human well-being.

A post-growth society thus need not be a no-growth one. For Hamilton, the key is that "working life, the natural environment and the public sector would no longer be sacrificed in order to push up the rate of growth."[29] The sum of the measures advocated in these chapters would undoubtedly slow GDP growth considerably in the United States. Perhaps the economy would evolve to a steady state, where a declining labor force and shorter work hours are offset by rising productivity.[30] But as Keynes, Galbraith, Daly, and many others have noted, that is not the end of the world but the beginning of a new one. As John Stuart Mill noted long ago, there would still be "as much scope as ever for all kinds of mental culture, and moral and social progress; as much room for improving the Art of living, and much more likelihood of it being improved."[31]

Per capita GDP in 2006 was thirty-five thousand dollars a year in Germany and France, thirty-nine thousand dollars a year in the United Kingdom, and forty-four thousand dollars a year in the United States. Shortage of money is not the problem. What America really needs is new priorities. We should stop looking at GDP growth as our savior and instead seek to solve our problems by addressing them directly, with ways that will actually work. It is to this alternative approach that we now turn.

6 Real Growth: Promoting the Well-Being of People and Nature

Has America's pursuit of growth and ever-greater material abundance brought true happiness and satisfaction in life?

Happiness is a complicated subject. Almost everyone wants to be happy and lead a life of genuine satisfaction. Yet many major works of art and literature and many of the deepest insights have in fact been products of unhappy, even tormented minds. Moreover, happiness can and does have many meanings. Concepts of happiness range all the way from a shallow, hedonistic pursuit of instant gratification to the Buddhist emphasis on finding happiness in recognizing the futility of striving and in the movement beyond self to compassion. Most of the great philosophers from antiquity forward have wrestled with happiness. What are the wellsprings of true happiness? Where does happiness fit into the pantheon of goals worthy of our species?

Darrin McMahon, in his wonderful book *Happiness: A History*, traces these questions down through the centuries. McMahon finds the origins of the "right to happiness" in the Enlightenment. The Enlightenment, he writes, sought "to create space of happiness on earth. To dance, to sing, to enjoy our food, to revel in our bodies and the company of others—in short, to delight in a world of our own making—was not to defy God's will but to live as nature had intended. This was our earthly purpose. . . . 'Does not everyone have a right to happiness?' asked . . . the entry on that subject in the French encyclopedia edited by Denis Diderot. Judged by the standards of the preceding millennium and a half, the question was extraordinary: a *right* to happiness? And yet it was posed rhetorically, in full confidence of the nodding assent of enlightened minds."[1]

It was in 1776, the year of the Declaration of Independence, that Jeremy Bentham would write his famous principle of utility: "It is the greatest happiness of the greatest number that is the measure of right and wrong."

Thus, when Thomas Jefferson drafted the declaration in June 1776, the words "the pursuit of happiness" came naturally to him, and the language sailed through the debates of June and July without dissent. McMahon believes this lack of controversy stemmed in part from the fact that the "pursuit of happiness" phrase combined ambiguously two very different notions: the idea from John Locke and Jeremy Bentham that happiness was the pursuit of personal pleasure and the older Stoic idea that happiness derived from active devotion to the public good and from civic virtue, which have little to do with personal pleasure.

"The 'pursuit of happiness,'" McMahon writes, "was launched in different, and potentially conflicting, directions from the start, with private pleasure and public welfare coexisting in the same phrase. For Jefferson, so quintessentially in this respect a man of the Enlightenment, the coexistence was not a problem." But Jefferson's formula almost immediately lost its double meaning, in practice, McMahon notes, and the right of citizens to pursue their personal interests and joy won out. This victory was confirmed by waves of immigrants to America's shores, for whom America was truly the land of opportunity. "To pursue happiness in such a land was quite rightly to pursue prosperity, to pursue pleasure, to pursue wealth."[2]

It is in this jettisoning of the civic virtue concept of happiness in favor of the self-gratification side that McMahon finds the link between the pursuit of happiness and the rise of American capitalism in the nineteenth and twentieth centuries. Happiness, he writes, "continued to entice with attractive force, providing a justification for work and sacrifice, a basis for meaning and hope that only loomed larger on the horizon of Western democracies." Daniel Bell, McMahon notes, described the monumental transformation that occurred: "the shift from production to consumption as the fulcrum of capitalism" that brought "luxury to the masses" and made "marketing and hedonism . . . motor forces of capitalism." "If economic growth was now a secular religion," McMahon observes, "the pursuit of happiness remained its central creed, with greater opportunities than ever before to pursue pleasure in comfort and things."[3] Max Weber saw this transformation firsthand. "Material goods," he observed in *The Protestant Ethic and the Spirit of Capitalism,* "have gained an increasing and finally an inexorable power over the lives of men as at no previous period in history."[4]

The story of the pursuit of happiness in America is thus a story of its close alliance with capitalism and consumerism. But in recent years, many researchers have begun to see this relationship as one of misplaced allegiance. Has the pursuit of happiness through growth in material abundance and possessions actually brought Americans happiness? That is a question more for science than for philosophy, and the good news is that social scientists have in fact recently turned abundantly to the subject.[5] A new field, positive psychology, the study of happiness and subjective well-being, has been invented, and there is now even a professional *Journal of Happiness Studies.*[6]

Why is this outpouring of happiness studies "good news"? Imagine, if you will, two very different alternatives for affluent societies. In one, economic growth, prosperity, and affluence bring steadily increasing human happiness, well-being, and satisfaction. In a second, prosperity and happiness are not correlated, and indeed, prosperity, beyond a certain point, is associated with the growth of important social pathologies. If the first scenario more closely resembles reality, then the possibility of sustaining the environment by confronting capitalism, growth, and consumption is powerfully constrained. Sustaining the environment would be at odds with the march of human happiness. On the other hand, if the second scenario provides the better fit to reality, then there are well-founded grounds for hope, for in that case sustaining the environment and the pursuit of happiness are not at odds.

So what the social scientists in this new field are telling us is of fundamental importance. Let us turn now to their findings. Two of the leaders in the field, Ed Diener and Martin Seligman, reviewed the now-voluminous literature on well-being in their 2004 article, "Beyond Money: Toward an Economy of Well-Being."[7] In what follows, I draw on this article, supplementing it with other research.

Happiness and Money

The overall concept that is gaining acceptance among researchers is "subjective well being," that is, a person's own opinion of his or her well-being. Diener and Seligman note that well-being includes three things: pleasure, engagement, and meaning.[8] A pleasant life is characterized by positive emotions and disposition. Engagement involves absorption in what one is doing—sometimes described as flow. Boredom is the opposite of engagement. Meaning is belonging to and serving something larger than oneself. All three seem to play a role in life satisfaction. Subjects in surveys are frequently asked, on a scale of one to ten, how satisfied are you with your life? Most well-being surveys today ask individuals how happy or satisfied they are with their lives in general, how satisfied they are in particular contexts (for example, work, marriage), how much they trust others, and so on.

Although available data on subjective well-being are not as complete or systematic as one would like, they are extensive, and findings based on them tend to be robust and internally consistent.[9] Researchers have found high correlations between self-reported measures of happiness and life satisfaction on one hand and, on the other, an index of psychological well-being that includes purpose in life, autonomy, positive relationships, personal growth, and self-acceptance. Thus, when social scientists measure happiness and life satisfaction, they are measuring important things, not superficial ones.

A good place to begin is with studies that compare levels of happiness and life satisfaction among nations at different stages of economic development. They find that the citizens of wealthier countries do report higher levels of life satisfaction, although the correlation is rather poor and is even poorer when such factors as quality of government are statistically controlled. Moreover, this positive relationship between national well-being and national per capita income virtually disappears when one looks only at countries with GDP per capita over ten thousand per year.[10] In short, once a country achieves a moderate level of income, further growth does not significantly improve perceived well-being (fig. 1).[11]

Diener and Seligman report that peoples with the highest well-being are not those in the richest countries but those who live where political institutions are effective and human rights are protected, where corruption is low and mutual trust is high. Other factors positively associated with a sense of well-being at the national level are low divorce rates, high participation in voluntary associations, and strong religious affiliations.[12]

Even more challenging to the idea that well-being increases with higher incomes is extensive time series data showing that throughout almost the entire post–World War II period, as incomes skyrocketed in the United States and other advanced economies, reported life satisfaction and happiness levels stagnated or even declined slightly (fig. 2).[13] The consistency of this finding across a range of economically advanced societies is rather startling.

But that is not all. Diener and Seligman note, "Even more disparity [between income and well-being] shows up when ill-being measures are considered. For instance, depression rates have increased 10-fold over

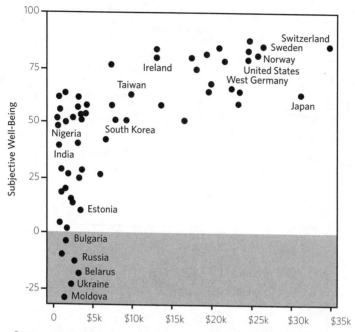

Figure 1. Subjective well-being versus GNP in various nations in 1998 (Source: Leiserowitz et al., "Sustainability Values, Attitudes and Behaviors," 2006)

the same 50-year period, and rates of anxiety are also rising. . . . [T]he average American child in the 1980s reported greater anxiety than the average child receiving psychiatric treatment in the 1950s. There is [also] a decreasing level of social connectedness in society, as evidenced by declining levels of trust in other people and in governmental institutions. Because trust is an important predictor of societal stability and quality of life, the decreases are of considerable concern."[14]

There is, however, a seemingly paradoxical finding—namely, surveys show that within countries at any one time, richer individuals tend to be happier than poorer ones. In *Happiness: Lessons from a New Science,* Richard Layard reports that in the United States, 45 percent of those in the top quarter of incomes say they are "very happy,"

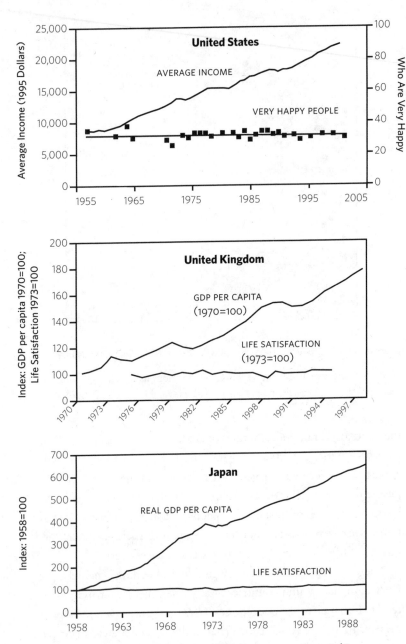

Figure 2. Trends in life satisfaction and happiness versus per capital income in affluent societies (Sources: *United States,* Porritt, *Capitalism as If the World Matters,* 2005; *United Kingdom,* Donovan and Halpern, *Life Satisfaction,* 2002; *Japan,* Frey and Stutzer, *Happiness and Economics,* 2002)

whereas only 33 percent of those in the bottom quarter are very happy. In Britain the numbers are 40 percent versus 29 percent.[15]

How can one explain this? There is, first, good evidence that happier people are more successful and do better financially. The causation thus seems to run in both directions. Second, wealthy individuals have a smaller gap between their incomes and their desires. But how do we account for the fact that richer people within societies are happier while societies that get richer don't get happier? Two factors are at play: social positioning and habituation. People constantly compare themselves with others, and if everyone is better off financially, then no one is any happier. If comparative position is what counts, not absolute income, then rising incomes can leave just as many unhappy comparisons. You may be able to buy a new Dodge, but your neighbor just bought a Lexus. You're moving up to a larger house, but so is everyone else. This human tendency to compare ourselves with others has not escaped the attention of humorists. Ambrose Bierce's *Devil's Dictionary* defined happiness as "an agreeable sensation arising from contemplating the misery of another." And then there's the one about the Russian peasant whose neighbor had a cow while he did not. When God asked how he could help, the peasant replied, "Kill the cow!" Numerous studies confirm that happiness levels depend inversely on one's neighbors' prosperity.[16]

A second factor is what is called habituation or the hedonic treadmill. People adapt or habituate to their new incomes. Layard explains this in *Happiness:* "When I get a new home or a new car, I am excited at first. But then I get used to it, and my mood tends to revert to where it was before. Now I feel I *need* the bigger house and the better car. If I went back to the old house and car, I would be much less happy than I was before I had experienced something better. . . . Once your situation becomes stable again, you will revert to your 'set-point' level of happiness.

"The things that we get used to most easily and most take for granted are our material possessions—our car, our house. Advertisers understand this and invite us to 'feed our addiction' with more and more spending. However, other experiences do not pale in the same way—the time we spend with our family and friends, and the quality and security of our job."[17]

So how do we sum up matters thus far? "Those who say money can't buy happiness just don't know where to shop!" goes the joke, but the truth is that the data indicate that money can't buy happiness or satisfaction in life among the more affluent. Study after study shows that there is a sharply declining marginal utility to extra income. As Diener and Seligman put it: "Economic growth seems to have topped out in its capacity to produce more well-being in developed nations. . . . [E]fforts and policies to raise income in wealthy nations are un-likely to increase well-being and might even undermine factors (such as rewarding social relationships or other cherished values) that have higher leverage for producing enhanced well-being.

"Thus, when the sciences of economics and of well-being come face-to-face, they sometimes conflict. If the well-being findings simply mirrored those for income and money—with richer people invariably being much happier than poorer people—one would hardly need to measure well-being, or make policy to enhance it directly. But income, a good surrogate historically when basic needs were unmet, is now a weak surrogate for well-being in wealthy nations."[18]

The Wellsprings

If incomes are such weak generators of well-being in our more affluent societies, what things do produce happiness and unhappiness? Most important, it appears that our genes do. Some of us are just congeni-tally happy or unhappy. Our genes seem to account for about half the variation in individual happiness.

Regarding things that can be changed, unemployment—getting laid off—is devastating to one's sense of well-being. For many, even finding a new job does not restore well-being to former levels. Self-reported good health also correlates with well-being, and mental disorders are an increasingly widespread source of human misery. Diener and Seligman also stress the importance of relationships: "The quality of people's social relationships is crucial to their well-being. People need supportive, positive relationships and social belonging to sustain well-being. . . . [T]he need to belong, to have close and long-term social relationships, is a fundamental human need. . . . People need social bonds in committed relationships, not simply interactions with strangers, to experience well-being."[19]

Layard has summed up the factors neatly: "What doesn't matter: We can begin with five features that on average have a negligible effect on happiness. The first is age: if we trace people through their life, average happiness is remarkably stable, despite the ups and then downs of income, and despite increasing ill-health. The second is gender: in nearly every country men and women are roughly equally happy. Looks too make little difference. Likewise, IQ is only weakly correlated with happiness, as are physical and mental energy (self-rated). Finally, education has only a small direct effect on happiness. . . . So what really does affect us? Seven factors stand out: our family relationships, our financial situation, our work, our community and friends, our health, our personal freedom and our personal values. Except for health and income, they are all concerned with the quality of our relationships."[20] An earlier study by Diener and Seligman found that the most important characteristic shared by the happiest students were their strong ties to friends and family.[21]

Other authorities have put a finer point on the problem of why we're not getting happier and instead are getting more depressed and anxious. Sociologist Robert Lane sees a pattern of lock-in and overshoot. In *The Loss of Happiness in Market Democracies*, he notes that "we get happiness primarily from people; it is their affection or dislike, their good or bad opinion of us, their acceptance or rejection that most influence our moods. . . .

"My hypothesis is that there is a kind of famine of warm interpersonal relations, of easy-to-reach neighbors, of encircling, inclusive member-ships, and of solidary family life. There is much evidence that for people lacking in social support of this kind, unemployment has more serious effects, illnesses are more deadly, disappointment with one's children is harder to bear, bouts of depression last longer, and frustra-tion and failed expectations of all kinds are more traumatic. . . .

"Something has gone wrong. The economism that made Americans both rich and happy at one point in history is misleading them, is of-fering more money, which does not make them happy, instead of more companionship, which probably would. . . .

"Western societies kept on course too long. . . . [T]he economic development that improved [subjective well-being] over the millennia is no longer a major source of well-being in the United States. Like other goods, money income and the commodities it buys have declin-ing marginal outcome utility while companionship has, at the moment, rising marginal utility. . . .

"What went wrong, then, is that the guiding disciplines failed to reconsider the ends that really mattered. It is not quite an accident of intellectual history that gave to economics the custody of how to think about well-being, for during the long period of its intellectual gestation the most important values were, first, survival and then de-liverance from poverty. Thanks to technology as well as economics, the advanced countries of the world have solved the first problem and are hesitantly moving toward solving the second. It is this very success that raises to rival importance the value of the most urgent competing good, companionship. But this rival good is an externality to market economics: because it is not priced, the market is not sensitive to its fluctuating values."[22]

Another acute observer of the American scene is Peter Whybrow, a psychiatrist and director of the Institute of Neuroscience and Human Behavior at the University of California at Los Angeles. In *American Mania*, Whybrow sees a perversion of America's search for happi-ness: "For many Americans the hallowed search for happiness has been hijacked by a discomforting and frenzied activity. As a practicing psychiatrist I find much in this frenetic chase that is reminiscent of mania, a dysfunctional state of mind that begins with a joyous sense of excitement and high productivity but escalates into reckless pursuit, irritability, and confusion, before cycling down into depression. . . . [I]n psychiatric parlance, mania is the *dysphoric* state of activity . . . that begins with happiness *but lies beyond it* in a tumult of anxiety, competition, and social disruption. By analogy, one can look on America's increasing frenzy as evidence of a national stumbling into something akin to this dysphoric state. Unwittingly, in our relentless pursuit of happiness we have overshot the target and spawned a manic society with an insatiable appetite for more. America's dream of a Utopian social order—fueled from the beginning by the twin beliefs that material success equates with personal satisfaction . . . and that technical advance is the key to social progress—has become mired in a confusing mix of manic desire and depressive discomfort."[23]

In recent decades, then, economic output per person in the United States has risen sharply, but there has been no increase in life satisfaction, while levels of distrust and depression have increased substantially. Lane, Whybrow, and others depict American society as having gone astray and lost its way. Patterns that once brought happiness now do just the opposite. One of our most perceptive national observers, author Bill McKibben, has reached a similar conclusion. He notes that "our single-minded focus on increasing wealth has succeeded in driving the planet's ecological systems to the brink of failure, even as it's failed to make us happier." How did it happen? he asks. "The answer is pretty obvious—we kept doing something past the point that it worked. Since happiness had increased with income in the past, we assumed it would inevitably do so in the future." Instead, McKibben notes, it had led us to becoming more thoroughly individualistic than we really wanted to be, increasing social isolation and undermining our sense of community.[24]

Psychologist David Myers sees this pattern of soaring wealth and shrinking spirit as "the American paradox." He observes that at the beginning of the twenty-first century, Americans found themselves "with big houses and broken homes, high incomes and low morale, secured rights and diminished civility. We were excelling at making a living but too often failing at making a life. We celebrated our prosperity but yearned for purpose. We cherished our freedoms but longed for connection. In an age of plenty, we were feeling spiritual hunger. These facts of life lead us to a startling conclusion: Our becoming better off materially has not made us better off psychologically."[25]

Well-Being in America

If American society has lost its way following the compass provided by GDP, it is not surprising that many observers have sought to identify the shortcomings of that measure and to develop alternatives that more faithfully gauge human and environmental well-being. First, the system of national economic accounts that gives us GDP has been under attack by analysts who believe that GDP is badly flawed even as a system for measuring economic welfare.[26] They point out a series of shortcomings in GDP as currently measured—shortcomings that are in fact widely conceded.

GDP includes everything that can be sold or has monetary value, even if it adds nothing to human well-being or welfare. Imagine a society that spends 20 percent of its GDP on prisons and police, on cleaning up pollution, and on the consequences of traffic accidents. Now imagine another society that has no need for these defensive expenditures, for example, because its citizens don't pollute or drive recklessly and are law-abiding. This second society instead allocates that 20 percent of GDP to better schools, on improving life expectancy, and on alleviating the problems of the poor. GDP is the same in both countries, but welfare is much higher in the latter case.

Second, GDP does not count the costs and benefits that occur outside the market. For example, a country can consume its natural capital, but that shows up in national income accounts not as capital depreciation but as income. As economist Robert Repetto has written, "A country could exhaust its mineral resources, cut down its forests, erode its soils, pollute its aquifers, and hunt its wildlife and fisheries to extinction, but measured income would not be affected as these assets disappeared. . . . [The] difference in the treatment of natural resources and other tangible assets confuses the depletion of valuable assets with the generation of income. . . . The result can be illusory gains in income and permanent losses in wealth."[27] GDP also neglects to count the real welfare benefits generated by volunteer and household labor.

And third, GDP fails to take into account the distribution of the income measured, even though for most societies welfare could be improved by shifting disposable incomes from the very rich to the very poor, where the marginal utility of income is almost certainly higher.

The shortcomings of GDP as a measure of social and environmental conditions have stimulated a proliferation of measures and indicators that seek to improve our understanding of actual conditions. Some of these measures seek mainly to bring a range of environmental considerations into the national accounts.[28] Other approaches seek to measure human welfare by combining measures of purchasing power with indicators of health and education. The Human Development Index we developed at UNDP takes this approach. It shows, for example, that countries with similar levels of GDP per capita can and do have very different levels of human development and welfare.[29]

The most interesting efforts to date have been those seeking to create comprehensive alternatives to GDP. One of the first of these is the Index of Sustainable Economic Welfare (ISEW). It begins with national private consumption expenditures and adjusts that for distributional inequalities. It then adds in nonmarket contributions to welfare, such as unpaid housework, and subtracts out defensive expenditures such as police protection and pollution control, as well as the depreciation of natural resources and environmental assets.

When adjustments such as these are made for six major industrial

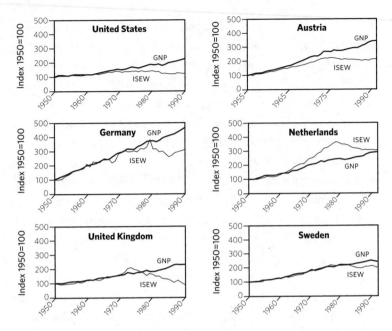

Figure 3. Trends in sustainable economic welfare per capita and GNP per capita in affluent societies (Source: Jackson and Stymne, *Sustainable Economic Welfare in Sweden*, 1996)

economies, the results show a pattern (fig. 3).[30] ISEW increases with GDP only for a period, and then it stagnates and can begin to decline, despite continuing increases in GDP. Beyond this point, growth in GDP is outweighed by increased environmental and social costs, and growth can actually reduce welfare. A threshold is reached beyond which growth no longer improves the quality of life.[31]

The ISEW has continued with improvements under the new label of Genuine Progress Indicator (GPI). In the United States, the GPI suggests that Americans on average are no better off today than they were in 1970 even though GDP per capita has grown greatly during that period (fig. 4).[32]

It should be stressed that alternative measures like ISEW and GPI employ major methodological and data assumptions that are open to

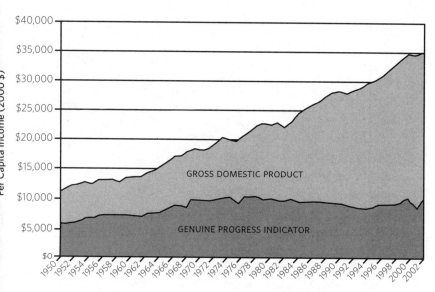

Figure 4. Trends in GPI per capita and GDP per capita in the United States
(Source: Venetoulis and Cobb, *The Genuine Progress Indicator*, 2004)

dispute, and to improvement. Yet they build on pioneering work of
the best economists, including James Tobin and William Nordhaus;
they are serious efforts, and they do tell us something.[33] In short, the
GPI tells us that since the early 1970s, growth's positive impact on the
welfare of Americans has been far, far less than that suggested by
GDP.

Another approach to index development is to stop trying to express conditions in dollars and cents and instead construct composite
indicators based on objective, measurable social and environmental
conditions. Again, there is an arbitrary element, but we can still learn
important things. Daniel Esty and his colleagues have developed an
index that evaluates nations' environmental performance. Among 133
countries Esty ranked, the United States was down the list at twenty-
eighth. New Zealand was number one, as all *Lord of the Rings* movie

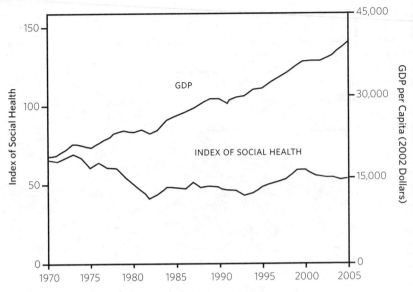

Figure 5. Trends in the Index of Social Health and GDP per capita in the United States, 1970–2005 (Source: Miringoff and Opdycke, *America's Social Health: Putting Social Issues Back on the Public Agenda*, 2007)

fans know.[34] America's great wealth is not being translated into stellar environmental performance.

Turning to social conditions, trend information in the United States was collected into a composite index by Marc and Marque-Luisa Miringoff for the years 1970–2005. Their index combined sixteen measures of social well-being, including data on infant mortality, high school dropouts, poverty, child abuse, teenage suicide, crime, average weekly wages, drug use, alcoholism, unemployment, and so on. The Miringoffs' Index of Social Health shows somewhat deteriorating social conditions despite huge growth in GDP per capita (fig. 5).[35]

Richard Estes at the University of Pennsylvania has developed a Weighted Index of Social Progress for 163 countries going back to 1970. It captures objective measures of both social and environmental conditions. Estes reports that the pace of social development in the United States has been "on hold" since 1980. The overall ranking puts the United States far down the list of the world's countries, tied with Poland and Slovenia for twenty-seventh place. America's affluence is thus not being translated into outstanding environmental *or* social performance.[36]

The third type of alternative welfare measures are those advocated by Diener, Seligman, and other psychologists such as Nobel Laureate Daniel Kahneman at Princeton. They are urging a system of regular national indicators of subjective well-being and ill-being. In "Beyond Money," Diener and Seligman conclude, "Economic indicators were extremely important in the early stages of economic development, when the fulfillment of basic needs was the main issue. As societies grow wealthy, however, differences in well-being are less frequently due to income, and are more frequently due to factors such as social relationships and enjoyment at work. . . . In order to facilitate the use of well-being outcomes in shaping policy, we propose creating a national well-being index that systematically assesses key well-being variables for representative samples of the population. Variables measured should include positive and negative emotions, engagement, purpose and meaning, optimism and trust, and the broad construct of life satisfaction."[37] The case for such an index is compelling given the findings reported here.

One measure I find intriguing is the Happy Planet Index developed by the New Economics Foundation in Britain. The Happy Planet Index (HPI) uses both objective and subjective data. It measures human well-being by multiplying a country's life satisfaction score times its life expectancy. And it then divides this by the country's ecological footprint (discussed in Chapter 1). It thus measures how well a country converts the earth's finite resources into the well-being of its citizens. The longer the people of a country lead happy lives with minimal environmental impact, the higher the score. The HPI is now available for most countries. The United States is near the bottom of the world list, below the nations of Western Europe, Asia, and Latin America. Costa Rica is near the top of the HPI; Zimbabwe is at the bottom.[38] Bhutan, by the way, has a very high HPI score—thirteenth in the world and second in Asia. Bhutan is serious about developing a system of objective and subjective measures that carry forward its commitment to Gross National Happiness as an alternative to Gross National Product.[39] It has been noted that the HPI is a good place to check in deciding where to vacation.

Well-Being Priorities

Taken together, these results suggest the need for a radical rethinking and reordering of priorities. Right now, the reigning policy orientation and mindset hold that the way to address social needs and achieve better, happier lives is to grow—to expand the economy. Productivity, wages, profits, the stock market, employment, and consumption must all go up. Growth is good. So good that it is worth all the costs. The Ruthless Economy can undermine families, jobs, communities, the environment, a sense of place and continuity, even mental health, because in the end, it is said, we'll somehow be better off. And we measure growth by calculating GDP at the national level and sales and profits at the company level. And we get what we measure.

But what the data and the analysts reviewed here are saying is that it is just not so. Aggregate economic growth—GDP growth—is no longer making us better off, and the data suggest that in many ways it is making us worse off, environmentally, socially, and psychologically. We are substituting GDP growth and more consumption for dealing with the real issues—for doing things that would truly make us better off. Those who preach the gospel of growth undoubtedly believe what they preach. But for those in government, business, and the media who call us to worship at the altar of GDP, this incessant demand for ever-more aggregate growth is largely self-serving, and therefore they rarely look beyond the quarterly economic reports to see what they are missing. The result is that society is being misled, literally.

There are huge lessons for public policy in the analyses reviewed here. It is time to chart a new course for the United States. Clearly, GDP growth has been a poor, sometimes counterproductive way to generate solutions to social problems. We need instead to address these problems directly and thoughtfully, with compassion and with generosity. A whole world of new and stronger policies is needed— measures that strengthen our families and our communities, address the breakdown of social connectedness, and favor rootedness over mobility; measures that guarantee good, well-paying jobs, increase employee satisfaction, minimize layoffs and job insecurity, and provide for adequate retirement incomes; measures that introduce more family-friendly policies at work, including flex time and easy access to good-quality child care; measures that give us more time for leisure, informal education, the arts, music, drama, sports, hobbies, volunteering, community work, outdoor recreation, exposure to nature, and play; measures that provide for universal health care and alleviate the devastating effects of mental illness; measures that give everyone a good education, for life as well as for productivity; measures that provide care and companionship for the chronically ill and incapacitated; measures that address prejudice, exclusion, and ostracism; measures that recognize our duties to the half of humanity who live in poverty, duties now reflected in the Millennium Development Goals; measures that regulate advertising, prohibit advertising to children, and provide free airtime for people to talk back; measures that sharply improve income distribution and tax luxury consumption, excessive work, and environmental damage and put the proceeds into our starved public sector and into strengthened income support and social programs for those at the bottom.[40]

These are among the things America should be striving to increase. These are directions that need to be emphasized in public investments and elsewhere. They are a big part of the alternative to the destructive path we are on, and as such, they should be seen as environmental measures as well as social ones. My hope is that all Americans who care about the environment will come to embrace these measures—these hallmarks of a caring community and a good society—as necessary to moving us beyond money to sustainability and community. Sustaining people, sustaining nature—it is one cause, inseparable.

7 Consumption: Living with Enough, Not Always More

Consumerism is a pillar of modern capitalism. It involves a powerful, socially sanctioned commitment to ever-increasing purchase of goods and services on the market. Consumerism in this sense is paired with materialism, an approach to life and social well-being that elevates the material conditions of life over the spiritual and social dimensions.

A consumer society is one in which consumerism and materialism are central aspects of the dominant culture, where goods and services are acquired not only to satisfy common needs but also to secure identity and meaning. A consumer society can also be thought of as one where consumer sovereignty reigns, but this expression is misleading. Consumption patterns are powerfully shaped by forces other than a preformed set of individual preferences—forces such as advertising, cultural norms, social pressures, and psychological associations.

Consumer spending has been a leading driver of environmental decline. It could hardly be otherwise. Private consumption expenditures in the United States, for example, are about 70 percent of Gross Domestic Product, and consumer spending is the principal driver of the economy and its expansion. In exploring "Why Americans Must Keep Spending," the *New York Times* summarized the dual reality of consumption: "Households perceive an endless stream of needs," it reports, "and besides the economy depends on it."[1]

When the *Financial Times* observes, "The stamina of shoppers will be crucial for global growth," the emphasis is on consumers serving the economy, not the other way around.[2] The stamina of the American consumer in particular is appreciated in business circles the world over. Despite stagnant real wages, American consumer spending has continued to rise, as has household debt. Consumer debt in the United States climbed from $525 billion in 1970 to $2,225 billion in 2004. Americans may be going into the red and losing their homes, but as of 2007 they were keeping the economy humming along.

Some of the new spending is optional, but the big increase has been driven by the rising costs of the basics—housing, health care, food, and education—up 11 percent between 2001 and 2004, when real wages went up zero.[3] This situation provides a vivid reminder that efforts to curb discretionary and extravagant consumption must be combined with equally powerful efforts to meet the real economic needs of low-income Americans who are "nickeled and dimed to death."

In the modern environmental era, there has been too little environmental focus on consumption. This situation is changing, but most mainstream environmentalists have not wanted to suggest that the positions they advocate would require serious lifestyle changes, and environmental economists have been of the view that focusing on consumption was a distraction. From their perspective, the way to deal with both consumption and growth generally is to "get the prices right." That will shift consumption sharply away from environmentally harmful products and services and toward those that are easy on the environment. The economists are undoubtedly correct about this shift, but as discussed previously, their approach, though valuable, is insufficient.

This reluctance to challenge consumption directly has been a big mistake, given the mounting environmental and social costs of American affluence. Since 1970 the size of a new house has gone up about 50 percent, electricity consumption per person rose more than 70 percent, and municipal solid wastes generated per person went up 33 percent. Eighty percent of all new homes since 1994 have been exurban, and more than half the lots have been ten acres or more. Yet even the larger homes and lots are too small to contain all the accumulating possessions. The self-storage industry didn't begin until the early 1970s but has grown so rapidly that its buildings now cover more than seventy square miles, an area the size of Manhattan and San Francisco combined.[4]

Not all consumption trends in the United States have been negative. Water withdrawals per capita have gone down somewhat from the peak in 1975. Oil use has grown at just about the same rate as population. But the use of water, oil, and other resources remains extraordinarily high and extravagantly wasteful. Despite the new environmental era that began in the 1970s, America's growing affluence and flawed politics have combined to degrade the environment steadily across a wide front.[5]

The good news is that the reluctance to face the consumption issue is beginning to change. The effort to challenge consumerism is occurring at two levels of seriousness, both traveling under the banner of "sustainable consumption," and both in need of much more support. First, there is the emergence of what I will call green consumerism. Green consumerism does not stress reducing consumption overall, but it does want consumers to buy green products and it wants corporations to produce them.

The second and more fundamental challenge argues that current levels of consumption are both environmentally and socially damaging and that better lives and a better environment can be found by reducing consumption. In the past, most environmental attention has been given to delinking output from resource inputs, thus "dematerializing" the economy with more efficient use of resources. Now attention is turning to delinking social welfare from output.

Buying Green

Green consumerism has considerable potential—but only if consumers have adequate information, are insistent and willing to pay a bit more, and have strong government backing. Individual consumers and households exercise real power in the marketplace, and they can shift their preferences with remarkable speed, as fashion fads and the unfortunate rise of sports utility vehicles make plain. A sustainable food campaign could help transform agribusiness and the fishing industry. A consumer commitment to sustainable energy could force changes in energy production while helping protect the climate, and a commitment to toxic-free home and workplace environments could push the chemical industry toward new, safer products.

Even at levels of consumption that are high and growing, consumers can at least insist on two green things. First, they can shift purchases to products and services where the making and the use of the product are carried out in a more environmentally friendly way. And second, they can insist that provisions be made for the recycling and reuse of consumer products. When the consumer is done with the television, fridge, range, or computer, the manufacturer should take it back and see that it is reused, recycled, or disposed of in an environmentally responsible manner. This system is called "extended producer responsibility," and it is more advanced in Europe than in the United States. These closely related goals can be promoted through both consumer campaigns and legislation.

There are hopeful signs in these areas, including increasing support from environmental and consumer groups. Ecolabeling and product biographies are a start.[6] Notable developments include the Forest Stewardship Council's efforts promoting the certification and labeling of wood products as having been produced in sustainably managed forests and the Marine Stewardship Council's program certifying sustainable fishery practices. The Green Building Council's certification of the environmental performance of new buildings is gaining wide acceptance and use. Consumers are beginning to vote green in the marketplace, and that is driving change. In Europe and Japan, the extended producer responsibility laws that require that the product be returned to the producer, "cradle to cradle," has the effect of encouraging the producer to think about reuse of components and materials from the outset.[7] The European Parliament has adopted laws obliging manufacturers to pay for the recycling of electrical appliances such as shavers, refrigerators, and computers. In 2002, Dell, responding to consumer pressure, broke new ground with a voluntary program of computer recycling. Now four states, including Washington and California, have e-waste recycling laws.

An important report prepared in 2003 for a group of U.S. foundations, the Environmental Grantmakers Association, encouraged investment in five areas to promote green consumption. Its recommendations are addressed to private foundations, but they need to be taken up by governments, environmental groups, and others.

- *Increase consumer awareness and choice.* "Grantmakers need to underwrite communications campaigns, school curricula, and other investments in cultural currency to raise awareness and engage citizens and consumers for this cause. Consumers also need to understand how to buy environmentally friendly products, and how to signal to producers that a growing constituency of green consumers is on the move."
- *Promote innovative policies.* "This grant-making approach involves increasing the political support for sustainability initiatives. . . . There are many new, innovative policies that can provide incentives, assess more accurate prices (tax policy) and eliminate subsidies of wasteful or unsustainable practices."
- *Accelerate demand for green products.* "Businesses, governments, universities and other institutions are major consumers of goods and services. This purchasing power is a fundamental lever for change because suppliers must listen to their customers. . . . When billions

of dollars—from governments, universities, and companies—are redirected to sustainably harvested and produced products, the market responds and producers change their practices."

- *Demand corporate accountability.* "One key lever for change focuses on emerging corporate campaigns and initiatives that spur companies to be accountable to their socially responsible investors and customers. Consumer campaigns, boycotts and shareholder advocacy are effective ways to influence corporate behavior, because corporations want to protect their brand value and company reputation."

- *Encourage sustainable business practices.* "NGOs, governments and others can help companies 'green' their products and services—through such means as mapping their environmental footprints; re-thinking resource extraction, use and recycling; sustainable re-design of products; and analysis of supply-chains and their environmental impacts."[8]

This is an excellent agenda for action and deserves extensive support far beyond the grant-making community.

There is evidence that American consumers are changing. The percentage of Americans who say they are willing to make significant sacrifices—meaning giving up time, money, or effort—for the environment has climbed from 45 percent in 2000 to 61 percent in 2006. Hybrid car sales climbed 267 percent from 2004 to 2005; consumers saved more than twelve billion dollars in utility bills by buying Energy Star qualified products; compact fluorescent light bulb sales climbed 22 percent between 2004 and 2005; and the market for organic foods doubled between 2001 and 2006, when it was a five-billion-dollar a year business.[9]

Despite these gains, "green" still remains a small share of market and consumer interest. More Americans express willingness to sacrifice for the environment, but 83 percent report that they do not take active steps to live green; 64 percent are unable to name a single green brand; and only 12 percent regularly buy green products.[10]

Green consumerism is more advanced in Europe, but even there, one acute observer and environmental leader, Jonathon Porritt, sees limits to green consumerism. He notes that the United Kingdom's Ethical Consumerism Report finds that only nine billion pounds were spent on ethical products and services in 2003, a small percentage of the market. Porritt believes that "consumer behaviour is the most problematic of all today's potential drivers for change." He notes that consumer campaigns have worked best when it's a question of stopping bad things from happening rather than one of making good things happen. "Far larger numbers of consumers can be mobilized for the former than for the latter."

"Beyond that minority of concerned consumers," Porritt observes, "many environmentally destructive activities and products seem to remain deeply attractive to the majority of consumers. At the glamorous end of 'conspicuous consumption,' which does so much to fuel mass consumer aspirations, environmentally friendly technologies are not going to find it easy to deliver the ever-expanding choice set involving speed, fashion, change, variety and luxury which the globalized affluent middle classes increasingly expect. At the more mundane level of mass consumption, there is, as yet, minimal consumer willingness to trade off the conventional consumer values of comfort, convenience and low prices against enhanced environmental or social performance. Even if it is technically possible to combine environmental sustainability and economic growth, it is by no means apparent that consumers are yet prepared to choose the kind of economic growth that this implies."[11]

In *Red Sky at Morning*, I admitted my personal attachment to consumption's benefits. I noted that "beyond meeting basic needs, consumption brings us pleasure and helps us to avoid pain and, worst of all, boredom and monotony. Consumption is stimulating, diverting, absorbing, defining, empowering, relaxing, fulfilling, educational, rewarding. If pressed, I would have to confess that I truly enjoy most of the things on which I spend money."[12]

There are a number of basic limits on the greening of consumption.

First, as stressed before in other contexts, the benefits of improved, greener consumption will tend to be overwhelmed by increased growth of consumption itself and even a strengthening of consumerism. John Lintott, in his article "Beyond the Economics of More," sees "establishment environmentalism" as a matter of making a profit from environmental problems through the introduction of new, cleaner products and the establishment of industries concerned with environmental cleanup. "Reducing consumption, much less the desire to consume, is emphatically not part of the programme," he notes. "The reason, or pretext, for this is the alleged reduction of welfare this would entail, and hence its political infeasibility. The result, although some specific improvements may occur, is overall a strengthening of the consumer society, and of the trend towards greater environmental damage."[13] Green has become fashionable in some circles, but even greened products and services have environmental costs and require throughput.

The second problem with the green consumerism approach is that it can suggest that *individual* consumer decisions are the problem when, in fact, there are bigger issues. Michael Maniates has described this result forcefully: "A proverbial fork in the road looms large for those who would seek to cement consumption into the environmental agenda. One path of easy walking leads to a future where 'consumption' in its environmentally undesirable forms . . . has found a place in environmental debates. Environmental groups will work hard to 'educate' the citizenry about the need to buy green and consume less [but] the . . . responsibility for and power over the environmental problems will remain obscure. Consumption, ironically, could continue to expand as the privatization of the environmental crisis encourages upwardly spiraling consumption, so long as this consumption is 'green.' This is the path of business-as-usual. The other road, a rocky one, winds towards a future where environmentally concerned citizens come to understand, by virtue of spirited debate and animated conversation, the 'consumption problem.' They would see that their individual consumption choices *are* environmentally important, but that their control over these choices is constrained, shaped, and framed by institutions and political forces that can be remade only through collective citizen action, as opposed to individual consumer behavior."[14]

A third problem with green consumerism is what has come to be called the "rebound effect." Rebound effects occur when the savings, say in utility bills from energy efficiency, get spent in ways that tend to undermine the environmental gain, say by keeping one's house warmer or buying more energy-consuming appliances.

Last, there is the tremendous potential for manipulating green consumers and perverting the process. "Greenwash" is already common in today's advertising and public relations campaigns. Paul Hawken and others have pointed out that many environmentally screened mutual funds don't look very different from the nonscreened ones.[15] If you aspire to green consumerism, beware: the professional marketers are coming at you, and they are exceedingly clever. You are already part of a targeted demographic segment. The Marketing Leadership Council's issue brief "Targeting the LOHAS Segment" states: "A large proportion of adults have sought an alternative lifestyle based on simple principles of health and ecological sustainability. This group, referred to as . . . the Lifestyle of Health and Sustainability (LOHAS) segment, places high value on holistic health, environmental preservation, social justice, personal fulfillment, and sustainable living. . . .

"Despite this potential, the segment proves very difficult to market to, as the majority distrust traditional media and exhibit suspicion towards companies they fear will exploit their values for profit. This issue brief explores the demographic and psychographic characteristics of the LOHAS segment, their communication preferences, and the tactics companies utilize to effectively market to this group."[16] Madison Avenue is hard at work figuring out how to sell more and more green products.[17]

With all this in mind, just what is the long-term potential for green products and green consumerism? It could be quite large if government drives it powerfully, and it will be quite small if government stays on the sidelines. For example, government measures advocated by economists—environmental and ecological—would make a huge difference, as would more direct prescription of new technology (as in energy efficiency requirements and renewable energy mandates) and requirements for extended producer responsibility. When there are clear, mandatory requirements, uniformly and fairly applied to all, green consumerism will be both more effective and more widely accepted. But the view from the mall is that it would be foolhardy to count on major change from the voluntary consumer choices of individuals.

Slimming Down

Beyond green consumerism, there is the second, more fundamental area for action—a focus on reducing consumption, not just on improving it. Personal consumption expenditures are two-thirds of GDP, so the environmental case for reducing overall consumption in the rich countries is roughly the same as the case for reducing throughput.

Consumption has costs and benefits. The full costs of consumption beyond market prices are hard to determine and hard to see, and they are typically underestimated. The benefits of consumption, by contrast, are immediate and tangible, and they are typically overestimated, thanks in part to an enormous and enormously sophisticated marketing apparatus. This asymmetry contributes to our overconsumption.

Yet there are diminishing returns to consumption as one moves from meeting basic needs to consumer satiation. And there are rising costs—environmental and social as well as economic. So consumption should proceed until the rising costs at the margin equal the declining benefits—then stop. Just as we can have uneconomic growth, we can have overconsumption—a realm where life as consumer is cutting too deeply into other aspects of life. In the United States we are beyond the point where we should have stopped—not every individual, of course, but in aggregate.

The good news, as discussed in Chapter 6, is that ample research demonstrates that market-based consumption is not tightly coupled with human welfare and life satisfaction. So the possibility of a double dividend presents itself. If today's hyperconsumption is damaging both psychologically and environmentally, we can improve our lives and our environment by doing with less of it. The bad news is that consumption remains a powerful aspiration, even addiction, of people everywhere. We are hooked on it. To explore reducing consumption and becoming less consumerist and materialistic, we had first better understand how and why these forces lock us so tightly in their grip.

The wellsprings of our consumerism are nicely summarized in an article by Tim Jackson in the *Journal of Industrial Ecology*'s 2005 issue on consumption.[18] The literature on this subject is vast, but Jackson identifies four main lines of analysis.

First, there are those who see consumer culture as a form of social pathology. Prominent names in this school include Thorsten Veblen, Eric Fromm, Ivan Illich, Tibor Scitovsky, Herbert Marcuse, and Ernest Becker. Jackson notes: "Fromm (1976) was alarmed at the alienation and passivity that pervaded modern life, and placed the blame squarely on an economic system predicated on increasing levels of consumption. Ivan Illich (1977) attacked the ideology that equates progress with affluence and needs with commodities. In attempting to discover why 'unprecedented and fast-moving prosperity had left its beneficiaries unsatisfied,' Scitovsky (1976) highlighted the addictive nature of consumer behavior and its failure to mirror the complexity of human motivation and experience."[19] Such views have found empirical support in the growing number of studies showing the failure of reported levels of well-being to match the growth in incomes.[20]

Tim Kasser and his colleagues find the origins of materialism in exposure to social models exalting consumption and material values and in experiences that increase personal insecurity. A vicious cycle is set in motion. Personal insecurities and social pressures lead people to become more attached to material goods ("I'm depressed; I think I'll go shopping"). Yet when they do, their basic psychological needs go further unmet, so more possessions are sought in compensation. Consumption increases, but personal well-being doesn't. Kasser believes that modern capitalism increases both personal insecurities and the social priority of consumption. Capitalism therefore furthers materialism. He also points out that those with high orientation to materialistic values are both more susceptible to advertising and less inclined to support environmental protection.[21]

"Materialism is toxic for happiness," Ed Diener believes.[22] Yet it is on the rise in America. In the American Council on Education survey of a quarter million entering college freshmen, the proportion saying they considered it very important to become "very well off financially" rose in the 1970s and 1980s from 40 percent to 74 percent, while the number saying they considered it very important to "develop a meaningful philosophy of life" declined sharply.[23]

In *Denial of Death* and other books, Ernest Becker sees all of us striving to deny our own death and to transcend our mortality—some of us through our children, our students, our books, or our religion, and most of us through amassing ever-more material goods, wealth, and power. In this view, attachment to consumption is another pathological pattern of managing the terror of our own death.[24] Percy Bysshe Shelley's "Ozymandias" addresses the futility of seeking to deny death through wealth and power:

> *I met a traveler from an antique land*
> *Who said: Two vast and trunkless legs of stone*
> *Stand in the desert. Near them, on the sand,*
> *Half sunk, a shattered visage lies, whose frown,*
> *And wrinkled lip, and sneer of cold command,*
> *Tell that its sculptor well those passions read*
> *Which yet survive, stamped on these lifeless things,*
> *The hand that mocked them, and the heart that fed;*
> *And on the pedestal these words appear:*

'My name is Ozymandias, king of kings:
Look on my works, ye Mighty, and despair!'
Nothing beside remains. Round the decay
Of that colossal wreck, boundless and bare
The lone and level sands stretch far away.

Psychologists see people as hardwired to find security by both "sticking out" and "fitting in." Consumption serves both goals; the culture of capitalism and commercialism emphasize both "sticking out" and "fitting in" through possessions and their display. This culture shifts the balance away from "fitting in" through belonging to a community, social empathy, and connecting with nature.

A second school of analysis sees consumer behavior as an evolutionary adaptation. Evolutionary psychologists believe that our attachment to consumption was essential to our ancestors' genetic success. In particular, they see us conditioned to strive to position ourselves in relation to the opposite sex and to establish our status, power, and social position. Visible consumption behaviors meet these strivings. "Positional goods" allow us to position ourselves better with respect to others, who may be competitors. Advertisers know this well, of course. Sex sells.

A third school is composed of those who stress, more prosaically, that a lot of consumer spending is in fact locked in by social convention and manipulation by business. They refer to this as "inconspicuous consumption" to contrast it with Veblen's "conspicuous consumption." The mortgage. Health care costs. Education. Energy prices. Here the pathology is located not in the individual but within the institutional architecture of everyday choice.

A fourth and final school stresses the symbolic role of consumer goods. Our possessions give us meaning and identity; they speak loudly, to ourselves and to others. Jackson notes, "The most important lesson from this huge body of work is rather clear: material commodities are important to us, not just for what they do, but for what they signify (about us and about our lives, loves, desires, successes, and failings) both to others and to ourselves. Material commodities are not just artifacts. Nor do they offer purely functional benefits. They derive their importance, in part at least, from their symbolic role in mediating and communicating personal, social, and cultural meaning."[25]

Here is how Clive Hamilton describes the marketing of margarine: "In the marketing of margarine, the product's contribution to the wellbeing of the consumer is wholly divorced from any of its physical properties. The actual usefulness of the product has become irrelevant so that the consumer does not buy something to spread on bread, but a concatenation of feelings associated with idealized family relationships. The complex, clever symbolism of the advertisement is designed to convince the viewer that a tub of vegetable fat that is identical to half a dozen other brands of other vegetable fat can give us something very special, something we really need. In a world of social disintegration, modern consumers have a powerful need for family warmth, and humans, just like Pavlov's dogs, make unconscious associations. Unmet emotional needs and unconscious association are the twin psychological pillars of the marketing society."[26] And now we know there was another problem as well. The margarine manufacturers neglected to test the health effects of the trans fat they were selling.

Challenging Consumption

All these factors—from all four schools—are at work. This is why our commitment to consumption is so powerful. Powerful, yes, but unassailable? The assault on the citadel of consumption will be difficult, to be sure, but not doomed by any means.

Consider the following. As the social pathology school stresses, today's consumption is not meeting social and psychological needs. If the opposite were the case, if extra consumption truly did improve life satisfaction and well-being, then we would be in big trouble on the environmental front. But that is not the case. And more and more people are sensing the shallowness of constantly shifting identities manufactured out of advertising pitches. People are searching for something more real and lasting and authentic. They may be looking in the wrong places sometimes, but they are looking. They are tired of the rat race and trying to keep up with the Joneses. There's a wonderful sketch in the book *Affluenza:* "You're watching TV, in the middle of a program, when the screen goes black for a moment. The scene cuts to a breaking news story. A large crowd is gathered outside an expensive home with some equally pricey cars parked out front. A well-dressed family of four stands on the stairs, looking grim. One of the children is holding a white flag. The reporter, in hushed tones, speaks into his microphone: 'We're here live at the home of the Joneses —Jerry and Janet Jones—the family we've all been trying to keep up with for years. Well, you can stop trying right now, because they have surrendered. Let's eavesdrop for a moment.' The shot changes, revealing a tired-looking Janet Jones, her husband's hand resting on her shoulder. Her voice cracks as she speaks: 'It's just not worth it. We never see each other anymore. We're working like dogs. We're always worried about our kids, and we have so much debt we won't be able to pay it off for years. We give up. So please, stop trying to keep up with us.' From the crowd someone yells, 'So what will you do now?' 'We're just going to try to live better on less,' Janet replies. 'So there you have it. The Joneses surrender,' says the reporter. 'And now for a commercial break.'"[27]

More and more people sense at some level that there's a great misdirection of life's energy. We have channeled our desires, our insecurities, our need to demonstrate our worth and our success, our wanting to fit in and to stand out increasingly into material things—into bigger homes, fancier cars, grander appliances, exotic vacations. But in the background we cannot help but know that "the best things in life are free" and that "money can't buy love." We know we're slighting the precious things that no market can provide—that truly make life worthwhile. We sense that we are hollowing out whole areas of life, individual and social autonomy, and of nature and that, if we don't wake up, we will soon lose the chance to return, to reclaim ourselves, our neglected society, our battered world, because if we are not more careful soon, there will be nothing left to reclaim, nothing left to return to.

We sense that possibility and we shudder. We reject it or, at least, we aspire in our best moments to transcend it. In one survey, 83 percent of Americans say society is not focused on the right priorities; 81 percent say America is too focused on shopping and spending; 88 percent say American society is too materialistic; 74 percent believe excessive materialism is causing harm to the environment.[28] If these numbers are anywhere near correct, there is a powerful base on which to build.

In the bookstores, the shelves are full of how to "take back your life," how to cope with "spiritual hunger in an age of plenty," how to overcome "nature deficit disorder," how to live more simply, more slowly.[29] On the Internet, dozens of Web sites can tell you how to live a more environmentally sound life; how to downshift; what we can do to save the planet and stop global warming.[30]

Tune in on Patagonia, one company I still believe in. "Don't buy this shirt unless you need it," Yvon Chouinard, the CEO, says. "In an economy of abundance, there is enough. Not too much. Not too little. Enough. Most important, there is enough time for the things that matter: relationships, delicious food, art, games and rest. Most of us in the United States live in what is thought to be abundance, with plenty all around us, but it is only an illusion, not the real thing. The economy we live in is marked by 'not enough.' . . . In the economy of abundance, wild salmon are given back rivers in which to run. Trees grow to their natural height. Water is clean. A sense of mystery and enchantment is restored to the world. We humans live within our means and, best of all, we have the time to enjoy what we have."[31]

Here's a revolutionary new product that is trying to make it in the marketplace: Nothing: "Guaranteed not to put you in debt . . . 100 percent nontoxic . . . sweatshop-free . . . zero waste . . . doesn't contribute to global warming ... family-friendly ... fun and creative!" The young women who were selling Nothing in shopping malls refused to leave and were arrested![32] Good for them. Humor is a powerful way to change the system—intelligent, irreverent debunking of pretension and artificiality.

Many people are now trying to fight back against consumerism and commercialization.[33] They invite us to a new style of life and a new struggle. They say to us: Confront consumption. Practice sufficiency. Work less. Reclaim your time—it's all you have. Turn off technology. Join No Shopping Day. Buy Nothing. No logo. Practice mindfulness, and playfulness. Live in the natural world; let nature nurture. Create social environments where overconsumption is viewed as silly, wasteful, ostentatious. Create commercial-free zones. Buy local. Eat slow food. Simplify your life. Shed possessions. Downshift. Create a local currency. Build consumer-owned cooperatives. Take back America.[34]

Sign Wendell Berry's "Manifesto":[35]

When they want you to buy something
they will call you. When they want you
to die for profit they will let you know.
So, friends, every day do something
that won't compute. Love the Lord.
Love the world. Work for nothing.
Take all that you have and be poor.
Love someone who does not deserve it.
Denounce the government and embrace
the flag. Hope to live in that free
republic for which it stands ...
Expect the end of the world. Laugh.
Laughter is immeasurable. Be joyful
though you have considered all the facts.
So long as women do not go cheap

for power, please women more than men,
Ask yourself: Will this satisfy
a woman satisfied to bear a child?. . .
As soon as the generals and the politicos
can predict the motions of your mind,
lose it. Leave it as a sign
to mark the false trail, the way
you didn't go. Be like the fox
who makes more tracks than necessary,
some in the wrong direction.
Practice resurrection.

8 The Corporation: Changing the Fundamental Dynamics

Corporations are the principal actors on capitalism's stage. They are capitalism's most important institutions, perhaps the most important institutions of our time. If capitalism is a growth machine, corporations are doing the growing. If growth is destroying the environment, then corporations are doing most of the destroying. In the United States, growth and capitalism have few critics. But corporations, in contrast, are fair game. They have been in the crosshairs of social critics for generations, and for good reason.

Of course, there is a positive side. Corporations also do tremendous good in the world. They made my TiVo, built my hybrid cars and the photovoltaic energy system I purchased, keep me more or less informed, do my banking, and make my blood pressure medication. I am grateful for all of these, and much more. And today there's a lot of genuine corporate greening going on. In 1970 I would not have recommended a career in business to students concerned about the environment; I do that often now. But still, in a world where the environment is in as much trouble as today's and corporations are such a dominant force, something major must be done.

Modern Corporation

The modern corporation is a relatively recent invention, dating from the mid-nineteenth century, but its rise has been rapid. Corporations comprise only about 20 percent of U.S. firms; most businesses are proprietorships and partnerships. But the corporate sector accounts for 85 percent of U.S. business revenue. On a global scale, the thousand largest corporations produce about 80 percent of the world's output. The corporation has several defining characteristics that dramatically affect its behavior:

1. *The separation of ownership from management.* Shareholders own the corporation, but it is managed by the company's directors and the officers they hire. Adam Smith warned long ago that the directors "being managers of other people's money . . . cannot well be expected [to] watch over it with the same anxious vigilance they would their own money."[1]

2. *Limited liability.* Unlike proprietorships and partnerships, corporate owners can lose their investment, but that's all. Corporate owners, the shareholders, are not personally liable to the firm's creditors. Limited liability is one reason corporations must be chartered by some government authority—states in the United States—and the chartering authority has the right to supervise and regulate the corporations, though this is rarely done in practice.

3. *Personhood.* The story of how corporations became people enjoying the protection of constitutional provisions intended to guarantee rights to individuals is fascinating. In the 1886 Supreme Court case of *Santa Clara County v. Southern Pacific Railroad,* the chief justice merely said from the bench during oral argument that Southern Pacific was entitled to the protection of the Fourteenth Amendment. This comment, irrelevant to the Court's disposition of the case, made it into the clerk's notes on the case, not the decision itself, and the rest is history.[2] And the history continues. In June 2007,

the Supreme Court struck down a provision of the 2002 McCain-Feingold campaign finance law, one restricting political ads, on the ground that it violated a corporation's First Amendment rights. And in February 2007, the Supreme Court threw out a jury verdict against a cigarette manufacturer on the grounds that the punitive damages award violated the company's constitutional right to due process.

4. *The "best interest of the corporation" principle.* This principle, a key part of corporate law, states that directors and managers have a duty to act in the best interest of the corporation, which has been interpreted as a duty to maximize the wealth of shareholders. This principle—shareholder primacy—is a huge obstacle to corporate evolution toward a more socially responsible institution. Joel Bakan, in his book *The Corporation,* explains the result: "A corporation can do good only to help itself do well, a profound limit on just how much good it can do. . . . The people who run corporations are, for the most part, good people, moral people. They are mothers and fathers, lovers and friends, and upstanding citizens in their communities. . . . Despite their personal qualities and ambitions . . . their duty as corporate executives is clear: they must always put their corporation's best interests first and not act out of concern for anyone or anything else (unless the expression of such concern can somehow be justified as advancing the corporation's own interests)."[3]

5. *Externalization of costs.* We explored earlier the corporation's powerful drive to maximize profits in a capitalist system, a drive we now see has legal backing as well, in the principle just discussed. Bakan describes how this drive makes the corporation into an externalizing machine: "Nothing in its legal makeup limits what it can do to others in pursuit of its selfish ends, and it is compelled to cause harm when the benefits of doing so outweigh the costs. Only pragmatic concern for its own interests and the laws of the land constrain the corporation's predatory instincts, and often that is not enough to stop it from destroying lives, damaging communities,

ıd endangering the planet as a whole. . . . All the bad things that
ppen to people and the environment as a result of corporations' relentless and legally compelled pursuit of self-interest are
. . . neatly categorized by economists as externalities—literally,
other people's problems. . . . [I]t is no exaggeration to say that the
corporation's built-in compulsion to externalize its costs is at the
root of many of the world's social and environmental ills. That
makes the corporation a profoundly dangerous institution."[4]

Another prominent feature of corporate capitalism is the limits it
places on democratic control. Everyone knows there is a tug of war
between corporate power and citizen power, and in the day-to-day
world of politics, it is generally not an equal match. First, business
leaders can exert great power directly in the political process—through
lobbying, campaign contributions, and in other ways. In 1968 there
were fewer than a thousand lobbyists in Washington. Today there
are about thirty-five thousand.[5] Corporate political action committee
(PAC) spending increased almost fifteenfold over the past three decades, from fifteen million dollars in 1974 to $222 million in 2005.[6] Of
the one hundred largest lobbying efforts in Washington between 1998
and 2004, ninety-two were corporations and their trade associations.
The U.S. Chamber of Commerce was the largest.[7]

Second, corporations can shape public opinion and the policy debate. Business owns the media, and even public broadcasting depends
significantly on corporate donations. Expensive issue advertising,
support for business-oriented think tanks, well-funded studies, and
policy entrepreneurs are all tools of the trade. Business leaders sit on
nonprofit boards and contribute to their fundraising efforts. Business
supports university and other research. Its influence can be strong or
subtle, but it is there.

Third, there is economic power. Labor can strike, but so can capital.
It can leave an area or refuse to invest there if the "business climate"
is not right. As long as regions and nations are hell-bent on attracting

investment and growth, and competing with each other, corporate interests will be served.

Last, there is an asymmetry in access to information. It is often in the corporation's interest to hold back information that the government and the public can obtain only with difficulty, if at all.

As a result, corporations are not merely the dominant economic actors, they are the dominant political actors as well. William Domhoff is now into the fifth edition of his well-known and provocative book *Who Rules America?* His answer to his title's question: the corporate community. His analysis shows how "the owners and top-level managers in large companies work together to maintain themselves as the core of the dominant power group. . . . [Despite] highly visible policy conflicts among rival corporate leaders . . . the corporate community is cohesive on the policy issues that affect its general welfare, which is often at stake when political challenges are made by organized workers, liberals, or strong environmentalists."

In Domhoff's view, "The corporate community's ability to transform its economic power into policy influence and political access, along with its capacity to enter into a coalition with middle-class social and religious conservatives, makes it the most important influence on the federal government." He notes that corporate leaders are regularly appointed to top positions in the executive branch and that the policy recommendations of corporate experts are listened to carefully in Congress. "This combination of economic power, policy expertise, and continuing political success makes the corporate owners and executives a dominant class, not in the sense of complete and absolute power, but in the sense that they have the power to shape the economic and political frameworks within which other groups and classes must operate."[8]

All of this was on display in June 2007 as the U.S. Senate took up its sprawling energy bill. The *New York Times* reported that the proposed legislation "kicked off an epic lobbying war by huge industries, some of them in conflict with one another; car companies, oil companies, electric utilities, coal producers and corn farmers, to name a few."[9] In

d, the Senate passed a classic compromise: improved auto fuel
ny standards were adopted but, thanks in part to opposition from
electric utilities, a national renewable energy goal was not.

Corporations and Globalization

Many corporations have grown to become giants, and, increasingly,
they bestride the narrow world. Of the hundred largest economies in
the world, fifty-three are corporations. Exxon alone is larger than more
than 180 nations. In 1970 there were seven thousand multinationals;
by 2007 there were at least sixty-three thousand. These sixty-three
thousand companies directly employ about ninety million people and
contribute a quarter of gross world product. They are driving the processes of economic globalization. In 1975 world trade was less than a
trillion dollars; by 2000 it was over five trillion dollars. The world stock
of foreign direct investment in 1975 was two hundred billion dollars;
by 2005 it was over six trillion dollars. In 2006, the thirty members of
the OECD made foreign direct investments of more than a trillion
dollars. Cross-border mergers and acquisitions have also skyrocketed,
reaching over one trillion dollars in 2000. So the global corporation
has flown the national coop and has replaced the transnational corporation, just as the global economy has replaced a network of trading
national economies. And of course, these multinationals have a huge
impact on the global environment, generating, for example, half the
gases responsible for global warming. They also control half of the
world's oil, gas, and coal mining and refining.[10] Globalization is indeed
occurring, but it is the globalization of market failure.

Economic globalization and the rise of the global corporation have
both increased corporate power and weakened the capacity to control
it. One analysis concluded that "with their vast resources and technical
capabilities and without the responsibilities of nationhood, the corporation can move quickly when challenge or opportunity strikes. When
unfettered by national or international laws, ecological understanding,

or social responsibility, this freedom can lead to enormously destructive acts. At the same time, their agility and access to capital and resources allow them to innovate, produce goods and services, and influence the world on a scale and at a speed the world has never seen before."[11]

Much of the recent criticism of corporations has been directed at the multinationals and the globalization process.[12] John Cavanagh, Jerry Mander, and the other authors of *Alternatives to Economic Globalization: A Better World Is Possible* present a sustained critique of the ascendancy of what they call the "corporate globalists."[13] These authors, brought together by the International Forum on Globalization, are the intellectual leaders of what is often called the antiglobalization movement. Agree with them or disagree, they offer a coherent perspective on what is wrong, why the environment is under such threat, and what should be done about it. The antiglobalization movement is thought by some to be confused, self-contradictory, and even anarchistic. My reading of their 2002 book and other writings suggests that they are none of these things. Although I agree with them on many points and disagree on others, I think what they actually are is idealistic, and that's not such a bad thing.

Their assault is aimed squarely at the dominant structures of the modern economy and polity: "Since World War II, the driving forces behind economic globalization have been several hundred global corporations and banks that have increasingly woven webs of production, consumption, finance, and culture across borders. . . .

"These corporations have been aided by global bureaucracies that have emerged over the last half-century, with the overall result being a concentration of economic and political power that is increasingly unaccountable to governments, people, or the planet. . . .

"Together these instruments are bringing about the most fundamental redesign of the planet's social, economic, and political arrangements since the Industrial Revolution. They are engineering a power shift of stunning proportions, moving real economic and political power away from national, state, and local governments and communities toward

:edented centralization of power for global corporations, bank-
l global bureaucracies. . . .

ı ne first tenet of the globalization design is to give primary importance to the achievement of ever-more rapid, never-ending corporate economic growth—hypergrowth—fueled by the constant search
for access to new resources, new and cheaper labor sources, and new
markets . . . To achieve hypergrowth, the emphasis is on the ideological heart of the model—free trade—accompanied by deregulation of
corporate activity. The idea is to remove as many impediments as possible to expanded corporate activity."[14]

Environmental deterioration is placed unambiguously at the doorstep of these forces: "Economic globalization is intrinsically harmful
to the environment because it is based on ever-increasing consumption, exploitation of resources, and waste disposal problems. One of its
primary features, export-oriented production, is especially damaging
because it is responsible for increasing global transport activity . . .
while requiring very costly and ecologically damaging new infrastructures such as ports, airports, dams, canals, and so on."

Placing themselves in the camp of the social greens, they argue
that not much can be done about negative environmental trends ab-
sent far-reaching changes in the way economic and political power is
distributed in modern society. The antiglobalization critique, then, is
fundamentally political: "The current and future well-being of humanity depends on transforming the relationships of power within and
between societies toward more democratic and mutually accountable
modes of managing human affairs."[15]

In response they offer a different vision: "The corporate globalists
who meet in posh gatherings to chart the course of corporate globalization in the name of private profits, and the citizen movements that organize to thwart them in the name of democracy, are separated by deep
differences in values, worldview, and definitions of progress. At times
it seems that they must be living in wholly different worlds—which,
in fact, in many respects they are. . . .

"Citizen movements see a very different reality. Focused on people and the environment, they see the world in a crisis of such magnitude that it threatens the fabric of civilization and the survival of the species—a world of rapidly growing inequality, erosion of relationships of trust and caring, and failing planetary life support systems. Where corporate globalists see the spread of democracy and vibrant market economies, citizen movements see the power to govern shifting away from people and communities to financial speculators and global corporations replacing democracies of people with democracies of money, replacing self-organizing markets with centrally planned corporate economies, and replacing diverse cultures with cultures of greed and materialism."[16]

To address these concerns, the authors of *Alternatives to Economic Globalization* and similar critics are clear that the corporation must be the main object of transformative change: "At the dawn of the twenty-first century, the global corporation stands as the dominant institutional force at the center of human activity and the planet itself. . . . We must dramatically change the publicly traded, limited liability global corporation, just as previous generations set out to eliminate or control the monarchy."[17]

This is a powerful critique of corporate capitalism as we know it. Tone it down, and it is still a powerful critique. And there are many others.[18] What, then, should be done to tame the corporation—to make it an instrument of environmental protection rather than a force for environmental destruction? And what are the prospects for such measures, given the power relationships just reviewed?

Action can be envisioned at three levels—three arenas of change, each more far-reaching than the former. First, steps can be taken to encourage voluntary corporate initiatives. Second, corporate accountability can be promoted through regulation and other governmental controls at both national and international levels. And, third, the nature of the corporation itself can be changed.

rate Greening

On the first, voluntary initiatives front, corporations are clearly taking steps to green their operations and products in ways not required by government. Some would say the level of activity is unprecedented, and environmental groups deserve much credit for moving these changes forward. The business press today is crammed with stories:

Business Week, "Green is Good for Business" (May 8, 2006)
Financial Times, "Companies See the Gains of Going Green" (October 2, 2006)
New York Times, "Now Looking Green Is Looking Good" (December 28, 2006)

The green trend is driven by many factors, but prominent among them is a clear-eyed focus on the bottom line. There are more green consumers today, and green is good for corporate image and brand-name products. The *Financial Times* reports, "A string of household names—including General Electric, Wal-Mart, and Unilever—have been lining up to show off their green credentials in an effort to woo customers, at least at the high end of the market. . . . The UK's Institute of Grocery Distribution reports that sales of 'ethical' products are increasing by 7.5 percent a year, compared with 4.2 percent for conventional products."[19] *Business Week* in 2007 carried a major story on companies that are "doing well by doing good."[20]

Demand is also growing for new, solution-oriented technologies and products. GE's wind machine business is booming, as is its overall "Ecomagination" line.[21] Daniel Esty and Andrew Winston's 2007 book *Green to Gold* analyzes these developments in detail. They report, "In a world of constrained natural resources and pollution pressures, the business case for environmental stewardship grows stronger every day. Pressures on companies now come not only from screaming eco-radicals, but also from traditional 'white-shoe' bankers and others asking tough-minded questions about environmental risk and liability.

Those who offer solutions to society's environmental problems both mute their potential critics and find expanding markets."[22] Companies that successfully anticipate emerging new directions in public policy and regulatory risk will be ahead of the competition, securing early market share for new products and services and building the institutional know-how required in a changed setting.

As Esty and Winston indicate, keeping critics and government regulators at bay is a factor, too. Corporate worry here is not misplaced. A recent survey of public attitudes in twenty countries found that huge majorities in every country, including the United States, favored tougher regulation to protect the environment. The average level of support for more regulation in the twenty countries was 75 percent. Two-thirds of Americans report that they would like to see major corporations have less influence in the nation, and the number of Americans who see big business as the "biggest threat to the future of this country" has reached the highest point (38 percent) in forty-eight years of polling, although even more Americans fear big government.[23]

Another factor driving change is the emergence of what has been called the "new capitalists." In 1970, a relatively modest number of wealthy individuals controlled corporations. Today, a variety of funds—pension funds, mutual funds, and so on—own more than half of all U.S. stock, up from 19 percent in 1970. These institutional investors seek top returns to be sure, but they have also been increasingly assertive on responsible management and sustainability issues.[24]

Reflecting the trend in business toward embracing the "sustainable enterprise" concept, with its triple bottom line of economy, environment, and society, "corporate social responsibility" has become a catchphrase and CSR an established acronym.[25] CSR can refer to both not-for-profit and for-profit corporate initiatives, provided the for-profit initiatives seem to have a strong social or environmental component. Counted here are the rapidly mounting number of voluntary

f conduct and product certification schemes operating at both
ɔnal and international levels: the Global Reporting Initiative's
ɡ ⸺ɩɩnes for corporate reporting on sustainability; the LEED certification of new green buildings; the Forest Stewardship Council and the
Marine Stewardship Council programs for certifying and ecolabeling
forest and fish products; the environmental performance principles
adopted by major banks; the U.N. Global Compact aimed at promoting
good corporate behavior on labor, environmental, and human rights
issues; the ISO 14000 program; and numerous others. Environmental
groups, other nongovernmental organizations and engaged academics
have all pressed these issues vigorously.

The threat of global warming is a key driving force important in all
these processes of corporate greening and accounts for a large share of
the change occurring. Corporations see the handwriting on the wall,
foretelling a future of tough national and international regulation and
a wave of new products to meet them. Companies are already feeling
climate-inspired pressures from their investors, bankers, and insurers,
and they know that legal actions to establish liability for climate change
damages have begun. And at least some corporate leaders are aware
that a world of unchecked climate change will be very disruptive for
their operations.[26]

Corporate greening is thus driven by green consumerism; by lenders, investors, and insurers worried about risks both environmental and
financial; by the blame and shame campaigns of NGOs; by existing
government regulation and the prospect of future regulation at home
and abroad; by sales opportunities opened up by new green products
and technology; and by the general need to improve corporate standing
as good citizens. In the old days, the model was simple: government
regulated, corporations complied. Now there are multiple stakeholder
pressures on the corporation. They open up a range of better outcomes beyond simple compliance, including fewer problems requiring
regulation, new products for sustainability markets, and better corporate behavior in policy and political arenas.

Encouraging change is thus occurring in the corporate sector today, but how reliable and extensive will these changes be? Two studies of voluntary initiatives and CSR raise doubts regarding their potential. Berkeley business professor David Vogel reaches the following conclusions in his book *The Market for Virtue:* "There are important limits to the market for virtue. The main constraint on the market's ability to increase the supply of corporate virtue is the market itself. There is a business case for CSR, but it is much less important or influential than many proponents . . . believe. CSR is best understood as a niche rather than a generic strategy: it makes business sense for some firms in some areas under some circumstances. . . .

"CSR reflects both the strengths and the shortcomings of market capitalism. On the one hand, it promotes social and environmental innovation by business, prompting many firms to adopt new policies, strategies, and products, many of which create social benefits and some of which even boost profits by reducing costs, creating new markets, or improving employee morale. . . .

"On the other hand, precisely because CSR is voluntary and market-driven, companies will engage in CSR only to the extent that it makes business sense for them to do so. [It] has proven capable of forcing *some* companies to internalize *some* of the negative externalities associated with *some* of their economic activities. But CSR can reduce only some market failures. It often cannot effectively address the opportunistic behaviors such as free riding that can undermine the effectiveness of private or self-regulation. Unlike government regulation, it cannot force companies to make unprofitable but socially beneficial decisions. In most cases, CSR only makes business sense if the costs of more virtuous behavior remain modest."[27]

In their recent book *Reality Check,* economists at Resources for the Future assess the results of a long series of voluntary environmental programs in the United States, Europe, and Japan. They conclude that "voluntary programs can affect behavior and offer environmental gains but in a limited way. . . . [N]one of the case study authors found

nvincing evidence of dramatic environmental improvements.
re, we find it hard to argue for voluntary programs where there
...clear desire for major change in behavior."[28]

Reliably Green

It would thus be a mistake to count too heavily on CSR and voluntary
initiatives, as both Vogel and the RFF economists have warned, and
they are not alone in their skepticism.[29] Much depends on the continued
strengthening of the drivers of corporate greening just mentioned.
The big gorilla in the room—the main force driving corporate greening in the past and in the future—is government action, actual and
anticipated, domestic and foreign.[30] To change corporate dynamics,
government action is needed across a wide front. First of all, there
are the governmental actions urged in previous chapters. Their main
target, of course, is the corporation. A reliably green company is one
that is required to be green by law. Even the best-intentioned man-
ager will avoid actions that are desirable but costly when faced by a
competitor lacking a conscience. These environmental regulations and
other controls must be promoted at the international level as well as
at the national and state levels. My earlier book *Red Sky at Morning*
contains a set of prescriptions on what the international community
needs to do to make the world of environmental treaties and protocols
succeed, which they are not now doing for the most part. One initiative
urged there, the creation of a World Environment Organization, got a
boost recently when France and forty other countries championed the
concept, but the United States promptly objected.

The arena of needed government action also includes an array of
worthwhile measures that are not strictly environmental:

1. *Revoke corporate charters.* Most corporate law statutes contain provisions allowing government to revoke charters if the corporation
   has grossly violated the public interest. Making this threat alive and

real could have very salutary effects. One way to do this would be to require periodic public reviews and rechartering.

2. *Exclude or expel unwanted corporations.* This tactic has been used extensively in India, for example, by the farmers and consumers who organized the "Monsanto: Quit India" campaign. In the United States there have been campaigns to block Wal-Mart and other giant retailers from various sites.

3. *Roll back limited liability.* Corporate directors and top managers should be personally liable for gross negligence and other major failings. Eventually, personal liability should extend to shareholders in certain cases. That would make buying a company's stock a rather more serious affair and would make management far more circumspect on environmental, labor, and human rights issues.

4. *Eliminate corporate personhood.* There is a nascent movement in the United States to do just that. Spurred by local corporate abuses and corporate claims of due process and First Amendment rights, Porter Township, Pennsylvania, and Arcata, California, both passed (largely symbolic) measures aimed at stripping corporations of the legal fiction of personhood and thus their ability to claim constitutional rights intended for people. Short of outright reversal of a long string of Supreme Court decisions, modification of Supreme Court rulings protecting corporate speech and advertising are overdue.

5. *Get corporations out of politics.* This can best be done by moving to publicly financed elections.[31] The "clean elections" cause is gathering some support. A further step would be to impose tighter restrictions on conflicts of interest by limiting the revolving door between government and corporations and by attending with great care to the process of confirming proposed political appointees.

6. *Reform corporate lobbying.* Environmental economist Robert Repetto has urged some important initial steps in this direction. "Should corporate management lobby on public policy issues with broad societal implications, using shareholders' money, with no oversight by shareholders' representatives on the board of directors?"

Repetto asks rhetorically in his paper. Repetto notes, "If lobbying on public policy issues is an intrinsic and important aspect of a company's business, then boards of directors, as part of their fiduciary 'duty of care,' have a responsibility to be informed about the company's lobbying activities and positions and to oversee them." He argues in favor of oversight of corporate policy positions and lobbying expenditures by a committee of the corporate board of directors, the majority of whom would be "outside directors with a broad view of the economy and political horizon."[32]

Such ideas are beginning to catch on. In 2006, thirty shareholder resolutions on corporate lobbying were offered; they received average support of 21 percent at annual meetings, double the previous year's support. Further issues that need addressing are corporations that say one thing and lobby for another, sometimes letting trade associations do the dirty work.

The Corporation of the Future

These six points comprise a far-reaching agenda. Others could be added, such as mandating the Securities and Exchange Commission to require a truly sophisticated array of financial and environmental disclosures.[33] Some of the initiatives, like imposing personal liability in certain cases and abolishing corporate personhood, are sufficiently transformative that they could be considered in the third and final category of actions—those that seek to change the nature of the corporation itself. But the major change in the nature of the corporation that is needed now, and that will be essential in the future, is to change the legal mandate that requires the corporation strictly to pursue its own self-interest and to give primacy to maximizing shareholder wealth. The corporation must be, in Bakan's words, "reconstituted to serve, promote, and be accountable to broader domains of society than just themselves and their shareholders."[34]

Allen White of the Tellus Institute believes, correctly I think, that "shareholder primacy is the single greatest obstacle to corporate evolution toward a more equitable, humane and socially beneficial institution." He argues for "fundamental changes to the current privilege accorded capital providers and to the legal, regulatory, and financial market structures that enable such privilege to persist. The 'gladiatorial culture' that deifies competitive advantage, efficiency and, above all, shareholder returns is not a corporate culture that comports with [a sustainable economy and a humane society]. The behavior it induces and societal consequences it engenders lay at the heart of the low esteem and high distrust in which the public holds the business community."[35]

The corporation of the future, as envisioned by White and others, must be built around the idea that the wealth produced by the corporation is the joint product of all resource providers—shareholders, employees, unions, future generations, government, customers, communities, and suppliers. Each provides resources for wealth creation over time, and each has a right to expect returns for its contribution: "Framing the corporation as the beneficiary of multiple resource providers opens up horizons for transformation that shareholder primacy stifles. In this [new] framework, the diverse parties that contribute their resources to create goods and services are not simply secondary and dispensable contributors to the production process. Instead, they hold rightful claims to both the surplus generated by the firm as well as to accountability from its board and management. They are, in short, equals, not subordinates to capital providers. This reinterpretation of the nature of the corporation has profound implications for governance, charters and securities laws, as well as the means of corporate wealth distribution.

"Whereas scale, growth and profit-maximization were previously viewed as intrinsic goods and core goals of the corporation, the new corporation marches to a whole different set of principles; namely, those serving the public interest, sustainability, equity, participation and respect for the rights of human beings. Corporate forms [should include] a rich pluralism conforming to global norms that [would] govern business conduct regardless of place, sector or scale." White envisions "a multi-tiered structure in the form of global, regional and local agents, norms, and powers that enables the exercise of citizen rights and democratic control over the corporation. The public purpose of the corporation [should ascend] to preeminence, supported by policies, procedures and instruments that bring democratic process to the forefront of corporate governance."[36]

Is such a future realistic? Certainly, right now, the changes White and others envision are mostly beyond the reach of U.S. politics. But in the future, dissatisfaction with corporations and globalization, already high, is likely to grow. That dissatisfaction could even extend to an increasing number of corporate leaders who feel as trapped and frustrated and worried about the future as many of the rest of us.

It is sometimes said that there are no good answers to today's challenges. The rich array of options for transformative change presented here and in other chapters indicates otherwise. With the distrust of corporations and the stirrings already visible, motivation for change is building. What we need are opportunities for transformative change. It seems highly likely that such opportunities will come along, given our crisis-prone world and the dynamics that now govern corporate behavior. And of course, that day can be hastened by citizen demand.

9 Capitalism's Core: Advancing beyond Today's Capitalism

Today's capitalism seems an impregnable citadel. Marx's socialism, its tragic offspring, communist totalitarianism, and even the mild evolutionary version of socialism of Eduard Bernstein and others are today in either full defeat or fast retreat. But the challenge to capitalism has a long and rich history, and it is unlikely that we are at the end of history. As Gar Alperovitz puts it in *America beyond Capitalism*, "Fundamental change—indeed, radical systemic change—is as common as grass in world history."[1] As it has in the past, capitalism will evolve, and it may evolve into a new species altogether.

Robert Heilbroner in *The Nature and Logic of Capitalism* reminds us that many of the great economists have long envisioned capitalism's evolution into something else. "Its span of life cannot be precisely predicted, but its eventual demise or supersession by another social order is universally foreseen. Adam Smith describes the system as reaching a plateau, when the accumulation of riches will be 'complete,' bringing about a deep and lengthy decline. John Stuart Mill expects the momentary arrival of a 'stationary state,' when accumulation will cease and capitalism will become the staging ground for a kind of associationalist socialism. Marx anticipates a sequence of worsening crises produced by the internal contradictions of accumulation—each crisis clearing away the obstacles of the moment but hastening the day when the system will no longer be able to manage its self-generated tensions. Keynes thought the future would require a 'somewhat comprehensive socialization of investment'; Schumpeter thought it would evolve into managerial socialism."[2]

Looking beyond Today

A number of contemporary scholars also see an eventual end to capitalism, or at least capitalism as we know it. It is instructive to understand why they see that day coming. Samuel Bowles and his colleagues in *Understanding Capitalism* present a mild version of this thesis. They write that "changes in science and technology are likely either to bring about fundamental changes in the institutions of capitalism . . . or to lead to the emergence of a qualitatively different economic system. . . . Over the coming decades changes in technology, especially the information revolution, and the accelerating impact of humans on our natural environment, especially global warming, will confront us with challenges utterly without precedent in human history."[3]

But Bowles cautions that needed changes in the system are not inevitable: "Today there are many people throughout the world who have done very well within capitalism as we know it. They appear to be reluctant to risk losing their privileged status by experimenting with new institutional structures that might be more suitable for dealing with the challenges of the information economy, controlling the encroachment of humans on our natural environment, and closing the gaps between rich and poor within and among nations. If established elites resist such institutional change, the next stop in our historical journey could well be a world plagued by economic irrationality, buffeted by environmental crisis, and divided into increasingly hostile camps of haves and have-nots."[4]

Immanuel Wallerstein, the father of World System Analysis, believes that modern capitalism is driving the world to the point where there is a choice: either costly environmental measures that "could well serve as the coup de grace to the viability of the capitalist world economy" or "various ecological catastrophes" brought on by the ceaseless accumulation of capital and growth inherent in capitalism. "The political economy of the current situation is that historical capitalism is in fact in crisis precisely because it cannot find reasonable solutions to its current dilemmas, of which the inability to contain ecological destruction is a major one, if not the only one." Wallerstein believes that "the present historical system is in fact in terminal crisis. The issue before us is what will replace it. This is the central political debate of the next 25–50 years. The issue of ecological degradation, but not of course only this issue, is a central locus of this debate."[5]

Political theorist John Dryzek's analysis is similar. Like Bowles and Wallerstein, he sees environmental problems as a key driver of change: "Ecological problems are sufficiently widespread and serious to constitute an acid test for all actual and proposed political and economic arrangements and for all processes of institutional reconstruction, be they incremental or revolutionary." Dryzek believes that the combination of capitalism, interest group politics, and the bureaucratic state will prove "thoroughly inept when it comes to ecology" and "that any redeeming features are to be found only in the possibilities that they open up for their own transformation."[6]

Dryzek sees a new system as necessary, but he sounds a note of caution: "Historically, the outcomes of revolutions have generally borne little relation to the intentions of revolutionaries. . . . Rather than speculate about grandiose possibilities for sweeping structural transformation, it seems more sensible to locate the real possibilities for change at vulnerable locations in the political economy. Such possibilities exist either where there is significant opposition to dominant structures and their imperatives, or where contradiction and confusion in dominant structures renders them vulnerable to action on behalf of some alternative institutional order."[7] He sees significant opposition coming from a wide variety of issues and oppressed groups and believes that the confrontation of these groups against the state and corporate power can be a major force for change in capitalism.

In *A Theory of Global Capitalism*, William Robinson also sees global capitalism as headed for crisis: "In my view, the crisis that beset global capitalism at the turn of the [twenty-first] century involved four interrelated aspects: (1) overproduction or underconsumption, or what alternatively is known as overaccumulation; (2) global social polarization; (3) the crisis of state legitimacy and political authority; (4) the crisis of sustainability. The last of these . . . raises profound theoretical, historical, and practical issues for humanity."[8]

Robinson contends that fundamental change becomes possible when an organic crisis occurs. "An organic crisis is one in which the system faces both a structural (objective) crisis and a crisis of legitimacy or hegemony (subjective). An organic crisis [itself] is not enough to bring about fundamental, progressive change in a social order; indeed, in the past it has led to social breakdown, authoritarianism, and fascism. A [positive] outcome to an organic crisis also requires that there be a viable alternative that is in hegemonic ascendance, that is, an alternative to the existing order that is viable and that is seen as viable and preferable by a majority of society." Robinson concludes that "global capitalism was not experiencing an organic crisis in the early twenty-first century" but that "the prospect for such a crisis to develop was more palpably on the horizon at the turn of the century than at any time since perhaps 1968."[9]

Like many others, Robinson sees the possibility of change arising from the growing strength of social and resistance movements around the world. Our mainstream media in the United States give scant coverage to these movements and their issues; most Americans are unaware of what's going on.[10] Participants in what might be called the "global justice movement" gather annually now, usually in Porto Alegre, Brazil, at the World Social Forum, an event intended to be the alternative to the World Economic Forum in Davos, Switzerland. To give a flavor of their positions, here are excerpts from their final statements in 2001 and 2002: "We are women and men, farmers, workers, unemployed, professionals, students, blacks and indigenous peoples, coming from the South and from the North, committed to struggle for peoples' rights, freedom, security, employment and education. We are fighting against the hegemony of finance, the destruction of our cultures, the monopolization of knowledge, mass media, and communications, the degradation of nature, and the destruction of the quality of life by multinational corporations and antidemocratic policies. Participative democratic experiences—like that of Porto Alegre—show us that a concrete alternative is possible. We reaffirm the supremacy of human, ecological and social rights over the demands of finance and investors."

"In the face of continuing deterioration in the living conditions of people, we, social movements from all around the world, have come together in the tens of thousands at the second World Social Forum in Porto Alegre. We are here in spite of the attempts to break our solidarity. We come together again to continue our struggles against neoliberalism and war, to confirm the agreements of the last Forum and to reaffirm that another world is possible.

"We are a global solidarity movement, united in our determination to fight against the concentration of wealth, the proliferation of poverty and inequalities, and the destruction of our earth. We are living and constructing alternative systems, and using creative ways to promote them. We are building a large alliance from our struggles and resistance against a system based on sexism, racism and violence, which privileges the interests of capital and patriarchy over the needs and aspirations of people.

"The system produces a daily drama of women, children, and the elderly dying because of hunger, lack of health care and preventable diseases. Families are forced to leave their homes because of wars, the impact of 'big development,' landlessness and environmental disasters, unemployment, attacks on public services and the destruction of social solidarity. Both in the South and in the North, vibrant struggles and resistance to uphold the dignity of life are flourishing."[11]

I have never been to Porto Alegre, but a number of my students have, and I have talked with them. As best I can tell, they are seriously committed to their slogan: "a better world is possible." They are truly out to change the world.

Alperovitz believes America has entered a period of "systemic crisis—an era of history in which the political-economic system must slowly lose legitimacy because the realities it produces contradict the values it proclaims." He acknowledges that this situation is still difficult for most people to appreciate, but he reviews an extraordinary range of new ideas and initiatives that are germinating "just below the surface level of media attention" and that begin to offer "a radically different system-wide political-economic model." Among the forces driving this system crisis, in Alperovitz's view, is the "overriding issue of ecological sustainability."[12]

Significantly, what these authors are saying is that capitalism's inability to sustain the environment is one of the biggest threats to its future, perhaps the biggest threat. They all see current environmental challenges as contributing to crises that delegitimize an existing order that is unable to cope. None of them think the outcome of such crisis is predetermined. Indeed, the eventual outcome is ground for contestation and struggle. But the struggle offers promise, says Wallerstein, "which is the most we can ever expect."[13]

Of course, the big problem facing all discussions of alternatives to capitalism is that there do not seem to be any alternatives. Throughout the Cold War, the alternative was state socialism or communism, but it is fading fast around the globe. Asked about alternatives to capitalism today, most people draw a blank. Some would add, for good reason. It is therefore worth noting the diversity of economic systems both within capitalism and within socialism, a point stressed by the Tellus Institute.[14] Within capitalism, a variety of national economic systems exist, where the key variable is the degree of engagement of government in determining economic priorities and social conditions. At one end of the spectrum, the so-called Anglo-American model approximates laissez-faire. Here, the market tends to dominate the state. In Scandinavia and elsewhere on the Continent, one finds varieties of social democratic capitalism.[15] Social democratic nations exert greater public control over capital investment and have created more comprehensive social programs including higher minimum wages and unemployment compensation, greater protections against layoffs, free or near-free health care and schooling, and so on. In these countries the market and the state are seen as partners. In Japan and elsewhere in Asia, there are systems that can be described as state capitalism, where there is heavy government involvement in directing the economy and where the state tends to dominate the market.

Just as there are types of capitalism, there are at least two main branches of socialism, both involving heavy state ownership. In the state socialism of the former Soviet bloc, government bureaucracy set production targets based on a multiyear plan for the economy. The state also established most prices and wages. Under market socialism, government set investment priorities and state-owned businesses participated in markets for most goods and services, in part to avoid many of the coordination and efficiency problems of central planning.

As this brief review suggests, there are many options and gradations in organizing economic activity. As for the socialist alternative, hardly anyone wants a return to state socialism. The democratic market socialist alternative is still part of political discourse in Europe, but it is not faring well. Two sociologists, Lawrence Peter King and Ivan Szelenyi, summed up the current situation: "We are perfectly aware that, despite a revival of theoretical interest in new ideas about socialism, and despite the electoral success of various new social democratic parties, there is no social movement on the horizon. The ideas are there, but at present there is no political force that could make these ideas a reality."[16]

The important question is no longer the future of socialism; rather, it is to identify the contours of a new *nonsocialist* operating system that can transform capitalism as we know it. One vision of such a new system is that offered by Clive Hamilton in his book *Growth Fetish*. Hamilton argues that what will animate the new system is not the old struggle to replace capitalism with socialism. "Capitalism is so called because the motivating force of production and social organization is ownership of private capital; socialism is so called because it is centered on social ownership of the means of production. Political philosophies whose competing claims have defined the history of the world for the last two centuries have been at one in identifying the central social problem—how to produce and distribute material wealth. But now that in rich countries the economic problem has been solved, the axis of political debate and social change must move away from the production sphere and the forms of ownership of the means of production."[17]

Hamilton believes the focus of policy should be to promote "the full realization of human potential through, in the first instance, proper appreciation of the sources of wellbeing. While [such a program] would, if taken up, represent a profound challenge to capitalism as we know it, it cannot be characterized as socialist. It reaffirms a necessary role for public ownership, but it does not propose any expropriation of private property. It is, however, anti-capitalist in the sense that it argues that society and governments should no longer cede special significance to the objectives or moral claims of the owners of capital."

In this critique of today's "growth fetish" and his call for strengthening the sources of human and environmental well-being, Hamilton has identified important features of a nonsocialist alternative to today's capitalism. "We need to recover the security and integration of premodern societies," he writes, "societies in which the unity of work and life, of society and community, of the individual and the collective, of culture and politics, of economy and morality, is re-established."[18]

Seeds of Change

Recently, two able American thinkers have also turned attention to the possible contours of a new operating system. I refer to Alperovitz's *America beyond Capitalism* and to William Greider's *Soul of Capitalism*. Their ideas are similar in several ways, and their books are quintessentially American. Greider and Alperovitz are optimistic and brimming with concrete proposals for change. Best of all, their ideas are grounded in things that are actually happening in America today. Interestingly, they both disagree with Hamilton to some degree, because they both see ownership of capital and enterprise as still important. As Alperovitz puts it, "Systemic change above all involves questions of how property is owned and controlled—the locus of real power in most political economies."[19] This disagreement may be more apparent than real, however. What Hamilton is decrying is the continuation of the old capitalism versus socialism debate, not innovations that broaden property ownership and control and make it more responsive to civic needs.

Both Greider and Alperovitz see the seeds of change being planted within today's capitalist system, seeds that can grow and transform the system. Here is how Greider puts it: "The idea of reinventing American capitalism sounds far-fetched . . . and especially improbable considering the market-centered orthodoxy that reigns in conventional thinking. I can report, nevertheless, that many Americans are already at work on the idea in various scattered ways (though usually not with such sweeping declarations of intent). They are experimenting in localized settings—tinkering with the ways in which the system operates—and are convinced that alternatives are possible, not utopian schemes but self-interested and practical changes that can serve broader purposes. This approach seems quite remote from the current preoccupations of big politics and big business, but this is where the society's deepest reforms usually have originated in the American past."[20]

Greider, a long-term Washington observer, sees little hope that

Washington will drive major change. "The larger point . . . is that the collision between society and capitalism has endured over many years, despite the laws and shifting political sensibilities, because it is essentially a clash of two different value systems. Government has not succeeded in reconciling the clash because, though it issues many rules of dos and don'ts for enterprise to follow, it does not attempt to alter the underlying values that shape capitalism's behavior. To be enduring, that change has to occur inside capitalism, like altering the gene system of a plant or animal."[21]

Remember Bowles's definition of capitalism: an economic system in which employers—the owners of capital—hire workers to produce goods and services for the owners' profit. A key change that both Greider and Alperovitz observe is the beginning of an erosion of this system through new forms of ownership and control. They believe that conscious promotion of these developments can hasten that erosion.

One pattern is employee ownership—people owning their own work. Greider reports that "at the start of this new century, around 10 million Americans are worker-owners in some 11,000 employee-owned companies."[22] Much of this worker ownership stems from the idea—first put forward in 1958 by Louis Kelso—of Employee Stock Ownership Plans, or ESOPs. The ESOP approach resembles a leveraged buyout: employees borrow capital to buy the company's stock, take a controlling position, and pay back the creditors from the profit they earn. Worker ownership in the United States reached eight hundred billion dollars in 2002, roughly 8 percent of all U.S. corporate stock.

Jeff Gates, in his pathbreaking book *The Ownership Solution*, notes that the ESOP concept is being extended. It can be extended to RESOP (Related Enterprise Share Ownership Plans), where employees of smaller companies can gain an ownership stake in larger, more established companies, and to CSOPs (Customer Stock Ownership Plans), where customers acquire a major stake in the operation.[23]

The CSOP is akin to another growing pattern of ownership—the co-op. Alperovitz notes that "it is rarely realized that there are more than 48,000 co-ops operating in the United States—and that 120 million Americans are co-op members. Roughly 10,000 credit unions (with total assets of over $600 billion) supply financial services to 83 million members; 36 million Americans purchase their electricity from rural electric cooperatives; more than a thousand mutual insurance companies (with more than $80 billion in assets) are owned by their policyholders; and approximately 30 percent of farm products are marketed through cooperatives."[24]

At the grandest level, state and national ownership funds—public trusts—could be established to benefit citizens and the environment. These funds would operate on fiduciary trust principles. Capital could be generated through the proceeds of natural resource sales (for example, oil revenue, as with the Alaska Permanent Fund) or from the auction of carbon dioxide emission rights or from Kelso-type loan guarantee strategies. These ideas have been creatively developed by Peter Barnes in his new book, *Capitalism 3.0.*[25]

Several other groundbreaking patterns of ownership and control are emerging and worthy of note:

- The top one thousand pension funds in the United States own nearly five trillion dollars in assets, and they and other participants in fiduciary capitalism are becoming far more assertive on social and environmental issues.[26]
- Cities and states are becoming owners and direct actors in the business arena—chartering municipal development corporations, providing health services and environmental management, and other revenue-generating activities.
- Charities and other nonprofit organizations are also getting into business, blurring the distinction between the for-profit and the not-for-profit sector. Well over sixty billion dollars is earned annually by the fourteen thousand largest U.S. nonprofits. Businesses and nonprofits are spawning a wide variety of corporate hybrids.[27]

All of these trends in what Alperovitz calls the "democratization of wealth" break with traditional capitalist patterns. They involve ownership by workers, public ownership, and public and private enterprises that do not seek traditional profits. They offer opportunities for greater local control, more sensitivity to employee, public, and consumer interests, and heightened environmental performance. Collectively, they signal the emergence of a new sector—a public or independent sector—that has the potential to be a countervailing center of power to today's capitalism.[28]

In sum, the rough contours of a nonsocialist alternative to today's capitalism can be glimpsed in the prescriptions of earlier chapters and in the ideas promoted by Greider, Alperovitz, Barnes, and others. A large array of initiatives has been identified to transform the market and consumerism, redesign corporations, and focus growth on high-priority human and environmental needs. If pursued, they would change modern-day capitalism in fundamental ways. We would no longer have capitalism as we know it. The question whether this something new is beyond capitalism or is a reinvented capitalism is largely definitional. And, as Hamilton suggests, the answer is no longer very important.

The remaining issue is whether all these prognostications are just interesting speculation or whether the system we know as today's capitalism is actually more vulnerable than we imagine. I would like to conclude this chapter by making the best case I can that something new will be born, though its gestation period will not be short. The case rests on six propositions:

Proposition 1: that today's system of political economy, referred to here as modern capitalism, is destructive of the environment, and not in a minor way but in a way that profoundly threatens the planet; people will therefore demand solutions, and the current system will not be able to accommodate them; so the system will be forced to change, perhaps in the unfortunate context of some type of environmental crisis or breakdown;

Proposition 2: that the affluent societies have reached or soon will reach the point where, as Keynes put it, the economic problem has been solved; the long era of ceaseless striving to overcome hardship and deprivation can soon be over; there is enough to go around;

Proposition 3: that in the more affluent societies, modern capitalism is no longer enhancing human well-being, either objective or subjective well-being, and is instead producing a stressed and ultimately unsatisfactory social reality; people are increasingly dissatisfied and looking for something more meaningful; this dissatisfaction will grow and force change;

Proposition 4: that the international social movement for change— which refers to itself as "the irresistible rise of global anti-capitalism" —is stronger than many imagine and will grow stronger; there is a coalescing of forces: peace, social justice, community, ecology, feminism—a movement of movements; meanwhile, America's weakened democracy and failed environmental politics are themselves ripe for transformation;

Proposition 5: that people and groups are busily planting the seeds of change through a host of alternative arrangements, and still other attractive directions for upgrading to a new operating system have been identified; these innovations can transform the current system, and they will grow;

And proposition 6: that the end of the Cold War and the West's long struggle against communism opens the door—creates the political space—for the questioning of today's capitalism.

These six propositions suggest the potential for major change. Perhaps there are others. Are they sufficient, or, better? Will they eventually be? I believe they are, and for the sake of the young people of our world, I surely hope they are.

Part Three　　Seedbeds of Transformation

IO   A New Consciousness

Throughout this book I have sought to identify the profound changes that will be needed to sustain natural and human communities—changes in public policy and changes in individual and social behavior. Most of these changes are difficult and far-reaching by today's standards. They are not the next steps. The next steps involve urgent efforts to apply the approaches of today's environmentalism to address climate change and other challenges where serious action is long overdue. But the prescriptions of previous chapters are the next, next steps. What new circumstances might make these "impossible" prescriptions "inevitable," as Milton Friedman put it? This question cannot be answered with certainty, to say the least, but two additional and allied transformations will be involved: a transformation in consciousness and a transformation in politics.

Many of our deepest thinkers and many of those most familiar with the scale of the challenges we face have concluded that the transitions required can be achieved only in the context of what I will call the rise of a new consciousness. For some, it is a spiritual awakening—a transformation of the human heart. For others it is a more intellectual process of coming to see the world anew and deeply embracing the emerging ethic of the environment and the old ethic of what it means to love thy neighbor as thyself. But for all it involves major cultural change and a reorientation of what society values and prizes most highly.

Voices for Change

Vaclav Havel has stated beautifully the fundamental shift that is needed. "It's fascinating to me," he writes, "how preoccupied people are today with catastrophic prognoses, how books containing evidence of impending crises become bestsellers, but how very little account we take of these threats in our everyday activities. . . . What could change the direction of today's civilization? It is my deep conviction that the only option is a change in the sphere of the spirit, in the sphere of human conscience. It's not enough to invent new machines, new regulations, new institutions. We must develop a new understanding of the true purpose of our existence on this Earth. Only by making such a fundamental shift will we be able to create new models of behaviour and a new set of values for the planet."[1] For Havel and many others, the environmental crisis is a crisis of the spirit.

The father of the land ethic, Aldo Leopold, came to believe that "there is a basic antagonism between the philosophy of the industrial age and the philosophy of the conservationist." Remarkably, he wrote to a friend that he doubted anything could be done about conservation "without creating a new kind of people."[2]

Two leading scientists, Stanford's Paul Ehrlich and Donald Kennedy, note that "it is the collective actions of individuals that lie at the heart of the [environmental] dilemma," and that "analysis of individual motives and values should be critical to the solution." They call for a Millennium Assessment of Human Behavior "to conduct an ongoing examination and public airing of what is known about how human cultures (especially their ethics) evolve, and about what kinds of changes might permit transition to an ecologically sustainable, peaceful, and equitable global society. . . . What we are asking for is a cultural change; we know that cultures evolve, and our hope is that the very process of debate will speed that process and encourage change in a positive direction."[3]

Paul Raskin and his Global Scenario Group have developed many scenarios of world economic, social, and environmental conditions, including scenarios where there are no fundamental changes in consciousness and values. But without a change in values, all their scenarios run into big trouble. So they favor the New Sustainability worldview where society turns "to non-material dimensions of fulfillment . . . the quality of life, the quality of human solidarity and the quality of the earth. . . . Sustainability is the imperative that pushes the new agenda. Desire for a rich quality of life, strong human ties and a resonant connection to nature is the lure that pulls it toward the future."[4] The revolution Raskin and his colleagues envision is primarily a revolution in values and consciousness.

Peter Senge and his colleagues in their book *Presence* say that "if the future is going to be different, we have to go far beyond these little piecemeal gestures and begin to see the systems in which we're embedded. . . . What would it take to shift the whole? . . . When all is said and done, the only change that will make a difference is the transformation of the human heart."[5]

Two leading authorities on religion and ecology, Mary Evelyn Tucker and John Grim, believe that to meet the environmental crisis, "we are called to a new intergenerational consciousness and conscience" and that "values and ethics, religion and spirituality" are important factors in "transforming human consciousness and behavior for a sustainable future."[6]

Erich Fromm believed that the only hope was a "New Man" and called for "a radical change of the human heart." "The need for profound human change emerges not only as an ethical or religious demand, not only as a psychological demand arising from the pathogenic nature of our present social character, but also as a condition for the sheer survival of the human race. . . . [O]nly a fundamental change in human character from a preponderance of the having mode to a predominantly being mode of existence can save us."[7]

The cultural historian Thomas Berry has described forging a new consciousness as our "Great Work." "The deepest cause of the present devastation is found in a mode of consciousness that has established a radical discontinuity between the human and other modes of being and the bestowal of all rights on the humans. . . .

"Consistently we have difficulty in accepting the human as an integral part of the Earth community. We see ourselves as a transcendent mode of being. We don't really belong here. But if we are here by some strange destiny then we are the source of all rights and all values. All other earthly beings are instruments to be used or resources to be exploited for human benefit."

Berry believes what is required is "a profound reversal in our perspective on ourselves and on the universe about us. . . . What is demanded of us now is to change attitudes that are so deeply bound into our basic cultural patterns that they seem to us as an imperative of the very nature of our being."[8]

Many similar calls for profound reorientation of prevailing values and worldview could be cited, but I will conclude by relating a personal experience. In the late 1960s as a young law student at Yale, I had the pleasure of being a teaching and research assistant to Professor Charles Reich as he was writing *The Greening of America*, which was published first in the *New Yorker* in 1970 and then as a best-selling book. Reich coined the terms Consciousness I, II, and III. Consciousness I is "the traditional outlook of the American farmer, small businessman, or worker trying to get ahead." Reich saw it as most appropriate for the disappearing America of small towns, face-to-face relationships, and individual economic enterprise. Consciousness II is consciousness that was "formed by technological and corporate society, far removed from the realities of human needs. [It] represents the values of an organizational society."

In Reich's view, the combination of Consciousness I and Consciousness II "has proved utterly unable to manage, guide, or control the immense apparatus of technology and organization that America has built. In consequence, this apparatus of power has become a mindless juggernaut, destroying the environment, obliterating human values, and assuming domination over the lives and minds of its subjects. Faced with this threat to their very existence, the inhabitants of America have begun . . . to develop a new consciousness, appropriate to today's realities. . . . Consciousness III, which is spreading rapidly among wider and wider segments of youth, and by degrees to older people, is in the process of revolutionizing the structure of our society. . . . At the heart of everything is what must be called a change of consciousness. This means a new way of living—almost a new man. This is what the new generation has been searching for, and what it has started to achieve."

Like many social critics whose hopes get ahead of reality, Reich saw Consciousness III as expanding almost inevitably and transforming the country. "Consciousness III is capable of changing and of destroying the corporate state, without violence, without seizure of political power, without overthrow of any existing group of people. The new generation has shown the way to the one method of change that will work in today's post-industrial society: revolution by consciousness. No political revolution is possible in the Untied States right now, but no such revolution is needed.

"Revolution by consciousness requires two basic conditions. First, a process of change of consciousness must be under way in the population—a process that promises to continue until it reaches a majority of the people. Second, the existing order must depend for its power on an earlier consciousness, and therefore be unable to survive a change of consciousness. Both of these conditions now exist in the United States."[9]

Reich was a delightful friend and good mentor. Shy, brilliant, and irrepressible, he found the law school too confining and launched what became the most popular course in Yale College. For many years, I have had the opportunity to consider where he was right and where he went wrong. I believe Reich was right that a new consciousness is both possible and necessary. His seeing America in terms of three types of consciousness was useful in presenting a complex reality, and his core idea that a change in consciousness could transform American society and culture was, as we said then, "right on." But he was too enamored with the youth culture of the sixties, and he mistakenly concluded that it would spread, deepen, and mature. This led him to an unfounded optimism about change. In the end, as Robert Dahl has noted, the Counterculture faded in popularity among the young and left behind little change in the prevailing consumerist culture.[10]

What the authors previously cited and many others are now saying is that today's challenges require a rapid evolution to a new consciousness. That is a profound conclusion. It suggests that today's problems cannot be solved with today's mind. That should give us pause, for we know that changing minds can be slow and difficult. This entire area deserves much more investigation and research. Some psychologists contend that changing values is neither necessary nor sufficient for improved environmental behavior, but typically the behavioral changes they study do not extend to the deep and profound transformations sought by those quoted here.[11] In the end, it is hard to doubt the need for the new consciousness sought by Havel, Raskin, and others. Today's dominant worldview is simply too biased toward anthropocentrism, materialism, egocentrism, contempocentrism, reductionism, rationalism, and nationalism to sustain the changes needed. That being the case, two important questions emerge. First, what are the dimensions of the change in consciousness required by today's circumstance, and, second, what can be said about forces that can drive cultural and consciousness change of the type and on the scale needed?

A New Worldview

One excellent summation of the dimensionality of the needed cultural change is provided by Paul Raskin in his work on the Great Transition Initiative.[12] Raskin's device is to write from the vantage point of someone in the second half of this century looking back on the dominant value shifts that occurred earlier. His is a history of the future. Here is what he sees: "The emergence of a new suite of values is the foundation of the entire edifice of our planetary society. Consumerism, individualism, and domination of nature—the dominant values of yesteryear—have given way to a new triad: quality of life, human solidarity, and ecological sensibility.

"That the enhancement of the 'quality of life' should be the basis for development is now so self-evident, it must be remembered that, over the eons, the problem of scarcity and survival . . . dominated existence. Then, the industrial cornucopia, while unleashing an orgy of consumption among the privileged and desperation among the excluded, opened the historical possibility for our post-scarcity planetary civilization. People are as ambitious as ever. But fulfillment, not wealth, has become the primary measure of success and source of well-being.

"The second value—'human solidarity'—expresses a sense of connectedness with people who live in distant places and with the unborn who will live in a distant future. It is a manifestation of the capacity of reciprocity and empathy that lies deep in the human spirit and psyche, the 'golden rule' that is a common thread across many of the world's great religious traditions. As a secular doctrine, it is the basis for the democratic ideal and the great social struggles for tolerance, respect, equality, and rights.

"With their highly evolved 'ecological sensibility,' people today are both mystified and horrified by the feckless indifference of earlier generations to the natural world. Where the right to dominate nature was once sacrosanct, people today hold a deep reverence for the natural world, finding in it endless wonder and enjoyment. Love of nature is complemented by a deep sense of humanity's place in the web of life, and dependence on its bounty. Sustainability is a core part of the contemporary worldview, which would deem any compromise of the integrity of our planetary home both laughably idiotic and morally wrong."[13]

In Raskin's view, these "universal principles that underpin global society did not fall from the sky. They were shaped by our forebears in the great historical projects for human rights, peace, development, and environment."[14] Indeed, it is quite impossible to read together the Universal Declaration of Human Rights, the declarations of the major United Nations conferences of the 1990s, the U.N.'s Millennium Development Goals, the Earth Charter, the World Charter for Nature and other internationally agreed statements of humanity's values and goals and not be tremendously impressed by the qualities of these aspirations (and also depressed by the depth of our failure to meet them).

Like Raskin, David Korten in *The Great Turning* sees humanity at a turning point, a pivot in history, and puts new values front and center: "The Great Turning begins with a cultural and spiritual awakening—a turning in cultural values from money and material excess to life and spiritual fulfillment, from a belief in our limitations to a belief in our possibilities, and from fearing our differences to rejoicing in our diversity. It requires reframing the cultural stories by which we define our human nature, purpose, and possibilities. . . .

"The values shift of the cultural turning leads us to redefine wealth —to measure it by the health of our families, communities, and natural environment. It leads us from policies that raise those at the top to policies that raise those at the bottom, from hoarding to sharing, from concentrated to distributed ownership, and from the rights of ownership to the responsibilities of stewardship."[15]

The most serious and sustained effort to date to state a compelling ethical vision for the future is the Earth Charter, which is gaining wide endorsement and support around the world. The Earth Charter is an eloquent statement of the ethical principles needed to "bring forth a sustainable global society founded on respect for nature, universal human rights, economic justice, and a culture of peace." By 2005, more than two thousand organizations representing tens of millions of people had endorsed the Earth Charter. A key portion of the Charter is reprinted in this chapter.[16]

Another way of describing the values and worldview that are needed is to identify the transitions that are required to move successfully from today to tomorrow:

- from seeing humanity as something apart from nature, transcending and dominating it, to seeing ourselves as part of nature, offspring of its evolutionary process, close kin to wild things, and wholly dependent on its vitality and the finite services it provides;
- from seeing nature in strictly utilitarian terms, humanity's resource to exploit as it sees fit for economic and other purposes, to seeing the natural world as having both intrinsic value independent of people and rights that create the duty of ecological stewardship;
- from discounting the future, focusing severely on the near term, to empowering future generations economically, politically, and environmentally and recognizing duties to yet unborn human and natural communities well into the future;
- from hyperindividualism, narcissism, and social isolation to powerful community bonds reaching from the local to the cosmopolitan and to profound appreciation of interdependence both within and among countries;
- from parochialism, sexism, prejudice, and ethnocentrism to tolerance, cultural diversity, and human rights;
- from materialism, consumerism, getting, the primacy of possessions, and limitless hedonism to personal and family relationships, leisure play, experiencing nature, spirituality, giving, and living within limits;
- from gross economic, social, and political inequality to equity, social justice, and human solidarity.[17]

The Earth Charter Preamble

We stand at a critical moment in Earth's history, a time when humanity must choose its future. As the world becomes increasingly interdependent and fragile, the future at once holds great peril and great promise. To move forward we must recognize that in the midst of a magnificent diversity of cultures and life forms we are one human family and one Earth community with a common destiny. We must join together to bring forth a sustainable global society founded on respect for nature, universal human rights, economic justice, and a culture of peace. Towards this end, it is imperative that we, the peoples of Earth, declare our responsibility to one another, to the greater community of life, and to future generations.

Earth, Our Home

Humanity is part of a vast evolving universe. Earth, our home, is alive with a unique community of life. The forces of nature make existence a demanding and uncertain adventure, but Earth has provided the conditions essential to life's evolution. The resilience of the community of life and the well-being of humanity depend upon preserving a healthy biosphere with all its ecological systems, a rich variety of plants and animals, fertile soils, pure waters, and clean air. The global environment with its finite resources is a common concern of all peoples. The protection of Earth's vitality, diversity, and beauty is a sacred trust.

The Global Situation

The dominant patterns of production and consumption are causing environmental devastation, the depletion of resources, and a massive extinction of species. Communities are being undermined.

The benefits of development are not shared equitably and the gap between rich and poor is widening. Injustice, poverty, ignorance, and violent conflict are widespread and the cause of great suffering. An unprecedented rise in human population has overburdened ecological and social systems. The foundations of global security are threatened. These trends are perilous—but not inevitable.

The Challenges Ahead

The choice is ours: form a global partnership to care for Earth and one another or risk the destruction of ourselves and the diversity of life. Fundamental changes are needed in our values, institutions, and ways of living. We must realize that when basic needs have been met, human development is primarily about being more, not having more. We have the knowledge and technology to provide for all and to reduce our impacts on the environment. The emergence of a global civil society is creating new opportunities to build a democratic and humane world. Our environmental, economic, political, social, and spiritual challenges are interconnected, and together we can forge inclusive solutions.

Universal Responsibility

To realize these aspirations, we must decide to live with a sense of universal responsibility, identifying ourselves with the whole Earth community as well as our local communities. We are at once citizens of different nations and of one world in which the local and global are linked. Everyone shares responsibility for the present and future well-being of the human family and the larger living world. The spirit of human solidarity and kinship with all life is strengthened when we live with reverence for the mystery of being, gratitude for the gift of life, and humility regarding the human place in nature.

Overcoming human alienation from nature requires a reenchantment with the natural world, making it again a place of wonder, a magnificent stage for life's daily unfolding before us. Max Weber noted, with regret I think, that science and intellectualization had disenchanted the world for us. Yet George Levine, in his delightful book *Darwin Loves You*, notes that even that ultimate disenchanter of nature, Charles Darwin, "with all his pains, illnesses, losses, loved the earth and the natural world he gave his life to describing; he found value and meaning in it; he argued that the human sense of value, which he regarded as the world's highest achievement, grew out of the earth, and this genealogy, he believed, did not degrade but ennobled."[18]

Poets and indigenous peoples are best at finding a human place in nature.

> *UP! up! my Friend, and quit your books;*
> *Or surely you'll grow double:*
> *Up! up! my Friend, and clear your looks;*
> *Why all this toil and trouble?*
>
> *The sun, above the mountain's head,*
> *A freshening lustre mellow*
> *Through all the long green fields has spread,*
> *His first sweet evening yellow.*
>
> *Books! 'tis a dull and endless strife:*
> *Come, hear the woodland linnet,*
> *How sweet his music! on my life,*
> *There's more of wisdom in it.*[19]

Oren Lyons, faithkeeper of the Onondaga Nation, addressed the delegates of the United Nations with these words: "I do not see a delegation for the four-footed. I see no seat for the eagles. We forget and we consider ourselves superior, but we are after all a mere part of the Creation. And we must continue to understand where we are. And we stand between the mountain and the ant, somewhere and there only, as part and parcel of the Creation. It is our responsibility since we have been given the minds to take care of these things."[20]

Forces for Change

The very practical and very difficult question is what might spur human sensibilities in these directions? When one considers our world today, with its widespread ethnic hatreds, intrastate warfare, and immense violence, militarism, and terrorism, not to mention the dysfunctional values already addressed, the task can seem hopelessly idealistic. In truth, it is precisely because of these calamities, which are linked in many ways, that one must search for answers and hope desperately to find them.

There is a vast literature on cultural change and evolution. In what spirit, then, should we take up the question of spurring change? The goal must be forging cultural change, not waiting on it. Here, the insight of Daniel Patrick Moynihan is helpful: "The central conservative truth is that culture, not politics, determines the success of a society. The central liberal truth is that politics can change a culture and save it from itself."[21] Historian Harvey Nelsen has asked the right question: "How . . . can politics save a culture from itself?" "There is only one way," he answers, "through the development of new consciousness."[22] People have conversion experiences and epiphanies. Can an entire society have a conversion experience?

Unfortunately, the surest path to widespread cultural change is a cataclysmic event that profoundly affects shared values and delegitimizes the status quo and existing leadership. The Great Depression is a classic example. I believe that both 9/11 and Hurricane Katrina could have led to real cultural change in the United States, both for the better, but America lacked the inspired leadership needed.

The most thorough look at this issue from the perspective here is Thomas Homer-Dixon's *The Upside of Down*. He argues "that our circumstances today are surprisingly like Rome's in key ways. Our societies are also becoming steadily more complex and often more rigid. This is happening partly because we're trying to manage—often with limited success—stresses building inside our societies, including stresses arising from our gargantuan appetite for energy. . . . Eventually, as occurred in Rome, the stresses may become too extreme, and our societies too inflexible to respond, and some kind of economic or political breakdown will occur. . . .

"People often use the words 'breakdown' and 'collapse' synonymously. But in my view, although both breakdown and collapse produce a radical simplification of a system, they differ in their long-term consequences. Breakdown may be serious, but it's not catastrophic. Something can be salvaged after breakdown occurs and perhaps rebuilt better than before. Collapse, on the other hand, is far more harmful. . . .

"In coming years, I believe, foreshocks are likely to become larger and more frequent. Some could take the form of threshold events—like climate flips, large jumps in energy prices, boundary-crossing outbreaks of new infectious disease, or international financial crises."[23]

Homer-Dixon argues that foreshocks and breakdowns can lead to positive change if the ground is prepared. "We need to prepare to turn breakdown to our advantage when it happens—because it will," he says.[24] Homer-Dixon's point is critically important. Breakdowns, of course, do not necessarily lead to positive outcomes; authoritarian ones and Fortress World are also possibilities. Turning a breakdown to advantage will require both inspired leadership and a new story that articulates a positive vision grounded in what is best in the society's values and history.

A congressman is said to have told a citizens' group, "If you will lead, your leaders will follow." But it doesn't have to be that way. Harvard's Howard Gardner stresses this potential of true leadership in his book *Changing Minds:* "Whether they are heads of a nation or senior officials of the United Nations, leaders of large, disparate populations have enormous potential to change minds . . . and in the process they can change the course of history.

"I have suggested one way to capture the attention of a disparate population: by creating a compelling story, embodying that story in one's own life, and presenting the story in many different formats so that it can eventually topple the counterstories in one's culture. . . . [T]he story must be simple, easy to identify with, emotionally resonant, and evocative of positive experiences."[25]

There is evidence that Americans are ready for another story. As noted, large majorities of Americans, when polled, express disenchantment with today's lifestyles and offer support for values similar to those discussed here.[26] But these values are held along with other strongly felt and often conflicting values, and we are all pinned down by old habits, fears, insecurities, social pressures, and in other ways. A new story that helps people find their way out of this confusion and dissonance could help lead to real change.

Gardner's stress on story and narrative is thus important. Bill Moyers, a powerful force for good in our country, has written that "America needs a different story. . . . Everywhere you turn you'll find people who believe they have been written out of the story. Everywhere you turn there's a sense of insecurity grounded in a gnawing fear that freedom in America has come to mean the freedom of the rich to get richer even as millions of Americans are dumped from the Dream. So let me say what I think up front: The leaders and thinkers and activists who honestly tell that story and speak passionately of the moral and religious values it puts in play will be the first political generation since the New Deal to win power back for the people. . . . Here, in the first decade of the 21st century, the story that becomes America's dominant narrative will shape our collective imagination and hence our politics."[27]

If Moyers addresses the social aspects of our need for a new narrative, many other authors have begun to develop new stories of our relationship with nature—Thomas Berry in *The Dream of the Earth*, Carolyn Merchant in *Reinventing Eden*, Evan Eisenberg in *The Ecology of Eden*, Bill McKibben in *Deep Ecology*, and others.[28] One story that needs to be told is about a people who set out on a journey—a journey through time—to build a better world for themselves and their children. High-minded and full of hope as they began, they accomplished much in their quest. But they became so enamored of their successes, indeed captured by them, that they failed to see the signs that pointed in new directions, and they became lost. Now they must find their way back to the right path.[29]

Another source of value change is social movements. Social movements are all about raising consciousness and, if successful, can usher in a new consciousness. We speak casually about the environmental movement. We need a real one. One can hear echoes of Reich in Curtis White's book *The Spirit of Disobedience*. "Although the sixties counterculture has been much maligned and discredited, it attempted to provide what we still desperately need: a spirited culture of refusal, a counterlife to the reigning corporate culture of death. We don't need to return to that counterculture, but we do need to take up its challenge again. If the work we do produces mostly bad, ugly, and destructive things, those things in turn will tend to recreate us in their image.

"If we're concerned about the kind of human future we are creating, we must also be concerned with how we are living in the present. Unhappily, how we live is presently the near exclusive concern of corporations and media conglomerates which have, together, turned every Main Street into the same street and made the inside of every American head echo with the same vacuous music and movie/TV scenarios. This is the arena in which a spiritualized disobedience means most."[30]

Another way forward to a new consciousness should lie in the world's religions. Mary Evelyn Tucker has noted that "no other group of institutions can wield the particular moral authority of the religions" and that "the environmental crisis calls the religions of the world to respond by finding their voice within the larger Earth community. In so doing, the religions are now entering their ecological phase and finding their planetary expression."[31] The potential of faith communities is enormous. About 85 percent of the world's people belong to one of the ten thousand or so religions, and about two-thirds of the global population is Christian, Muslim, or Hindu. Religions played key roles in ending slavery, in the civil rights movement, and in overcoming apartheid in South Africa, and they are now turning attention with increasing strength to the environment.[32]

Last, there is the great importance of sustained efforts at education.[33] Here one should include education in the largest sense as embracing not only formal education but also day-to-day and experiential education. It includes education we get from personally experiencing nature in all its richness and diversity. My colleague Steve Kellert has stressed that such exposure, especially for children, is important to well-being and human development.[34] Education in this broad sense also includes the fast-developing field of social marketing. Social marketing has had notable successes in moving people away from bad behaviors such as smoking and drunk driving, and its approaches could be applied to larger themes as well.[35]

All of these forces for change are potentially complementary: a calamity or breakdown (or, ideally, the public anticipation of one brought on by many warnings and much evidence), occurring in the presence of wise leadership and a new narrative that helps make sense of it all and provides a positive vision, urged on by a demanding citizens' movement that fuses social and environmental causes, informed and broadened by well-conceived social marketing campaigns, joined by a contagious proliferation of real-world examples that point the way. It is not hard to envision such circumstances coming together. Except for a real calamity, they are within the power of citizens to make happen.

There was a calamity off Santa Barbara, California, in 1969—a huge oil leakage from the Union Oil Company's offshore drilling operation that turned beaches black, destroyed fish and wildlife, and, more than any single event, catalyzed the remarkable environmental progress of the 1970s. Drawing on what had just happened to them, citizens in Santa Barbara found a new consciousness and were inspired to write the Santa Barbara Declaration of Environmental Rights: "We, therefore, resolve to act. We propose a revolution in conduct toward an environment which is rising in revolt against us. Granted that ideas and institutions long established are not easily changed; yet today is the first day of the rest of our life on this planet. We will begin anew."

II A New Politics

The transformation of contemporary capitalism requires far-reaching and effective government action. How else can the market be made to work for the environment rather than against it? How else can corporate behavior be altered or programs built that meet real human and social needs? Government is the principal means available to citizens to collectively exercise their stewardship responsibility to leave the world a better place. Inevitably, then, the drive for transformative change leads to the political arena, where a vital, muscular democracy steered by an informed and engaged citizenry is needed.

Yet, for Americans, merely to state the matter this way suggests the enormity of the challenge. Democracy in America today is in deep trouble. Weak, shallow, dangerous, and corrupted, it is the best democracy that money can buy. The ascendancy of market fundamentalism and antiregulation, antigovernment ideology makes the current moment particularly frightening, but even the passing of these extreme ideas would leave deeper, longer-term deficiencies. It is unimaginable that American politics as we know it will deliver the transformative changes needed.

There are many reasons why government in Washington today is more problem than solution. It is hooked on GDP growth—for its revenues, for its constituencies, and for its influence abroad. It has been captured by the very corporations and concentration of wealth it should be seeking to regulate and revamp, a pattern that has now reached alarming proportions. And it is hobbled by an array of dysfunctional institutional arrangements, beginning with the way presidents are elected.

William Greider, in his book *The Soul of Capitalism*, expresses a proper skepticism that today's politics can address the underlying problems of capitalism. He writes, "If an activist president set out with good intentions to rewire the engine of capitalism—to alter its operating values or reorganize the terms for employment and investment or tamper with other important features—the initiative would very likely be chewed to pieces by the politics. Given the standard legislative habits of modern government, not to mention its close attachments to the powerful interests defending the status quo, the results would be marginal adjustments at best and might even make things worse."[1]

Peter Barnes explains the problem starkly in *Capitalism 3.0:* "The reason capitalism distorts democracy is simple. Democracy is an open system, and economic power can easily infect it. By contrast, capitalism is a gated system; its bastions aren't easily accessed by the masses. Capital's primacy thus isn't an accident, nor the fault of George W. Bush. It's what happens when capitalism inhabits democracy." Barnes notes that regulatory agencies have been co-opted by the industries they were intended to regulate. "And it's not just regulatory agencies that have been captured. Congress itself, which oversees the agencies and writes their controlling laws, has been badly infected. According to the Center for Public Integrity, the 'influence industry' in Washington now spends $6 billion a year and employs more than thirty-five thousand lobbyists. . . . [I]n a capitalist democracy, the state is a dispenser of many valuable prizes. Whoever amasses the most political power wins the most valuable prizes. The rewards include property rights, friendly regulators, subsidies, tax breaks, and free or cheap use of the commons. The notion that the state promotes 'the common good' is sadly naive. . . . We face a disheartening quandary here. Profit-maximizing corporations dominate our economy. . . . The only obvious counterweight is government, yet government is dominated by these same corporations."[2]

Another longtime analyst of our politics, Gar Alperovitz, explains how the corporate sector wields the influence it does. In *America beyond Capitalism*, he writes that "the large corporation regularly

1. Influences legislation and agenda setting through lobbying
2. Influences regulatory behavior through direct and indirect pressure
3. Influences elections via large-scale campaign contributions
4. Influences public attitudes through massive media campaigns
5. Influences local government choices through all of the above—and adds the implicit or explicit threat of withdrawing its plants, equipment, and jobs from specific locations."[3]

Another constraint on positive government action is an indirect one—the intense competition for political space and attention. One of my professors when I was a Yale student, Roger Masters, wrote a book entitled *The Nation Is Burdened*.[4] The title said it all. Like most of us, government cannot deal with too many issues at one time. Over the past quarter century it has proven damnably difficult to get the large-scale environmental issues that are the most troubling firmly on the U.S. political docket. It would seem that the climate issue is finally, and belatedly, making it. The problem of the preemption of political space is particularly acute when there are competing issues like the "war on terror" and the war in Iraq. The nation is indeed burdened.

Clearly, there are formidable barriers to political reform and action. One response might be to bypass Washington for now and concentrate elsewhere, for example, on building up small-scale counter-models in society. But it would be a great error to stop there. My conclusion from the problems just identified is that all of us concerned with environment se had better start moving fast to build a new politics. rmations reviewed in Part II require a transformation in politics.

The Shape of a New Democracy

The first step in such a transformation is to begin to envision the type of democracy that is needed. Some who place especially high value on sustaining the environment have stressed the revitalization of life and democracy at the local, community, or bioregional levels, as Kirkpatrick Sale did in his well-known *Dwellers in the Land: A Bioregional Vision.*[5] This preference for the local is also clear in the program of the antiglobalists in their book *Alternatives to Globalization: A Better World Is Possible.*[6]

In *The Land That Could Be,* William Shutkin discusses "civic environmentalism," where members of particular geographic or political communities work together to build a future that is environmentally healthy and economically vibrant at the local and regional levels: "Civic environmentalism entails a set of core concepts that embraces civic action and community planning on the part of a diverse group of stakeholders aimed at promoting both environmental protection and democratic renewal: participatory process, community and regional planning, environmental education, industrial ecology, environmental justice, and place."[7] A sense of place and geographic continuity are important in all these visions.

In *Global Environmental Politics,* Ronnie Lipschutz searches for approaches to global environmental protection that might succeed. In most areas he sees severe limitations. "The practice of global environmental politics," he writes, "must be centered elsewhere than the state system, international conferences, agencies, bureaucracies, and centers of corporate capital," all of which he sees as part of the problem. And neither is he happy with mainstream environmental organizations. "Those activities that use mainstream methods to accomplish their goals," he writes, "have done little to change the institutions and practices that are the cause of environmental problems in the first place."[8]

In the end, Lipschutz finds the wellspring of the new environmental politics he seeks in action at the local level: "Activists must still affect the beliefs and behaviors of real human beings, whose social relations are, for the most part, highly localized. Ideas do not fall from heaven or appear as light bulbs; they must resonate with conditions as experienced and understood by those real human beings, in the places that they live, work, and play. Moreover, it is in those local places that politics, activism, and social power are most intense and engage people most strongly."[9] For Lipschutz, then, even global responses must be rooted locally. This linking of global processes to local knowledge, experience, and participation is also important in the analysis of Harvard's Sheila Jasanoff.[10]

It is at the community and regional levels that it is easiest to envision what many see as the best model for democracy's future—deliberative or discursive democracy, what Benjamin Barber calls strong democracy. This is direct democracy—citizens debating the options, learning together, overcoming their differences, and coming to decision. It is far away from today's interest-group, representational democracy. In *Deliberative Environmental Politics,* Walter Baber and Robert Bartlett describe its growing support. "The deliberative democracy movement has been spawned by a growing realization that contemporary liberalism has lost its democratic character just as it has also sacrificed its ecological sustainability. Modern democracies, confronted with cultural pluralism, social complexity, vast inequities of wealth and influence, and ideological biases that discourage fundamental change, have allowed their political institutions to degenerate into arenas for strategic gamesmanship in which there is no possibility for genuine deliberation. Neither true democracy nor environmental protection is possible where citizens become mere competitors with no commitments beyond their own narrow self-interests. . . .

"Deliberative democrats presume that the essence of democracy is deliberation rather than voting, interest aggregation, or rights. Deliberative democracy has a distinguishing core set of propositions, namely: political equality of participants; interpersonal reasoning as the guiding political procedure; and the public giving, weighing, acceptance, or rejection of reasons."[11]

Efforts are now under way to identify ways to move deliberative democracy from theory to practice on a larger scale. These include identification of institutional arrangements that will require the direct participation of citizens and the types of dialogue mechanisms that can be used in the process. An important critique of deliberative approaches has come from those who stress that inherent power imbalances can skew its outcomes and who see a continuing need for activists' methods (demonstrations, boycotts, sit-ins, etc.). Both approaches are seen as having important roles.[12]

In his *Strong Democracy: Participatory Politics for a New Age,* Barber argues that participatory democracy does not require either the "antiquated republicanism" of the Greek polis or "face-to-face parochialism" of the town meeting. But it does require "self-government by citizens rather than representative government in the name of citizens. Active citizens govern themselves directly here, not necessarily at every level and in every instance, but frequently enough and in particular when basic policies are being decided and when significant power is being deployed. Self-government is carried on through institutions designed to facilitate ongoing civic participation in agenda-setting, deliberation, legislation, and policy implementation (in the form of 'common work'). Strong democracy does not place endless faith in the capacity of individuals to govern themselves, but it affirms with Machiavelli that the multitude will on the whole be as wise as or even wiser than princes and with Theodore Roosevelt that 'the majority of the plain people will day in and day out make fewer mistakes in governing themselves than any smaller body of men will make in trying to govern them.'"[13]

To implement these goals and make "every citizen his own politician," Barber lays out a series of innovative arrangements to institutionalize strong democracy in today's context, arrangements designed to "involve individuals at both the neighborhood and the national level in common talk, common decision-making and political judgment, and common action." At the top of his list is a uniform national system of local participation: "The first and most important reform in a strong democratic platform must be the introduction of a national system of *neighborhood assemblies* in every rural, suburban, and urban district in America. Political consciousness begins in the neighborhood."[14] He also favors a national initiative and referendum process, an improved version of the process in use today in many Western states.

In short, many of those who have given the future of our democracy the deepest thought have concluded that empowerment of citizens to decide matters of common concern and to legislate the results themselves is essential not just to better decisions but also to better citizens. Such empowerment would indeed be transformative of American politics.

A more global set of issues motivates those who see a necessary evolution toward cosmopolitanism. The "cosmopolitan project" as described by David Held and his colleagues in *Global Transformations* seeks to bring political accountability and democratic control to a range of international issues. To that end, they see the need for a "cosmopolitan citizen" who enjoys multiple citizenships—national, regional, and global. They believe that "democracy needs to be rethought as a 'double-sided process.' By a double-sided process—or process of double democratization—is meant not just the deepening of democracy within a national community . . . but also the extension of democratic forms and processes across territorial borders. Democracy for the new millennium must allow cosmopolitan citizens . . . to render accountable the social, economic and political processes and flows that cut across and transform their traditional community boundaries."[15]

There are thus advocates for localization of politics and advocates for political globalization. Seemingly at odds, the two positions are actually complementary. Globalization of many descriptions is eroding state sovereignty. The nation-state, it has been said, is too little for the big things and too big for the little things. "Glocalization" is emerging, with action shifting to local and global levels. In many places, especially in Europe, one can see psychological disinvestment in the nation-state and the strengthening of both local and transnational citizenship.

How can the global and the local be integrated into one political framework? Again, there is wisdom in the "report from the future" prepared by Paul Raskin and his colleagues in the Great Transition Initiative. In his epistle from the latter part of this century, his history of the future, Raskin begins by noting that "identity and citizenship has reached the level of the planet. Now, globalism is as deep-rooted as nationalism once was, perhaps more so." Raskin continues, explaining how global and local perspectives were combined: "The Great Transition political philosophy rests on what has come to be called the principle of constrained pluralism. It includes three complementary ideas: irreducibility, subsidiarity, and heterogeneity. The irreducibility principle states that the adjudication of certain issues is necessarily and properly retained at the global level of governance. Global society has the responsibility for ensuring universal rights, the integrity of the biosphere, the fair use of common planetary resources, and for the conduct of cultural and economic endeavors that cannot be effectively delegated to regions. The subsidiarity principle dictates that the scope of irreducible global authority be sharply limited. To promote effectiveness, transparency, and public participation, decision-making should be guided to the most local feasible level of government. The heterogeneity principle validates the rights of regions to pursue diverse forms of development and democratic decision-making constrained only by their obligations to conform to global responsibilities and principles. . . . These principles are enshrined in the world constitution and it would be difficult to find anyone who finds them objectionable."[16] Could I vote in this future world, I would not object.

Getting There from Here

Barber, Raskin, and others thus provide a long-term and hopeful vision of where an unfolding political transition should be headed—toward a revitalization of politics through direct citizen participation in governance, through decentralization of decision making, and through a powerful sense of global citizenship, interdependence, and shared responsibility. With this vision of the political future as background, the next question is how to begin the long march through history toward it. Raskin's vision is something today's young people may one day realize, but for the years and decades immediately ahead, we need a program to begin a far-reaching overhaul of American environmental politics. That overhaul should involve transformation in three major dimensions.

First, the new environmental politics must be broadened now so that environmental concern and advocacy extend to the full range of relevant issues. Efforts within the framework of today's environmentalism must continue; indeed, they must be strengthened. But the environmental agenda should expand to embrace a profound challenge to consumerism and commercialism and the lifestyles they offer, a healthy skepticism of growthmania and a sharp focus on what society should actually be striving to grow, a challenge to corporate dominance and a redefinition of the corporation and its goals, a commitment to deep change in both the functioning and the reach of the market, and a commitment to building what Alperovitz calls "the democratization of wealth" and Barnes calls "capitalism 3.0."

The new agenda should also incorporate advocacy of human rights as a central concern. Though environmental justice has gained a foothold in American environmentalism, it is not yet the priority it should be. Across much of the world social justice concerns and environmental concerns are fused as one cause, and many environmental leaders have been persecuted, jailed, and murdered. They are brothers and sisters, and their rights to life, speech, and democracy should be vigorously defended. Many established environmental issues must be seen as human rights issues—the right to water and sanitation, the right to sustainable development, the right to cultural survival, freedom from climatic disruption and ruin, freedom to live in a nontoxic environment, the rights of future generations.[17]

The new environmental politics should also embrace a program to address America's social problems directly and generously. Earlier I noted a long list of measures urgently needed to enhance social well-being—measures, for example, that address the need for good jobs, income security, and social and medical insurance. I pointed out that these were in fact environmental measures because they addressed human welfare directly and were the alternative to endlessly pumping up an environmentally destructive economy.[18] In particular, it is crucial for environmentalists to join with others in addressing the crisis of inequality now unraveling America's social fabric and undermining its democracy—a crisis of unprecedented profits, soaring executive pay, huge incomes, and increasingly concentrated wealth for a small minority occurring simultaneously with poverty rates near a thirty-year high, stagnant wages despite rising productivity, declining social mobility and opportunity, record levels of people without health insurance, failing schools, increased job insecurity, shrinking safety nets, and the longest work hours among the rich countries.[19]

America's gaping social and economic inequality poses a grave threat to democracy. Political scientist Robert Dahl believes it is "highly plausible" that "powerful international and domestic forces [could] push us toward an irreversible level of political inequality that so greatly impairs our present democratic institutions as to render the ideals of democracy and political equality virtually irrelevant."[20] The authors brought together by political analysts Lawrence Jacobs and Theda Skocpol in *Inequality and American Democracy* document the emergence of a vicious cycle: income disparities shift political access and influence to wealthy constituencies and businesses, which further imperils the potential of the democratic process to act to correct the growing disparities.[21] Among its many deleterious consequences, this process surely cannot be helpful to environmental goals in American politics.

A related issue to which the new environmental politics must turn major attention is the urgent need for political reforms—in campaign finance, elections, the regulation of lobbying, and much more. In their book *Off Center*, political scientists Jacob Hacker and Paul Pierson have developed an important and innovative agenda for political reform, including the revitalization of large-scale membership organizations that give citizens more leverage in the political process, measures that can increase voter turnout, open primaries, nonpartisan redistricting, a minimum free television and radio time for all federal candidates meeting basic requirements, reducing the perks of incumbency, bringing back the Fairness Doctrine requiring equal air time for competing political views, and more.[22] Hacker and Pierson are not optimistic about stemming the flow of money into politics, but Common Cause and others have developed a powerful case for clean and fair elections through public financing.[23] Lawrence Susskind at the Massachusetts Institute of Technology has observed that the Constitution does not require congressional districts as we know them. He believes better results and more accountability would be realized with at-large, multimember districts with election procedures akin to the proportional representation common in Europe.[24] In *Ten Steps to Repair American Democracy*, Steven Hill describes an innovative way to achieve direct election of the president without constitutional amendment.[25] Measures are also needed to reverse the appalling extent of media ownership consolidation. In short, an impressive set of ideas for reform of the American political process has emerged and needs support and action.

If the first watchword of the new environmental politics is "broaden the agenda," the second is "get political." Lawyering and lobbying are important, but what the new environmentalism must build now is a mighty force in electoral politics.[26] Building the necessary muscle will require major efforts at grassroots organizing; strengthening groups working at the state and community level; and developing messages, appeals, and stories that inspire and motivate because they speak in a language people can understand, resonating with what is best in both the American tradition and the public's values and presenting compelling visions of a future worth having for families and children. Perhaps above all, the new environmental politics must be broadly inclusive, reaching out to embrace union members and working families, minorities and people of color, religious organizations, the women's movement, and other communities of complementary interest and shared fate. And it is unfortunate but true that stronger alliances are still needed to overcome the "silo effect" that separates the environmental community from those working on domestic political reforms, the liberal social agenda, human rights, international peace, consumer issues, world health and population concerns, and world poverty and underdevelopment.

Environmental politics cannot succeed with only a narrowly defined environmental constituency.[27] The new environmentalism needs to reach out to many communities and support their causes not just to build the case for reciprocal support, and not just because the objectives are worthy, but also because environmental goals will not be realized unless these other causes succeed. In the end, they are all one cause and will rise or fall together. If, for example, someone says, "We can't help others abroad because we have got to take care of Americans first," know this: they will not take care of Americans either.

The final watchword of the new environmental politics is "build the movement."[28] Efforts to build environmental strength in America's electoral process and to join forces with a wider array of constituencies embracing a broader agenda should both contribute to the emergence of a powerful citizens' movement for change.

What we need now is an international movement of citizens and scientists, one capable of dramatically advancing the political and personal actions needed for the transition to sustainability. We have had movements against slavery, and many have participated in movements for civil rights and against apartheid and the Vietnam War. Environmentalists are often said to be part of "the environmental movement." We need a real one. It is time for we the people, as citizens and as consumers, to take charge.

The best hope we have for this new force is a coalescing of a wide array of civic, scientific, environmental, religious, student, and other organizations with enlightened business leaders, concerned families, and engaged communities, networked together, protesting, demanding action and accountability from governments and corporations, and taking steps as consumers and communities to realize sustainability in everyday life.

Young people will almost certainly be centrally involved in any movement for real change. They always have been. New dreams are born most easily when the world is seen with fresh eyes and confronted with impertinent questions. The Internet is empowering young people in an unprecedented way—not just by access to information but by access to each other, and to a wider world.

One goal should be to find the spark that can set off a period of rapid change, like the flowering of the domestic environmental agenda in the early 1970s. In the end, we need to trigger a response that in historical terms will come to be seen as revolutionary—the Environmental Revolution of the twenty-first century. Only such a response is likely to avert huge and even catastrophic environmental losses.

The passages in the preceding four paragraphs are taken from my book *Red Sky at Morning*.[29] Since writing them my views have changed in two important respects. I now believe there is more hope and more opportunity in a broad-gauged citizens' movement, one that includes social justice as well as environmental concerns. And I would now place this U.S. movement in the larger context of the emerging global movement well described by Paul Hawken in his *Blessed Unrest: How the Largest Movement in the World Came into Being and Why No One Saw It Coming*. Hawken has tried to estimate the number of organizations, mostly nonprofits, in this movement. He finally concluded that globally "there are over one—and maybe even two—million organizations working toward ecological sustainability and social justice." These groups engage tens of millions of people dedicated to change. "What is the intention of the movement?" he asks. "If you examine its values, missions, goals, and principles . . . you will see that at the core of all organizations are two principles, albeit unstated: first is the Golden Rule; second is the sacredness of all life, whether it be a creature, child, or culture." Hawken is optimistic about the movement's impact: "I believe this movement will prevail. . . . [T]he thinking that informs the movement's goals will reign. It will soon suffuse most institutions, but before then, it will change a sufficient number of people so as to begin the reversal of centuries of frenzied self-destructive behavior."[30]

Early Signs

Can one see the beginnings of a true citizens' movement in America? Perhaps like Charles Reich I am letting my hopes get the better of me, but I think we can. Its green side is visible, I think, in the remarkable surge of campus organizing and student mobilization occurring today, much of it coordinated by the student-led Energy Action Coalition.[31] It's visible also in the increasing activism of religious organizations, including many evangelical groups under the banner of Creation Care,[32] and in the rapid proliferation of community-based environmental initiatives.[33] It's there in the joining together of organized labor, environmental groups and progressive businesses in the Apollo Alliance[34] and in the Sierra Club's collaboration with the United Steelworkers, the largest industrial union in the United States.[35] It's visible too in the outpouring of effort to build on Al Gore's *An Inconvenient Truth*,[36] in the green consumer movement and in the consumer support for the efforts of the Rainforest Action Network to green the policies of the major U.S. banks.[37] It's there in the increasing number of teach-ins, demonstrations, marches, and protests, including the fourteen hundred events across the United States in 2007 inspired by Bill McKibben's "Step It Up!" stop global warming campaign. It is there in the constituency-building work of minority environmental leaders including African-Americans like Carl Anthony, Jerome Ringo, Marjora Carter, Van Jones, Dorceta Taylor, Michel Gelobter, and Steve Curwood.[38] It can be seen too in the strong presence of U.S. nonprofits in the various World Social Forums and in the convening of the first U.S. Social Forum in 2007.[39] It's just beginning, but it's there, and it will grow. Much of the new momentum is driven by the climate issue, for example, the 1Sky movement-building campaign.[40]

The welcome news is that the environmental community writ large is moving in these three directions delineated above—though more on the "get political" front than on "broaden the agenda" or "build the movement." Local and state environmental groups have grown in strength and number. There is more engagement supporting environmentally friendly candidates through the League of Conservation Voters and a few other groups, and more work to reach out to voters with political messages through authorized groups. The major national organizations have strengthened their links to local and state groups and established activist networks to support their lobbying activities. Still, there is a long, long way to go to build a new and vital environmental politics in America. As just one measure of the distance still to travel, Mark Hertsgaard reports that barely 10 percent of the support for environmental groups goes to local groups and most of that goes to land trusts.[41]

American politics today is failing not only the environment but also the American people and the world.[42] As Richard Falk reminds us, only an unremitting struggle will drive the changes that can sustain people and nature. If there is a model within American memory for what must be done, it is the Civil Rights Revolution of the 1960s. It had grievances, it knew what was causing them, and it also knew that that order had no legitimacy and that, acting together, they could redress those grievances. It was confrontational and disobedient, but it was nonviolent. It had a dream. And it had Martin Luther King, Jr.

King was murdered in 1968, as was Bobby Kennedy. In *1968: The Year That Rocked the World*, Mark Kurlansky writes, "The year 1968 was a terrible year and yet one for which many people feel nostalgia. Despite the thousands dead in Vietnam, the million starved in Biafra, the crushing of idealism in Poland and Czechoslovakia, the massacre in Mexico, the clubbings and brutalization of dissenters all over the world, the murder of the two Americans who most offered the world hope, to many it was a year of great possibilities and is missed. As Camus wrote in *The Rebel*, those who long for peaceful times are longing for 'not the alleviation but the silencing of misery.' The thrilling thing about the year 1968 was that it was a time when significant segments of population all over the globe refused to be silent about the many things that were wrong with the world. They could not be silenced. There were too many of them, and if they were given no other opportunity, they would stand in the street and shout about them. And this gave the world a sense of hope that it has rarely had, a sense that where there is wrong, there are always people who will expose it and try to change it."[43]

It is amazing what can be accomplished if citizens are ready to march, in the footsteps of Dr. King. It is again time to give the world a sense of hope.

12 The Bridge at the Edge of the World

For those of my generation, the quest for answers to the challenges addressed in this book is nearing its end, but for today's young people it is just beginning. We do indeed borrow the earth from our children. If only my generation could say that we are returning it to them a better place than we found it. In truth, we have continued to purchase prosperity at an enormous cost to the natural world and to our human solidarity as well.

But what's past is past. It cannot be undone or remade. The future, though, is something else entirely. It can be remade—made very differently from what it would otherwise be. That is the Great Work ahead.

It is easy to push these challenges out of one's mind. Life for many of us is comfortable, and dwelling on such disturbing material is painful. Indeed, one still hears with regularity that it is a mistake to stress these gloomy and doomy realities if one wants to motivate people. In *The Death of Environmentalism*, Michael Shellenberger and Ted Nordhaus remind us, for example, that Martin Luther King, Jr., did not proclaim, "I have a nightmare." My reply to them was that he did not need to say it—his people were living a nightmare. They needed a dream. But we, I fear, are living a dream. We need to be reminded of the nightmare ahead. Here is the truth as I see it: we will never do the things that are needed unless we know the full extent of our predicament.

Having faced up to the perils ahead, we must also remind ourselves and others that solutions exist, abundantly. We have just reviewed a small library of them, and there are many more. There are, moreover, solid grounds for hope. Scientific understanding is greatly improved. Population growth is slowing, and the number of the world's people in poverty is being reduced. Technologies that can bring a vast environmental improvement in manufacturing, energy, transportation, construction, and agriculture are either available or close at hand. Environmental and other civil society organizations have developed new capacities for leadership and effectiveness and are beginning to build strengths in areas that have been too long neglected. Business is seeing gold in greening. A global civil society is emerging as like-minded organizations in many countries come together.

The seriousness of looming environmental threats is slowly sinking in, driven largely by the climate issue but also informed by the outpouring of serious books and articles pointing out that various breakdowns and collapses are actually possible. In the right hands, crises and calamities related to environment can generate positive change, as Hurricane Katrina could have. We can also see the beginnings of social change in the efforts of some consumers to downshift and go green, in the anti-corporate-abuse stirrings of some communities, and in the proliferation of initiatives involving new forms of business ownership and management. Polls suggest that the public is distressed by runaway materialism, and there are signs that student activism is reawakening and that faith communities are taking up environmental causes. Religion can help us see that the challenges we face are moral and spiritual and that sin is not strictly individual but is also social and institutional, and it can call us to reflection, repentance, and resistance.

And there is growing strength in the worldwide social movement described by Paul Hawken in *Blessed Unrest*. From huge nonprofits to home-based causes, the groups in this movement are emerging as a creative and influential global force. And, of course, there is the hope that springs from today's young people. We see their commitment in the demand for the greening of our colleges and universities and in the growing student activism and political mobilization. Concerns have been expressed that they are the "quiet generation," too on-line, but climate threats and social justice issues are now spurring a new, activist youth-led movement for change.

In the past, leadership most often came from scientists, economists, and lawyers like myself. Today we need especially the preachers, the philosophers, the psychologists, and the poets. There's an upsurge of interest in Aldo Leopold and his writings now. In 2007, as I was writing, I made a pilgrimage to Aldo Leopold's shack in rural Wisconsin, where in the 1940s *A Sand County Almanac* was written and environmental ethics were born. Ken Brower has written that "the shack sits just above a sandy flood channel of the Wisconsin River, at a fork in the evolution of our regard for the land."[1] And there it was, just a shack, still there: a place of the new consciousness. We are hearing the new consciousness now more and more from other voices. In one poem, W. S. Merwin said, "On the last day of the world / I would want to plant a tree." And in another: "I want to tell you what the forests were like / I will have to speak a forgotten language." Most prominently, the new consciousness can be seen in the growing worldwide endorsement and adoption of the Earth Charter.

Last, we should remember that, as the expression goes, the impossible will take a little while. There is much to be done, and it will not be easy. The progress just noted, is, as Richard Falk observed, mostly a snapping at the heels of the system. Proposals for transformational change will be derided and, when they gain traction, resisted at every turn. It is true but too easy to say that the resistance will come from entrenched interests. It will also come from ourselves. We are the consumers and the employees, and we are easily seduced. Still, there is a world at stake, the world our children and grandchildren will inherit. We must all be out to save the world, literally.

In our journey down the path between two worlds, we are fast approaching a place where the path forks. We got to this fork through a long history dominated by two great and related struggles—the struggle against scarcity and the struggle to subdue nature. To win in these struggles we created a powerful technology and forged an organization of economy and society to deploy that technology extensively, rapidly, and, if need be, ruthlessly. And we succeeded at subduing nature and creating wealth far beyond our ancestors' imaginings. So successful were these systems and accomplishments that we were swept up in them, mesmerized by them, captivated, even addicted. We thus continued pell-mell ahead—ever-grander, ever-larger, ever-richer, doing what once made sense but no longer did. There were warning signs along the way, but we did not notice them, or when we did, we paid them no heed. These signs said things like:

being, not having
giving, not getting
needs, not wants
better, not richer
community, not individual
other, not self
connected, not separate
ecology, not economy
part of nature, not apart from nature
dependent, not transcendent
tomorrow, not today

We ignored these warnings to the point that, as we now approach the fork ahead, we are perilously close to losing the most precious things of all. We are rapidly hollowing out nature, ourselves, and our society.

Beyond the fork, down either path, is the end of the world as we have known it. One path beyond the fork continues us on our current trajectory. Presidential science adviser John Gibbons used to say with a wry smile that if we don't change direction, we'll end up where we're headed. And right now we're headed toward a ruined planet. That is one way the world as we know it could end, down that path and into the abyss.

But there is the other path, and it leads to a bridge across the abyss. We have been examining this bridge at the edge of the world and what is required to cross it. Of course, where the path forks will be the site of another struggle, a struggle that must be won even though we cannot see clearly what lies beyond the bridge. Yet in that struggle and in the crossing that will follow, we are carried forward by hope, a radical hope, that a better world is possible and that we can build it. "Another world is not only possible. She is on her way," says Arundhati Roy. "On a quiet day, I can hear her breathing."[2]

Notes

Preface

1. James Gustave Speth, *Red Sky at Morning: America and the Crisis of the Global Environment*, 2nd ed. (New Haven and London: Yale University Press, 2005). The quotation from *Time* is on the cover.

2. The World Resources Institute, the Natural Resources Defense Council, and Environmental Defense worked with a group of leading corporations to give birth to a pathbreaking initiative, the United States Climate Action Partnership, which calls for "prompt enactment of national legislation in the United States to slow, stop and reverse the growth of greenhouse gas (GHG) emissions over the shortest period of time reasonably achievable." See www.us-cap.org.

3. I am indebted here to Paul Raskin et al., *Great Transition* (Boston: Stockholm Environment Institute, 2002), which makes a similar point.

4. John Maynard Keynes, *The General Theory of Employment, Interest and Money* (New York: Harcourt, Brace, 1936), 383.

5. Milton Friedman, *Capitalism and Freedom* (Chicago: University of Chicago Press, 1962), Introduction.

6. See Speth, *Red Sky at Morning*, 152–157, 173–175, Afterword. Between the established rich and the desperately poor are the rapidly growing emerging economies, notably China and India, which will indeed be the sites of large economic expansion and environmental pressures projected for the decades ahead. Although much in *Red Sky at Morning* and portions of this volume bear

on how best to engage these countries constructively on environmental issues, that challenge deserves a volume of its own. See, e.g., Joseph Kahn and Jim Yardley, "As China Roars, Pollution Reaches Deadly Extremes," *New York Times,* August 26, 2007, A1.

7. Aldo Leopold, *A Sand County Almanac* (London: Oxford University Press, 1949), 204, 211.

Introduction

1. The graphs are from W. Steffen et al., *Global Change and the Earth System: A Planet under Pressure* (Berlin: Springer, 2005), 132–133 (with sources for the graphs cited therein).

2. Millennium Ecosystem Assessment (MEA), *Ecosystems and Human Well-Being: Synthesis* (Washington, D.C.: Island Press, 2005), 31–32.

3. Food and Agriculture Organization, *Global Forest Resources Assessment 2005* (Rome: FAO, 2006), 20. This calculation includes all net change in forest area in South America, Central America, Africa, and South and Southeast Asia; the total is about twenty-eight million acres lost per year between 2000 and 2005.

4. MEA, *Ecosystems and Human Well-Being: Synthesis,* 2; MEA, *Ecosystems and Human Well-Being,* vol. 1: *Current State and Trends* (Washington, D.C.: Island Press, 2005), 14–15. See also N. C. Duke et al., "A World without Mangroves?" *Science* 317 (2007): 41. And see Carmen Revenga et al., *Pilot Analysis of Global Ecosystems: Freshwater Systems* (Washington, D.C.: WRI, 2000), 3, 21–22; World Resources Institute et al., *World Resources, 2000–2001* (Washington, D.C.: WRI, 2000), 72, 107; and Lauretta Burke et al., *Pilot Analysis of Global Ecosystems: Coastal Ecosystems* (Washington, D.C.: WRI, 2001), 19.

5. Food and Agriculture Organization, *World Review of Fisheries and Aquaculture* (Rome: FAO, 2006), 29 (online at http://www.fao.org/docrep/009/A0699e/A0699e00.htm); Ransom A. Myers and Boris Worm, "Rapid World-wide Depletion of Predatory Fish Communities," *Nature* 423 (2003): 280. See also Fred Pearce, "Oceans Raped of Their Former Riches," *New Scientist,* 2 August 2003, 4.

6. MEA, *Ecosystems and Human Well-Being: Synthesis,* 2.

7. MEA, *Ecosystems and Human Well-Being: Synthesis,* 5, 36.

8. Tim Radford, "Scientist Warns of Sixth Great Extinction of Wildlife," *Guardian* (U.K.), 29 November 2001. See also Nigel C. A. Pitman and Peter M. Jorgensen, "Estimating the Size of the World's Threatened Flora," *Science* 298 (2002): 989; and F. Stuart Chapin III et al., "Consequences of Changing Biodiversity," *Nature* 405 (2000): 234.

9. U.N. Environment Programme, *Global Environment Outlook, 3* (London: Earth-

scan, 2002), 64–65. Drylands cover about 40 percent of the earth's land surface, and an estimated 10–20 percent suffer from "severe" degradation. James F. Reynolds et al., "Global Desertification: Building a Science for Dryland Development," *Science* 316 (2007): 847. See also "Key Facts about Desertification," Reuters/Planet Ark, 6 June 2006, summarizing U.N. estimates.

10. Fred Pearce, "Northern Exposure," *New Scientist,* 31 May 1997, 25; Martin Enserink, "For Precarious Populations, Pollutants Present New Perils," *Science* 299 (2003): 1642. See also the data reported in Joe Thornton, *Pandora's Poison* (Cambridge, Mass.: MIT Press, 2000), 1–55.

11. U.N. Environment Programme, *Global Outlook for Ice and Snow,* 4 June 2007, available online at http://www.unep.org/geo/geo_ice. See also http://www.geo.unizh.ch/wgms. See generally William Collins et al., "The Physical Science behind Climate Change," *Scientific American,* August 2007, 64.

12. "UN Reports Increasing 'Dead Zones' in Oceans," Associated Press, 20 October 2006. See generally Mark Shrope, "The Dead Zones," *New Scientist,* 9 December 2006, 38; and Laurence Mee, "Reviving Dead Zones," *Scientific American,* November 2006, 79. On nitrogen pollution, see Charles Driscoll et al., "Nitrogen Pollution," *Environment* 45, no. 7 (2003): 8.

13. Peter M. Vitousek et al., "Human Appropriation of the Products of Photosynthesis," *Bioscience* 36, no. 6 (1986): 368; S. Rojstaczer et al., "Human Appropriation of Photosynthesis Products," *Science* 294 (2001): 2549. See also Helmut Haberl et al., "Quantifying and Mapping the Human Appropriation of Net Primary Production in Earth's Terrestrial Ecosystems," *Proceedings of the National Academy of Sciences* (2007), available online at http://www.pnas.org/cgi/doi/10.1073/pnas.0704243104.

14. U.N. Environment Programme, "At a Glance: The World's Water Crisis," available online at http://www.ourplanet.com/imgversn/141/glance.html.

15. MEA, *Ecosystem and Human Well-Being: Synthesis,* 32.

16. William H. MacLeish, *The Day before America: Changing the Nature of a Continent* (Boston: Houghton Mifflin, 1994), 164–168.

17. Quoted in Stephen R. Kellert, *Kinship to Mastery: Biophilia in Human Evolution and Development* (Washington, D.C.: Island Press, 1997), 179–180.

18. Quoted in Kellert, *Kinship to Mastery,* 181–182.

19. Angus Maddison, *The World Economy: A Millennial Perspective* (Paris: OECD, 2001).

20. J. R. McNeill, *Something New under the Sun: An Environmental History of the Twentieth-Century World* (New York: W. W. Norton, 2000), 4, 16.

21. Among the many books written about the possibility of large-scale economic, environmental, and social breakdown are Jared Diamond, *Collapse: How Societies Choose to Fail or Succeed* (New York: Viking, 2005); Fred Pearce,

The Last Generation: How Nature Will Take Her Revenge for Climate Change (London: Transworld, 2006); Martin Rees, *Our Final Hour: A Scientist's Warning . . .* (New York: Basic Books, 2003); Richard A. Posner, *Catastrophe: Risk and Response* (New York: Oxford University Press, 2004); James Lovelock, *The Revenge of Gaia: Why the Earth Is Fighting Back—and How We Can Still Save Humanity* (London: Penguin, 2006); James Martin, *The Meaning of the Twenty-first Century* (New York: Penguin, 2006); Thomas Homer-Dixon, *The Upside of Down: Catastrophe, Creativity, and the Renewal of Civilization* (Washington, D.C.: Island Press, 2006); Mayer Hillman, *The Suicidal Planet: How to Prevent Global Climate Catastrophe* (New York: St. Martin's Press, 2007); James Howard Kunstler, *The Long Emergency: Surviving the Converging Catastrophes of the Twenty-first Century* (New York: Grove Press, 2005); Richard Heinberg, *Power Down: Options and Actions for a Post-Carbon World* (Gabriola Island, B.C.: New Society, 2004); Ronald Wright, *A Short History of Progress* (New York: Carroll and Graf, 2004); John Leslie, *The End of the World: The Science and Ethics of Human Extinction* (London: Routledge, 1996); Colin Mason, *The 2030 Spike* (London: Earthscan, 2003); Michael T. Klare, *Resource Wars: The New Landscape of Global Conflict* (New York: Henry Holt, 2001); and Roy Woodbridge, *The Next World War: Tribes, Cities, Nations, and Ecological Decline* (Toronto: University of Toronto Press, 2004).

22. Rees, *Our Final Hour*, 8.
23. Robert A. Dahl, *On Political Equality* (New Haven and London: Yale University Press, 2006), 105–106.
24. Paul Hawken et al., *Natural Capitalism: Creating the Next Industrial Revolution* (Boston: Little, Brown, 1999), 10–11.
25. See Chapters 10–12.

Chapter 1. Looking into the Abyss

1. Quoted in Shierry Weber Nicholsen, *The Love of Nature and the End of the World: The Unspoken Dimensions of Environmental Concern* (Cambridge, Mass.: MIT Press, 2002), 171.
2. U.S. Council on Environmental Quality and U.S. Department of State, *The Global 2000 Report to the President—Entering the Twenty-first Century*, 2 vols. (Washington, D.C.: Government Printing Office, 1980).
3. Foreword to Robert Repetto, ed., *The Global Possible: Resources, Development, and the New Century* (New Haven and London: Yale University Press, 1985), xiii–xiv.
4. There are a number of useful overviews of global-scale environmental conditions and trends. See, e.g., World Resources Institute et al., *World Resources*

(Washington, D.C.: WRI, biennial series); W. Steffen et al., *Global Change and the Earth System: A Planet under Pressure* (Berlin: Springer, 2005); U.N. Environment Programme, *Global Environmental Outlook 3* (London: Earthscan, 2002); Donald Kennedy, ed., *State of the Planet: 2006–2007* (Washington, D.C.: Island Press, 2006); Ron Nielsen, *The Little Green Handbook: Seven Trends Shaping the Future of Our Planet* (New York: Picador, 2006); Worldwatch Institute, *State of the World* (New York: W. W. Norton, annual series); and Speth, *Red Sky at Morning: America and the Crisis of the Global Environment*, 2nd ed. (New Haven: Yale University Press, 2005). See also "Crossroads for Planet Earth," *Scientific American*, September 2005 (special issue); U.N. Environment Programme et al., *Protecting Our Planet, Securing Our Future* (Washington, D.C.: World Bank, 1998); John Kerry and Teresa Heinz Kerry, *This Moment on Earth: Today's New Environmentalists and Their Vision for the Future* (New York: Public Affairs, 2007); and Paul R. Ehrlich and Anne H. Ehrlich, *One with Nineveh: Politics, Consumptions, and the Human Future* (Washington, D.C.: Island Press, 2004).

See also the discussion in James Gustave Speth and Peter M. Haas, *Global Environmental Governance* (Washington, D.C.: Island Press, 2006), 17–44. At several points in this chapter, the discussion draws on the authors' presentation there.

5. David A. King, "Climate Change Science: Adapt, Mitigate, or Ignore," *Science* 303 (2004): 176.

6. Richard B. Alley et al., *Contribution of Working Group I to the Fourth Assessment Report of the Intergovernmental Panel on Climate Change: Summary for Policymakers* (Intergovernmental Panel on Climate Change, 2007), 5, 7–10, available online at http://ipcc-wg1.ucar.edu/wg1/wg1-report.html.

7. Neil Adger et al., *Working Group II Contributions to the Intergovernmental Panel on Climate Change Fourth Assessment Report: Summary for Policymakers* (Intergovernmental Panel on Climate Change, 2007), 5–8, available online at http://www.ipcc-wg2.org. All the IPCC working group reports can be accessed through this site.

8. Adger et al., *Working Group II Contributions*, 7.

9. Alley et al., *Contribution of Working Group I*, 9.

10. Adger et al., *Working Group II Contributions*, 7.

11. Arctic Climate Impact Assessment, *Impacts of a Warming Arctic* (Cambridge: Cambridge University Press, 2004); Deborah Zabarenko, "Arctic Ice Cap Melting Thirty Years Ahead of Forecast," Reuters, 1 May 2007; Gilbert Chin, ed., "An Ice Free Arctic," *Science* 305 (2004): 919.

12. U.N. Environment Programme, *Global Outlook for Ice and Snow*, 4 June 2007, 12, available online at http://www.unep.org/geo/geo_ice. See also Ian M. Howat

et al., "Rapid Changes in Ice Discharge from Greenland Outlet Glaciers" *Science Express*, 8 February 2007, available online at http://www.scienceexpress.org/8February2007/Page1/10.1126/science.1138478. And see Diana Lawrence and Daniel Dombey, "Canada Joins Rush to Claim the Arctic," *Financial Times*, 9 August 2007, 1.

13. World Health Organization, "New Book Demonstrates How Climate Change Impacts on Health," Geneva, 11 December 2003; World Health Organization et al., *Climate Change and Human Health* (Geneva: WHO, 2003); Andrew Jack, "Climate Toll to Double within Twenty-five Years," *Financial Times*/FT.com, 24 April 2007.

14. See, e.g., Douglas Fox, "Back to the No-Analog Future," *Science* 316 (2007): 823.

15. U.S. National Assessment Synthesis Team, *Climate Change Impacts on the United States: The Potential Consequences of Climate Variability and Change* (Cambridge: Cambridge University Press, 2000), 116–117. See also L. R. Iverson and A. M. Prasad, "Potential Changes in Tree Species Richness and Forest Community Types following Climate Change," *Ecosystems* 4 (2001): 193.

16. Richard Seager et al., "Model Projections of an Imminent Transition to a More Arid Climate in Southwestern North America," *Science* 316 (2007): 1181.

17. Jessica Marshall, "More Than Just a Drop in the Lake," *New Scientist*, 2 June 2007, 8.

18. See generally Michael Kahn, "Sudden Sea Level Surge Threatens One Billion —Study," Reuters/Planet Ark, 20 April 2007; Richard Kerr, "Pushing the Scary Side of Global Warming," *Science* 316 (2007): 1412; J. E. Hansen, "Scientific Reticence and Sea Level Rise," *Environmental Research Letters* 2 (2007), available online at http://www.stacks.iop.org/ERL/2/024002.

19. See Kevin E. Trenberth, "Warmer Oceans, Stronger Hurricanes," *Scientific American*, July 2007, 45.

20. John Vidal, "Climate Change to Force Mass Migration," *Guardian* (U.K.), 14 May 2007: Jeffrey D. Sachs, "Climate Change Refugees," *Scientific American*, June 2007, 43; Elisabeth Rosenthal, "Likely Spread of Deserts to Fertile Land Requires Quick Response, U.N. Report Says," *New York Times*, 28 June 2007, A6.

21. See, e.g., Tom Athanasiou and Paul Baer, *Dead Heat: Global Justice and Global Warming* (New York: Seven Stories Press, 2002); Nicholas D. Kristof, "Our Gas Guzzlers, Their Lives," *New York Times*, 28 June 2007, A23.

22. National Research Council, *Abrupt Climate Change: Inevitable Surprises* (Washington, D.C.: National Academy Press, 2002), 1.

23. Jim Hansen, "State of the Wild: Perspective of a Climatologist," 10 April 2007, available online at http://www.giss.nasa.gov/~jhansen/preprints/

Wild.070410.pdf, forthcoming in E. Fearn and K. H. Redford, eds., *The State of the Wild 2008: A Global Portrait of Wildlife, Wildlands, and Oceans* (Washington, D.C.: Island Press, 2008). See also J. Hansen et al., "Climate Change and Trace Gases," *Philosophical Transactions of the Royal Society* A365 (2007): 1925; J. Hansen et al., "Dangerous Human-Made Interference with Climate: A GISS ModelE Study," *Atmospheric Chemistry and Physics* 7 (2007): 2287; and James Hansen, "Climate Catastrophe," *New Scientist*, 28 July 2007, 30.

24. See Al Gore, *An Inconvenient Truth* (Emmaus, Pa.: Rodale, 2006); Speth, *Red Sky at Morning*, 55–71, 203–229; Eugene Linden, *Winds of Change: Climate, Weather, and the Destruction of Civilizations* (New York: Simon and Schuster, 2007); Eugene Linden, "Cloudy with a Chance of Chaos," *Fortune*, 17 January 2006; Fred Pearce, *With Speed and Violence: Why Scientists Fear Tipping Points in Climate Change* (Boston: Beacon Press, 2007); Harvard Medical School, *Climate Change Futures* (Cambridge, Mass.: Harvard Medical School, 2005); Scientific Expert Group on Climate Change, *Confronting Climate Change* (Washington, D.C.: Sigma Xi and United Nations Foundation, 2007); Elizabeth Kolbert, *Field Notes from a Catastrophe: Man, Nature, and Climate Change* (New York: Bloomsbury, 2006); Joseph Romm, *Hell and High Water: Global Warming—the Solution and the Politics—and What We Should Do* (New York: William Morrow, 2007); Tim Flannery, *The Weather Makers: How Man Is Changing the Climate and What It Means for Life on Earth* (New York: Grove Press, 2006); George Monbiot, *Heat: How to Stop the Planet from Burning* (Cambridge, Mass.: South End Press, 2007); Mark Lynas, *Six Degrees: Our Future on a Hotter Planet* (London: Fourth Estate, 2007); Ross Gelbspan, *Boiling Point* (New York: Basic Books, 2004); and Kirstin Dow and Thomas E. Downing, *The Atlas of Climate Change: Mapping the World's Greatest Challenge* (Berkeley: University of California Press, 2006). See also Stephen H. Schneider and Michael D. Mastrandrea, "Probabilistic Assessment of 'Dangerous' Climate Change and Emission Pathways," *Proceedings of the National Academy of Sciences* 102 (2005): 15728; Camille Parmesan, "Ecological and Evolutionary Responses to Recent Climate Change," *Annual Review of Ecology, Evolution, and Systematics* 37 (2006): 637; and Stefan Rahmstorf et al., "Recent Climate Observations Compared to Projections," *Science* 316 (2007): 709.

25. Michael Raupach et al., "Global and Regional Drivers of Accelerating CO_2 Emissions," *Proceedings of the National Academy of Sciences* (2007), available online at http://www.pnas.org/cgi/doi/10.1073/pnas.0700609104.

26. International Energy Agency, *World Energy Outlook, 2006* (Paris: OECD/IEA, 2006), 493, 529.

27. See note 23 above. See also the discussion in Speth, *Red Sky at Morning*, 205–212.

28. Terry Barker et al., *Climate Change, 2007: Mitigation of Climate Change, Working Group III Contribution to the IPCC Fourth Assessment Report, Summary for Policymakers* (Intergovernmental Panel on Climate Change, 2007), 23. Working Group III reports can be accessed at http://www.ipcc-wg2.org.

29. Nicholas Stern, *The Economics of Climate Change* (Cambridge: Cambridge University Press, 2007), xvi.

30. Stern, *Economics of Climate Change*, xvii. See also the exchange between William Nordhaus, "Critical Assumptions in the Stern Review on Climate Change," *Science* 317 (2007): 201; and Nicholas Stern and Chris Taylor, "Climate Change: Risk, Ethics, and the Stern Review," *Science* 317 (2007): 203.

31. See, e.g., Wallace S. Broecker, "CO_2 Arithmetic," *Science* 315 (2007): 1371, and the comments at *Science* 316 (2007): 829; and Oliver Morton, "Is This What It Takes to Save the World?" *Nature* 447 (2007): 132.

   On climate protection strategy generally, see California Environmental Associates, *Design to Win* (San Francisco: California Environmental Associates, 2007).

32. See Introduction, notes 2 and 3.

33. International Tropical Timber Organization, *Status of Tropical Forest Management, 2005: Summary Report* (Yokohama: ITTO, 2006), 5.

34. Roddy Scheer, "Indonesia's Rainforests on the Chopping Block," MSNBC, 8 August 2006; Lisa M. Curran et al., "Impact of El Niño and Logging on Canopy Tree Recruitment in Borneo," *Science* 286 (1999): 2184.

35. Adhityani Arga, "Indonesia World's No. 3 Greenhouse Gas Emitter—Report," Reuters/Planet Ark, 6 May 2007.

36. Tansa Musa, "Two-thirds of Congo Basin Forests Could Disappear," Reuters, 15 December 2006. The article discusses a World Wildlife Fund report on Congo Basin deforestation.

37. G. P. Asner et al., "Selective Logging in the Brazilian Amazon," *Science* 310 (2005): 480.

38. Food and Agriculture Organization, *Global Forest Resources Assessment, 2005* (Rome: FAO, 2006), 20.

39. See Introduction, note 9. See also Zafar Adeel et al., "Overcoming One of the Greatest Environmental Challenges of Our Time: Rethinking Policies to Cope with Desertification" (Tokyo: United Nations University, December 2006).

40. John Mitchell, "The Coming Water Crisis," *Environment: Yale*, Spring 2007, 5. See generally, World Water Assessment Programme, *Water: A Shared Responsibility* (Paris: UNESCO, 2006); Fred Pearce, *When the Rivers Run Dry: Water—The Defining Crisis of the Twenty-First Century* (Boston: Beacon Press, 2006); Sandra Postel and Brian Richter, *Rivers for Life: Managing Water for People and Nature* (Washington, D.C.: Island Press, 2003); and Jeffrey Roth-

feder, *Every Drop for Sale: Our Desperate Battle over Water* (New York: Penguin, 2004).

41. Nels Johnson et al., "Managing Water for People and Nature," *Science* 292 (2001), 1071–72.

42. See Introduction, note 14. See also Peter H. Gleick, "Safeguarding Our Water: Making Every Drop Count," *Scientific American*, February 2001, 41.

43. See Introduction, note 14.

44. Fred Pearce, "Asian Farmers Suck the Continent Dry," *New Scientist*, 18 August 2004, 6–7; Fred Pearce, "The Parched Planet," *New Scientist*, 26 February 2006, 32. See also Michael Specter, "The Last Drop," *New Yorker*, 23 October 2006, 60.

45. John Vidal, "Running on Empty," *Guardian Weekly* (U.K.), 29 September 2006, 1. See also Fiona Harvey, "Shortages of Water Growing Faster Than Expected," *Financial Times*, 22 August 2006, 3.

46. Celia Dugger, "The Need for Water Could Double in Fifty Years, U.N. Study Finds," *New York Times*, 22 August 2006, A12. See also Rachel Nowak, "The Continent That Ran Dry," *New Scientist*, 16 June 2007, 8.

47. "World Likely to Miss Clean Water Goals," Environmental News Service, 6 September 2006; Alana Herro, "Water and Sanitation 'Most Neglected Public Health Danger,'" *Worldwatch*, September–October 2006, 4; Anna Dolgov, "Two in Five People around the World without Proper Sanitation," Associated Press, 29 September 2006.

48. Claudia H. Deutsch, "There's Money in Thirst," *New York Times*, 10 August 2006. See also Abby Goodnough, "Florida Slow to See the Need to Save Water or to Enforce Restrictions on Use," *New York Times*, 19 June 2007, A18.

49. See Introduction, note 5; and Reg Watson and Daniel Pauly, "Systematic Distortions in World Fisheries Catch Trends," *Nature* 414 (2001): 534. See also "Fishy Figures," *Economist*, 1 December 2001, 75. See generally Daniel Pauly and Reg Watson, "Counting the Last Fish," *Scientific American*, July 2003, 42, and the references cited therein.

50. Ransom A. Myers and Boris Worm, "Rapid Worldwide Depletion of Predatory Fish Communities," *Nature* 423 (2003): 280.

51. Boris Worm et al., "Impacts of Biodiversity Loss on Ocean Ecosystem Services," *Science* 314 (2006): 787. See also the exchanges in "Letters," *Science* 316 (2007): 1281–1285. See also Richard Ellis, *The Empty Ocean* (Washington, D.C.: Island Press, 2003).

52. "Marine Environment Plagued by Pollution, UN Says," Environment News Service, 4 October 2006.

53. See Introduction, note 6.

54. Aaron Pressman, "Fished Out," *Business Week*, 4 September 2006, 56. See also

"More Species Overfished in U.S. in 2006—Report," Reuters/Planet Ark, 25 June 2007; and Roddy Scheer, "Ocean Rescue: Can We Head Off a Marine Cataclysm?" *E—The Environment Magazine,* July–August 2005, 26.

55. See generally Paul Molyneaux, *Swimming in Circles* (New York: Thunder's Mouth Press, 2007).

56. Center for Children's Health and the Environment, Mount Sinai School of Medicine, "Multiple Low-Level Chemical Exposures," available online at http://www.childenvironment.org/position.htm.

57. Nancy J. White, "A Toxic Life," *Toronto Star,* 21 April 2006, E1.

58. See International Scientific Committee, "The Faroes Statement: Human Health Effects of Developmental Exposure to Environmental Toxicants," International Conference on Fetal Programming and Developmental Toxicity, May 20–24, 2007; Marla Cone, "Common Chemicals Pose Danger for Fetuses, Scientists Warn," *Los Angeles Times,* 25 May 2007. See also Maggie Fox, "Studies Line Up on Parkinson's-Pesticide Link," Reuters/Planet Ark, 23 April 2007; Marla Cone, "Common Chemicals Are Linked to Breast Cancer," *Los Angeles Times,* 14 May 2007; and Erik Stokstad, "New Autism Law Focuses on Patients, Environment," *Science* 315 (2007): 27. And see Paul D. Blanc, *How Everyday Products Make People Sick: Toxins at Home and in the Workplace* (Berkeley: University of California Press, 2007).

59. Center for Children's Health and the Environment, Mount Sinai School of Medicine, "Endocrine-Disrupting Chemicals Act like Drugs, but Are Not Regulated as Drugs," available online at http://www.childenvironment.org. The question of EDSs was first brought to wide public attention by Theo Colborn et al., *Our Stolen Future: Are We Threatening Our Fertility, Intelligence, and Survival? A Scientific Detective Story* (New York: Dutton, 1996). The issue is discussed in Sheldon Krimsky, "Hormone Disruptors: A Clue to Understanding the Environmental Causes of Disease," *Environment* 43, no. 5 (2001): 22. See also Darshak M. Sanghavi, "Preschool Puberty, and a Search for Causes," *New York Times,* 17 October 2006.

60. Worldwatch Institute, *Vital Signs 2002* (New York: W. W. Norton, 2002), 112.

61. Stephen M. Meyer, *The End of the Wild* (Cambridge, Mass.: MIT Press, 2006), 4–5.

62. U.N. Secretariat of the Convention on Biodiversity, *Global Biodiversity Outlook, 2* (Montreal: Secretariat of the Convention on Biodiversity, 2006), 2–3. See also Worldwide Fund for Nature (WWF), *Living Planet Report, 2006* (Gland, Switzerland: WWF, 2006).

63. Stuart L. Pimm and Peter H. Raven, "Extinction by Numbers," *Nature* 403 (2000): 843.

64. See Speth, *Red Sky at Morning*, 30–36, for a more detailed review.

65. See Introduction, note 7.

66. Duncan Graham-Rowe, "From the Poles to the Deserts, More and More Animals Face Extinction," *New Scientist*, 6 May 2006, 10.

67. Constance Holden, ed., "Racing with the Turtles," *Science* 316 (2007): 179.

68. Joseph R. Mendelson III et al., "Confronting Amphibian Declines and Extinctions," *Science* 313 (2006): 48.

69. Erika Check, "The Tiger's Retreat," *Nature* 441 (2006): 927; James Randerson, "Tigers on the Brink of Extinction," *Guardian Weekly* (U.K.), 28 July–3 August 2006, 8.

70. Greg Butcher, "Common Birds in Decline," *Audubon*, July–August 2007, 58; Felicity Barringer, "Meadow Birds in Precipitous Decline, Audubon Says," *New York Times*, 15 June 2007, A19.

71. See Introduction, note 12, and Federico Magnani et al., "The Human Footprint in the Carbon Cycle of Temperate and Boreal Forests," *Nature* 447 (2007): 848.

72. Jane Lubchenco, "Entering the Century of the Environment," *Science* 279 (1998): 492.

73. The statement is reprinted in *Renewable Resource Journal*, Summer 2001, 16.

74. Millennium Ecosystem Assessment, Statement from the Board, *Living beyond Our Means: Natural Assets and Human Well-Being*, March 2005, 5. See also Jonathan A. Foley et al., "Global Consequences of Land Use," *Science* 309 (2005): 570.

75. "The Clock Is Ticking," *New York Times*, 17 January 2007, A19. See also http://www.thebulletin.org.

76. Nicholas Stern, *Economics of Climate Change*, 162. See also the exchange between Stern and William Nordhaus referenced in note 30, above.

77. WWF, *Living Planet Report, 2006*, 2–3.

78. WWF, *Living Planet Report, 2006*, 28–29.

79. U.N. Development Programme, *Human Development Report, 1998* (New York: Oxford University Press, 1998), 2.

80. These scenarios and worldviews are developed in Paul Raskin et al., *Great Transition* (Boston: Stockholm Environment Institute, 2002), 13–19; Jennifer Clapp and Peter Dauvergne, *Paths to a Green World: The Political Economy of the Global Environment* (Cambridge, Mass.: MIT Press, 2005), 1–19; and Allen Hammond, *Which World? Scenarios for the Twenty-first Century* (Washington, D.C.: Island Press, 1998), 26–65. See also John Dryzek, *The Politics of the Earth: Environmental Discourses* (Oxford: Oxford University Press, 2005).

81. Speth and Haas, *Global Environmental Governance*, 126–127.

82. Thomas Berry, *The Great Work: Our Way into the Future* (New York: Bell Tower, 1999), 1–7.

Chapter 2. Modern Capitalism

1. Javier Blas and Scheherazade Daneshkhu, "IMF Warns of 'Severe Global Slowdown,'" *Financial Times*, 6 September 2006; James C. Cooper, "If Oil Keeps Flowing, Growth Will, Too," *Business Week*, 31 July 2006, 21; Kevin J. Delaney, "Google Sees Content Deal as Key to Long-Term Growth," *Wall Street Journal*, 14 August 2006, B1.

2. Daniel Bell, *The Cultural Contradictions of Capitalism* (New York: Basic Books, 1978), 237–38. For an interesting perspective on the social and political roles of growth, see Benjamin M. Friedman, *The Moral Consequences of Economic Growth* (New York: Alfred A. Knopf, 2005).

3. "Economic Focus: Venturesome Consumption," *Economist*, 29 July 2006, 70. On advertising expenditures, see Speth, *Red Sky at Morning*, 20–21.

4. James C. Cooper, "Count on Consumers to Keep Spending," *Business Week*, 1 January 2007, 29.

5. Alex Barker and Krishna Guha, "Sharp Rise in Consumer Spending Heralds Strong Rebound in U.S. Growth," *Financial Times*, 14 June 2007, 6.

6. See "Time to Arise from a Great Slump," *Economist*, 22 July 2006, 65; and "What Ails Japan," *Economist*, 20 April 2002, 3 (special section). See also Clive Hamilton, *Growth Fetish* (London: Pluto Press, 2004), 226–227. But see also Ian Rowley and Kenji Hall, "Japan's Lost Generation," *Business Week*, 28 May 2007, 40.

7. Paul A. Samuelson and William D. Nordhaus, *Macroeconomics*, 17th ed. (Boston: McGraw-Hill Irwin, 2001), 69–70, 221.

8. J. R. McNeill, *Something New under the Sun: An Environmental History of the Twentieth-Century World* (New York: W. W. Norton, 2000), 334–336 (emphasis added).

9. Richard Bernstein, "Political Paralysis: Europe Stalls on Road to Economic Change," *New York Times*, 14 April 2006, A8.

10. Samuelson and Nordhaus, *Macroeconomics*, 409.

11. Paul Ekins, *Economic Growth and Environmental Sustainability* (London: Routledge, 2000), 316–317. Even the most ardent advocates of growth acknowledge the potential environmental costs, some more fully than others. See, e.g., Benjamin M. Friedman, *The Moral Consequences of Economic Growth*, 369–395; and Martin Wolf, *Why Globalization Works* (New Haven and London: Yale University Press, 2004), 188–194.

12. McNeill, *Something New under the Sun*, 360.

13. The figures presented are derived from time series data maintained by the World Resources Institute (www.earthtrends.wri.org), the Worldwatch Institute (www.worldwatch.org/node/1066/print), and the U.S. Bureau of the Census (www.census.gov). These figures are part of a more complete data set of eighteen indicators covering two periods (1960–1980, 1980–2004), available online at http://environment.yale.edu/post/5046/global_trends_1960_2004 _table/.

14. Donella Meadows, "Things Getting Worse at a Slower Rate," *Progressive Populist* 6, no. 14 (2000): 10.

15. Wallace E. Oates, "An Economic Perspective on Environmental and Resource Management," in Wallace E. Oates, ed., *The RFF Reader in Environmental and Resource Management* (Washington, D.C.: RFF, 1999), xiv.

16. Norman Myers and Jennifer Kent, *Perverse Subsidies: How Tax Dollars Can Undercut the Environment and the Economy* (Washington, D.C.: Island Press, 2001), 4, 188. As one indication of the seriousness of the subsidy problem, in May 2007, a group of 125 international marine scientists called on the World Trade Organization to slash government subsidies to their fishing industries. Robert Evans, "Scientists Urge WTO to Slash Fishing Subsidies," Reuters, 24 May 2007. See also Doug Koplow and John Dernbach, "Federal Fossil Fuel Subsidies and Greenhouse Gas Emissions," available online at http://www.earthtrack .net/earthtrack/library/Fossil%20Subsidies%20and%20Transparency.pdf.

17. Thomas L. Friedman, *The Lexus and the Olive Tree: Understanding Globalization* (New York: Farrar, Straus and Giroux, 1999), 86–87.

18. Michael Mandel, "Can Anyone Steer This Economy?" *Business Week*, 20 November 2006, 56–58.

19. Emily Matthews et al., *The Weight of Nations: Material Outflows from Industrial Economies* (Washington, D.C.: World Resources Institute, 2000), xi.

20. Stefan Bringezu et al., "International Comparison of Resource Use and Its Relation to Economic Growth," *Ecological Economics* 51 (2004): 97, 99.

21. Cutler Cleveland and Matthias Ruth, "Indicators of Dematerialization and the Materials Intensity of Use," *Journal of Industrial Ecology* 2, no. 3 (1999): 15. This study also points out that there are many cases where "less" may not be less from an environmental perspective, for example, the substitution of aluminum for steel and plastic for lumber. See also Ester van der Voet et al., "Dematerialization: Not Just a Matter of Weight," *Journal of Industrial Ecology* 8, no. 4 (2004): 121.

22. Arnulf Grubler, "Doing More with Less," *Environment*, March 2006, 29, 35. Dematerialization and increased resource productivity can be promoted as policy objectives. These issues are discussed in Chapters 4 and 5.

23. Paul Ekins, *Economic Growth*, 210 (emphasis added). See also D. I. Stern et al., "Economic Growth and Environmental Degradation: The Environmental Kuznets Curve and Sustainable Development," *World Development* 24, no. 7 (1996): 1151; William R. Moomaw and Gregory C. Unruh, "Are Environmental Kuznets Curves Misleading Us? The Case of CO_2 Emissions," *Environment and Development Economics* 2 (1997): 451; M. A. Cole et al., "The Environmental Kuznets Cure: An Empirical Analysis," *Environment and Development Economics* 2 (1997): 401; S. M. deBruyn et al., "Economic Growth and Emissions: Reconsidering the Empirical Basis of Environmental Kuznets Curves," *Ecological Economics* 25 (1998): 161; Scott Barrett and Kathryn Graddy, "Freedom, Growth, and the Environment," *Environment and Development Economics* 5 (2000): 433; Neha Khanna and Florenz Plassmann, "The Demand for Environmental Quality and the Environmental Kuznets Curve Hypothesis," *Ecological Economics* 51 (2004): 225; and Soumyananda Dinda, "Environmental Kuznets Curve Hypothesis: A Survey," *Ecological Economics* 49 (2004): 431.

24. Samuel Bowles et al., *Understanding Capitalism: Competition, Command, and Change* (New York: Oxford University Press, 2005), 4. See also Peter A. Hall and David Soskice, eds., *Varieties of Capitalism* (Oxford: Oxford University Press, 2001); and Colin Cronch and Wolfgang Streeck, *Political Economy of Modern Capitalism* (London: Sage, 1997).

25. Bowles, *Understanding Capitalism*, 119, 148–149, 152.

26. William J. Baumol, *The Free Market Innovation Machine: Analyzing the Growth Miracle of Capitalism* (Princeton, N.J.: Princeton University Press, 2002), 1. See also William J. Baumol et al., *Good Capitalism, Bad Capitalism, and the Economics of Growth and Prosperity* (New Haven and London: Yale University Press, 2007). And see Richard Smith, "Capitalism and Collapse: Contradictions of Jared Diamond's Market Meliorist Strategy to Save the Humans," *Ecological Economics* 55 (2005): 294.

27. Karl Polanyi, *The Great Transformation* (Boston: Beacon Press, 1944), 3, 73, 131.

28. Medard Gabel and Henry Bruner, *Global Inc.—An Atlas of the Multinational Corporation* (New York: New Press, 2003), 2–3. See also Richard J. Barnet and Ronald E. Muller, *Global Reach* (New York: Simon and Schuster, 1974).

29. See Chapter 8. See also Peter Barnes, *Capitalism 3.0: A Guide to Reclaiming the Commons* (San Francisco: Berrett-Koehler, 2006), 33–48.

30. See Chapters 7 and 10.

31. See Joseph S. Nye, Jr., *Soft Power: The Means to Success in World Politics* (New York: Public Affairs, 2004); and Robert Gilpin, *The Political Economy of International Relations* (Princeton, N.J.: Princeton University Press, 1987). For an interesting discussion of capitalism, growth, and nationalism, see Liah Green-

feld, *The Spirit of Capitalism: Nationalism and Economic Growth* (Cambridge, Mass.: Harvard University Press, 2001).

32. Jan Aart Scholte, "Beyond the Buzzword: Towards a Critical Theory of Globalization," in Eleonore Kofman and Gillian Youngs, eds., *Globalization: Theory and Practice* (London: Pinter, 1996), 55.

33. John S. Dryzek, "Ecology and Discursive Democracy: Beyond Liberal Capitalism and the Administrative State," in Martin O'Connor, ed., *Is Capitalism Sustainable? Political Economy and the Politics of Ecology* (New York: Guilford Press, 1994), 176.

34. Richard Falk, *Explorations at the Edge of Time: The Prospects for World Order* (Philadelphia: Temple University Press, 1992), 9.

35. Falk, *Explorations at the Edge of Time*, 13. Peter G. Brown has also provided a far-reaching vision of political transformation in *Ethics, Economics and International Relations* (Edinburgh: Edinburgh University Press, 2000).

36. See, e.g., David G. Myers, *The American Paradox: Spiritual Hunger in an Age of Plenty* (New Haven and London: Yale University Press, 2000).

37. Richard Hofstadter, *The American Political Tradition and the Men Who Made It* (New York: Vintage Books, 1948), vii–ix.

Chapter 3. The Limits of Today's Environmentalism

1. See James Gustave Speth, *Red Sky at Morning: America and the Crisis of the Global Environment*, 2nd ed. (New Haven and London: Yale University Press, 2005), 91–108.

2. World Resources Institute, *The Crucial Decade: The 1990's and the Global Environmental Challenge* (Washington, D.C.: WRI, 1989).

3. Environmental and Energy Study Institute Task Force, *Partnership for Sustainable Development: A New U.S. Agenda for International Development and Environmental Security* (Washington, D.C.: EESI, 1991).

4. World Resources Institute, *A New Generation of Environmental Leadership: Action for the Environment and the Economy* (Washington, D.C.: WRI, 1993). See also National Commission on the Environment, *Choosing a Sustainable Future* (Washington, D.C.: Island Press, 1993).

5. President's Council on Sustainable Development, *Sustainable America: A New Consensus* (Washington, D.C.: U.S. GPO, 1996).

6. On this general approach to environmental protection, see John S. Dryzek, *The Politics of the Earth: Environmental Discourses*, 2nd ed. (Oxford: Oxford University Press, 2005), 73–120.

7. Speth, *Red Sky at Morning*, 77–116.

8. David Levy and Peter Newell, "Oceans Apart: Business Responses to Global

Environmental Issues in Europe and the United States," *Environment* 42, no. 9 (2000): 9.

9. U.S. Environmental Protection Agency, "Air Quality and Emissions—Progress Continues in 2006," 30 April 2007 (online at http://www.epa.gov/airtrends/econ-emissions.html), 1.

10. EPA places the net benefits of the Clean Air Act between 1970 and 1990 at almost twenty trillion dollars. EPA, "The Benefits and the Costs of the Clean Air Act, 1970 to 1990," http://yosemite.epa.gov/ee/epa/eerm.nsf/vwRepNumLookup/EE-0295?opendocument.

11. John Heilprin, "EPA Says One-Third of Rivers in Survey Too Polluted for Swimming, Fishing," Associated Press, 1 October 2002. See also EPA, "The Wadeable Streams Assessment," May 2005, reporting that 42 percent of America's streams and small rivers were found to be in "poor" condition.

12. U.S. Environmental Protection Agency, "National Estuary Program Coastal Condition Report," June 2007 (online at http://www.epa.gov/owow/oceans/nepccrcpccr/index.html).

13. Lucy Kafanov, "Record Number of U.S. Beaches Closed Last Year," E+E News, 7 August 2007, available online at http://www.eenews.net/eenewspm/print/2007/08/07/3.

14. Lucy Kafanov, "Great Lakes Problems Nearing a 'Tipping Point,' Experts Say," Environment and Energy Daily, 14 September 2006; Andrew Stern, "Great Lakes near Ecological Breakdown: Scientists," Reuters/Planet Ark, 12 September 2005; John Flesher, "Lake Superior Shrinking, Warming," Associated Press, 7 August 2007.

15. EPA, "Air Quality and Emissions," 2.

16. American Lung Association, *State of the Air: 2006* (New York: American Lung Association, 2006), 5–13.

17. John Eyles and Nicole Consitt, "What's at Risk? Environmental Influences on Human Health," *Environment* 46, no. 8 (2004): 32.

18. Cheryl Dorschner, "Acid Rain Damage Far Worse than Previously Believed, USA," Medical News Today, 17 July 2005; Charles T. Driscoll et al., "Acid Deposition in the Northeastern United States," *Bioscience* 51, no. 3 (2001): 180; Kevin Krajick, "Longterm Data Show Lingering Effects from Acid Rain," *Science* 292 (2001): 195; Charles T. Driscoll et al., *Acid Rain Revisited*, Hubbard Brook Research Foundation, Science Links Publications, 2001. See also John McCormick, "Acid Pollution: The International Community's Continuing Struggle," *Environment* 40, no. 3 (1998): 17.

19. J. Clarence Davies and Jan Mazurek, *Pollution Control in the United States: Evaluating the System* (Washington, D.C.: Resources for the Future, 1998), 269.

20. These data and other data reflecting equally disturbing trends were collected from a variety of readily available U.S. government and other sources by Jorge Figueroa, Yale School of Forestry and Environmental Studies, in "Threats to the American Land," 3 May 2007, available online at http://environment.yale .edu/post/4971/threats_to_the_american_land/.

21. See Felicity Barringer, "Fewer Marshes + More Manmade Ponds = Increased Wetlands," *New York Times*, 31 March 2006, A16, reporting a U.S. Fish and Wildlife Service estimate of loss of 524,000 acres of natural wetlands between 1998 and 2004. The estimate is conservative. American groundwaters are also threatened by extensive use and pollution. See, e.g., William Ashworth, *Ogallala Blue: Water and Life on the High Plains* (New York: W. W. Norton, 2006).

22. See Bruce A. Stein et al., eds., *Our Precious Heritage: The Status of Biodiversity in the United States* (New York: Oxford University Press, 2000). Other grim statistics on declines of U.S. fish and bird populations are reported in Chapter 1.

23. James Gustave Speth and Peter M. Haas, *Global Environmental Governance* (Washington, D.C.: Island Press, 2006), 17. See also *Grist*, 22 April 2005 (online at www.grist.org with original sources cited).

24. See generally the discussion and works cited in Speth and Haas, *Global Environmental Governance*, 37–39; and Speth, *Red Sky at Morning*, 46–50.

25. John Wargo, *Our Children's Toxic Legacy: How Science and Law Fail to Protect Us from Pesticides* (New Haven and London: Yale University Press, 1998), 3.

26. Paul R. Ehrlich and Anne H. Ehrlich, *Betrayal of Science and Reason: How Anti-Environmental Rhetoric Threatens Our Future* (Washington, D.C.: Island Press, 1996), 163–165.

27. U.S. Environmental Protection Agency, *2005 TRI Public Data Release Report*, March 2007, 1–5, available online at http://www.epa.gov/tri/tridata/trio5/ index.htm.

28. "Fish with Male and Female Characteristics Found in the Potomac River," Greenwire, 6 September 2006; Deborah Zabarenko, "Intersex Fish Raises Pollution Concerns in U.S.," Reuters/Planet Ark, 9 August 2006; Brian Westley, "EPA Chided over 'Intersex' Fish Concerns," Associated Press, 5 October 2006.

29. Victoria Markham, "America's Supersized Footprint," *Business Week*, 30 October 2006, 132.

30. Richard N. L. Andrews, "Learning from History: U.S. Environmental Politics, Policies, and the Common Good," *Environment* 48, no. 9 (November 2006): 30, 33. See also Richard N. L. Andrews, *Managing the Environment, Managing Ourselves: A History of American Environmental Policy* (New Haven and London: Yale University Press, 2006).

31. Ross Gelbspan, *Boiling Point* (New York: Basic Books, 2004), 67–85.

32. Gelbspan, *Boiling Point,* 81.

33. Gelbspan, *Boiling Point,* 82.

34. Mark Dowie, *Losing Ground: American Environmentalism at the Close of the Twentieth Century* (Cambridge, Mass.: MIT Press, 1995), xiii.

35. Michael Shellenberger and Ted Nordhaus, *The Death of Environmentalism: Global Warming Politics in a Post-Environmental World* (New York: Nathan Cummings Foundation, 2004), 6–7, 10. Their critique is directed principally at the main national environmental organizations, not those actually working at the grassroots. See, e.g., *The Soul of Environmentalism* at www.rprogress .org/soul. See the discussion in Chapter 11.

36. It is good to see the recent growth of the League of Conservation Voters and other political engagement of the environmental community at national, state, and local levels. These are steps in the right direction. See Chapter 11.

37. See Richard J. Lazarus, *The Making of Environmental Law* (Chicago: University of Chicago Press, 2004), 94–97. See also Jason DeParle, "Goals Reached, Donor on Right Closes up Shop," *New York Times,* 29 May 2005, A1; and John J. Miller, *The Gift of Freedom: How the John M. Olin Foundation Changed America* (San Francisco: Encounter Books, 2006). Many, many books have chronicled the rise of the American right. See, e.g., Daniel Bell, ed., *The Radical Right* (Garden City, N.Y.: Anchor, 1963); Alan Crawford, *Thunder on the Right: The "New Right" and the Politics of Resentment* (New York: Pantheon, 1980); John Micklethwait and Adrian Wooldridge, *The Right Nation: Conservative Power in America* (New York: Penguin, 2005); and Jacob Hacker and Paul Pierson, *Off Center: The Republican Revolution and the Erosion of American Democracy* (New Haven and London: Yale University Press, 2005).

38. Frederick Buell, *From Apocalypse to Way of Life: Environmental Crisis in the American Century* (New York: Routledge, 2004), 3–4, 10, 18. See also Sharon Begley, "Global Warming Deniers: A Well-Funded Machine," *Newsweek,* 13 August 2007.

39. See William Ruckelshaus and J. Clarence Davies, "An EPA for the Twenty-first Century," *Boston Globe,* 7 July 2007, A9; and Sakiko Fukuda-Parr, ed., *The Gene Revolution: GM Crops and Unequal Development* (London: Earthscan, 2007).

40. Mark Hertsgaard, *Earth Odyssey* (New York: Broadway Books, 1999), 273–277. See also Edmund L. Andrews, "As Congress Turns to Energy, Lobbyists Are Out in Force," *New York Times,* 12 June 2007, A14.

41. S. W. Pacala et al., "False Alarm over Environmental False Alarms," *Science* 310 (2003): 1188.

42. See Thomas Sterner et al., "Quick Fixes for the Environment: Part of the

Solution or Part of the Problem," *Environment* 48, no. 10 (December 2006): 22; and Richard Levine and Ernest Yanarella, "Don't Pick the Low-Lying Fruit," 29 November 2006 (online at http://www.uky.edu/~rlevine/don1.html1).

43. William Greider, *The Soul of Capitalism: Opening Paths to a Moral Economy* (New York: Simon and Schuster, 2003), 32.

Chapter 4. The Market

1. Robert Kuttner, *Everything for Sale: The Virtues and Limits of Markets* (Chicago: University of Chicago Press, 1999), 4. See also Douglas S. Massey, *Return of the "L" Word: A Liberal Vision for the New Century* (Princeton, N.J.: Princeton University Press, 2005), 37–63.

2. Quoted in Kuttner, *Everything for Sale*, 39.

3. Paul Hawken et al., *Natural Capitalism: Creating the Next Industrial Revolution* (Boston: Little, Brown, 1999), 261.

4. Wallace E. Oates, ed., *The RFF Reader in Environmental and Resource Management* (Washington, D.C.: RFF, 1999), xiii.

5. Theodore Pantayotou, *Instruments of Change: Motivating and Financing Sustainable Development* (London: Earthscan, 1998), 6.

6. Nathaniel O. Keohane and Sheila M. Olmstead, *Markets and the Environment* (Washington, D.C.: Island Press, 2007), 65–66.

7. Frederick R. Anderson et al., *Environmental Improvement through Economic Incentives* (Baltimore: Johns Hopkins University Press, 1977).

8. Paul R. Portney, "Market-Based Approaches to Environmental Policy," *Resources*, Summer 2003, 15, 18.

9. Organisation for Economic Co-operation and Development, *Environmentally Related Taxes in OECD Countries: Issues and Strategies* (Paris: OECD, 2001), 9.

10. See, e.g., Keohane and Olmstead, *Markets and the Environment*, 140.

11. Tom Tietenberg, *Environmental Economics and Policy* (Boston: Pearson Addison Wesley, 2004), 248.

12. David Pearce and Edward Barbier, *Blueprint for a Sustainable Economy* (London: Earthscan, 2000), 7. See also Maureen L. Cropper and Wallace E. Oates, "Environmental Economics: A Survey," in Robert N. Stavins, ed., *Economics of the Environment* (New York: W. W. Norton, 2000), 62.

13. Frank Ackerman and Lisa Heinzerling, *Priceless: On Knowing the Price of Everything and the Value of Nothing* (New York: New Press, 2004), 8–9, 164, 177. See also Mark Sagoff, *The Economy of the Earth: Philosophy, Law, and the Environment* (New York: Cambridge University Press, 1988); and Douglas A. Kysar, "Climate Change, Cultural Transformation and Comprehensive Rationality," *Boston College Environmental Affairs Law Review* 31, no. 3 (2004): 555.

14. See, e.g., Daniel W. Bromley and Jouni Paavola, eds., *Economics, Ethics and Environmental Policy* (Oxford: Blackwell, 2002).

15. Norman Myers and Jennifer Kent, *Perverse Subsidies: How Tax Dollars Can Undercut the Environment and the Economy* (Washington, D.C.: Island Press, 2001), 188.

16. Congressional Research Service to Representative Diana Degette, memorandum, 26 May 2007.

17. See, e.g., Panayotou, *Instruments of Change*, 15–116; Keohane and Olmstead, *Markets and the Environment*, 125–206; Robert Repetto, *Green Fees: How a Tax Shift Can Work for the Environment and the Economy* (Washington, D.C.: WRI, 1992).

18. See, e.g., William J. Baumol and Wallace E. Oates, *Economics, Environmental Policy, and the Quality of Life* (Englewood Cliffs, N.J.: Prentice Hall, 1979), 307–322.

19. See "Special Issue: Priorities for Environmental Product Policy," *Journal of Industrial Ecology* 10, no. 3 (2006).

20. Richard B. Howarth and Richard B. Norgaard, "Intergenerational Resource Rights, Efficiency and Social Optimality," *Land Economics* 66, no. 1 (1990): 1; and Richard B. Howarth and Richard B. Norgaard, "Environmental Valuation under Sustainable Development," *American Economic Review* 82, no. 2 (1992), 473. See also Richard B. Norgaard, "Sustainability as Intergenerational Equity," *Environmental Impact Assessment Review* 12 (1992): 85.

21. McKinsey Global Institute, *Productivity of Growing Global Energy Demand*, November 2006.

22. Emily Thornton, "Roads to Riches," *Business Week*, 7 May 2007, 50.

23. Daniel Brook, "The Mall of America," *Harper's*, July 2007, 62. Outsourcing in America now extends to the military. See Jeremy Scahill, *Blackwater: The Rise of the World's Most Powerful Mercenary Army* (New York: Nation Books, 2007).

24. Kuttner, *Everything for Sale*, 49. See also the discussions in Peter G. Brown, *Ethics, Economics, and International Relations* (Edinburgh: Edinburgh University Press, 2000), 90–98; and Ronnie D. Lipschutz, *Global Environmental Politics* (Washington, D.C.: CQ Press, 2004), 108–121.

25. See Chapter 2.

26. Sagoff, *Economy of the Earth*, 15–17.

Chapter 5. Economic Growth

1. John Maynard Keynes, "Economic Possibilities for Our Grandchildren," in Keynes, *Essays in Persuasion* [1933] (New York: W. W. Norton, 1963), 365–373 (emphasis in original).

2. United Nations Development Programme, *Human Development Report, 1996* (New York: Oxford University Press, 1996), 2–4. See also Todd J. Moss, "Is Wealthier Really Healthier?" *Foreign Policy,* March–April 2005, 87.

3. See Jan Vandemoortele, "Growth Alone Is Not the Answer to Poverty," *Financial Times,* 13 August 2003, 11.

4. See, e.g., James Gustave Speth, *Red Sky at Morning: America and the Crisis of the Global Environment* (New Haven and London: Yale University Press, 2004), 154–157.

5. See Paul Ekins, *Economic Growth and Environmental Sustainability: The Prospects for Green Growth* (London: Routledge, 2000), 57. Ekins adds environmental growth to this list.

6. J. R. McNeill, *Something New under the Sun: An Environmental History of the Twentieth-Century World* (New York: W. W. Norton, 2000), xxiv, 336.

7. See Marian R. Chertow, "The IPAT Equation and Its Variants," *Journal of Industrial Ecology* 4, no. 4 (2000), 13.

8. Speth, *Red Sky at Morning,* 157–161.

9. The extensive use of "carbon capture and storage" technologies would allow these rates of change to be somewhat lower.

10. See the related discussion of GDP growth's links to environmental decline in Chapter 2.

11. Quoted in Robert M. Collins, *More: The Politics of Economic Growth in Postwar America* (Oxford: Oxford University Press, 2000), 63. See also John Kenneth Galbraith, *The Affluent Society* (Boston: Houghton Mifflin, 1958).

12. Kenneth E. Boulding, "The Economics of the Coming Spaceship Earth," in Henry Jarrett, ed., *Environmental Quality in a Growing Economy* (Baltimore: Johns Hopkins University Press, 1966).

13. E. J. Mishan, *The Costs of Economic Growth* (Harmondsworth, U.K.: Penguin, 1967). See also Fred Hirsch, *Social Limits to Growth* (Cambridge, Mass.: Harvard University Press, 1976); and Garrett Hardin, *Living within Limits: Ecology, Economics, and Population Taboos* (New York: Oxford University Press, 1993).

14. Donella H. Meadows et al., *The Limits to Growth* (New York: Signet, 1972). The most recent contribution is Donella Meadows et al., *Limits to Growth: The Thirty-Year Update* (White River Junction, Vt.: Chelsea Green, 2004).

15. Clive Hamilton, *Growth Fetish* (London: Pluto Press, 2004), 3, 10–11, 112–113. See also Robert A. Dahl, *On Political Equality* (New Haven and London: Yale University Press, 2007), 106–114.

16. Herman E. Daly and Joshua Farley, *Ecological Economics* (Washington, D.C.: Island Press, 2004), 6, 23. See also Herman E. Daly, *Beyond Growth* (Boston: Beacon Press, 1996). On ecological economics generally, see Robert Costanza, ed., *Ecological Economics* (New York: Columbia University Press, 1991); and

Robert Costanza et al., *An Introduction to Ecological Economics* (Boca Raton, Fla.: St. Lucie Press, 1997). See also John Gowdy and Jon Erickson, "Ecological Economics at a Crossroads," *Ecological Economics* 53 (2005): 17; and Stefan Baumgartner et al., "Relative and Absolute Scarcity of Nature," *Ecological Economics* 59 (2006): 487. And see Philip A. Lawn, *Toward Sustainable Development: An Ecological Economics Approach* (Boca Raton, Fla.: Lewis, 2001); Philip A. Lawn, "Ecological Tax Reform," *Environment, Development and Sustainability* 2 (2000): 143; and Mohan Munasinghe et al., eds., *The Sustainability of Long-Term Growth* (Cheltenham, U.K.: Edward Elgar, 2001).

17. Daly and Farley, *Ecological Economics*, 121.

18. Economist Partha Dasgupta has shown that accounting for natural capital can make a substantial difference in even weak sustainability. See Partha Dasgupta, *Economics: A Very Short Introduction* (Oxford: Oxford University Press, 2007), 126–138.

19. Hamilton, *Growth Fetish*, 209. In *Red Sky at Morning,* I made a similar point: "Imagine a group of countries where citizens rank at the top among today's countries in terms of purchasing power, health, longevity, and educational attainment; where income inequality between the top and the bottom of society is low and poverty virtually eliminated; and where fertility rates are at replacement levels or below, and the challenge is not unemployment but deploying innovative technologies to remain competitive and increase the productivity of a shrinking labor force. Should these countries not declare victory on the economic growth front and concentrate instead on protecting current standards of living (that's very different from resting on one's laurels in today's fast-moving world) and on enjoying the nonmaterial things that peace, economic security, education, freedom, and environmental quality make possible?" Speth, *Red Sky at Morning,* 192.

20. Daniel Bell, *The Cultural Contradictions of Capitalism* (New York: Basic Books, 1978), 237–238.

21. Benjamin M. Friedman, *The Moral Consequences of Economic Growth* (New York: Alfred A. Knopf, 2005), 4. Growth has many defenders, of course. Two of the best are Friedman and Martin Wolf, *Why Globalization Works* (New Haven and London: Yale University Press, 2004).

22. Quoted and cited in Chapter 2.

23. Collins, *More*, x–xi.

24. Collins, *More*, 240.

25. Quoted and cited in the Introduction.

26. Andrew Taylor, "Global Growth to Fall Unless People Work Longer," *Financial Times,* 11 October 2005; and "Aging Populations Threaten to Overwhelm Public Finances," *Financial Times,* 11 October 2005.

27. Phillip Longman, "The Depopulation Bomb," *Conservation in Practice* 7, no. 3 (2006): 40–41.

28. See, e.g., Victor Mallet, "Procreation Does Not Result in Wealth Creation," *Financial Times*, 4 January 2007, 11; and "Suddenly the Old World Looks Younger," *Economist*, 16 June 2007, 29.

29. Hamilton, *Growth Fetish*, 225.

30. See note 19, above.

31. John Stuart Mill, *Principles of Political Economy* (London: Longmans, Green, 1923), 751.

Chapter 6. Real Growth

1. Darrin M. McMahon, *Happiness: A History* (New York: Atlantic Monthly Press, 2006), 200.

2. McMahon, *Happiness*, 330–331.

3. McMahon, *Happiness*, 358–359.

4. Max Weber, *The Protestant Ethic and the Spirit of Capitalism* (New York: Charles Scribner's Sons, 1976), 181.

5. Among the many notable books on happiness are Robert E. Lane, *The Loss of Happiness in Market Democracies* (New Haven and London: Yale University Press, 2000), and Robert E. Lane, *After the End of History: The Curious Fate of American Materialism* (Ann Arbor: University of Michigan Press, 2006); Jonathan Haidt, *The Happiness Hypothesis: Finding Modern Truth in Ancient Wisdom* (New York: Basic Books, 2006); Daniel Gilbert, *Stumbling on Happiness* (New York: Vintage Books, 2005); Richard Layard, *Happiness: Lessons from a New Science* (New York: Penguin, 2005); Daniel Nettle, *Happiness: The Science behind Your Smile* (Oxford: Oxford University Press, 2005); Avner Offer, *The Challenge of Affluence: Self-Control and Well-Being in the United States and Britain since 1950* (Oxford: Oxford University Press, 2006); Bruno S. Frey and Alois Stutzer, *Happiness and Economics: How the Economy and Institutions Affect Human Well-Being* (Princeton, N.J.: Princeton University Press, 2002); Peter C. Whybrow, *American Mania: When More Is Not Enough* (New York: W. W. Norton, 2005); Robert H. Frank, *Luxury Fever: Money and Happiness in an Era of Excess* (Princeton, N.J.: Princeton University Press, 1999); Daniel Kahneman et al., *Well-Being: The Foundations of Hedonic Psychology* (New York: Russell Sage, 1999); and Mihaly Csikszentmihalyi, *Flow* (New York: Harper and Row, 1990). See also Tibor Scitovsky, *The Joyless Economy: The Psychology of Human Satisfaction* (Oxford: Oxford University Press, 1976).

6. Published by Springer Netherlands.

7. Ed Diener and Martin E. P. Seligman, "Beyond Money: Toward an Economy of

Well-Being," *Psychological Science in the Public Interest* 5, no. 1 (2004), 1. Diener and Seligman were featured in *Time*'s cover story on happiness, both looking very happy. "The Science of Happiness," *Time*, 17 January 2005, A4–A5.

8. Diener and Seligman, "Beyond Money," 4.

9. See, e.g., the discussions in Daniel Kahneman and Alan B. Krueger, "Developments in the Measurement of Subjective Well-Being," *Journal of Economic Perspectives* 20, no. 1 (2006): 3–9; Richard A. Easterlin, "Income and Happiness: Toward a Unified Theory," *Economic Journal* 111 (July 2001): 465–467; David G. Myers and Ed Diener, "The Pursuit of Happiness," *Scientific American*, May 1996, 54–56; and Carol Graham, "The Economics of Happiness," in Steven Durlauf and Larry Blume, eds., *The New Palgrave Dictionary of Economics*, 2nd ed. (London: Palgrave Macmillan, 2008).

10. Diener and Seligman, "Beyond Money," 5; Offer, *Challenge of Affluence*, 15–38.

11. Figure 1 is from Anthony Leiserowitz et al., "Sustainability Values, Attitudes and Behaviors: A Review of Multi-National and Global Trends," *Annual Review of Environment and Resources* 31 (2006): 413, available online at http://arjournals.annualreviews.org/doi/pdf/10.1146annurev.energy.31.102505.133552.

12. Diener and Seligman, "Beyond Money," 507.

13. Sources for fig. 2: United States, Jonathon Porritt, *Capitalism as If the World Matters* (London: Earthscan, 2005), 54; United Kingdom, Nick Donovan and David Halpern, *Life Satisfaction: The State of Knowledge and the Implications for Government*, U.K. Cabinet Office Strategy Unit, December 2002, 17; Japan, Bruno S. Frey and Alois Stutzer, *Happiness and Economics: How the Economy and Institutions Affect Human Well-Being* (Princeton, N.J.: Princeton University Press, 2002), 9.

14. Diener and Seligman, "Beyond Money," 3.

15. Layard, *Happiness*, 31.

16. See Layard, *Happiness*, 43–48; Diener and Seligman, "Beyond Money," 10; and Andrew Oswald, "The Hippies Were Right All Along about Happiness," *Financial Times*, 19 January 2006, 17. See also Gary Rivlin, "The Millionaires Who Don't Feel Rich," *New York Times*, 5 August 2007, 1A.

17. Layard, *Happiness*, 48–49.

18. Diener and Seligman, "Beyond Money," 10. .

19. Diener and Seligman, "Beyond Money," 18–19.

20. Layard, *Happiness*, 62–63.

21. Reported in Claudia Walls, "The New Science of Happiness," *Time*, 17 January 2005, A6.

It is surprising how little of the recent literature on happiness focuses on people's outdoor experiences and relationship to nature. This omission is no doubt partly due to the lack of questions regarding the environment in some of the major well-being surveys. Sociologist Stephen Kellert's *Building for Life* reviews the literature and concludes that "even in our modern increasingly urban age, human physical and mental well-being continues to depend highly on the quality of people's experience of the natural environment." Stephen R. Kellert, *Building for Life: Designing and Understanding the Human-Nature Connection* (Washington, D.C.: Island Press, 2005), 45. See also Peter H. Kahn, Jr., and Stephen R. Kellert, eds., *Children and Nature: Psychological, Sociocultural, and Evolutionary Investigations* (Cambridge, Mass.: MIT Press, 2002); Richard Louv, *Last Child in the Woods: Saving Our Children from Nature Deficit Disorder* (Chapel Hill, N.C.: Algonquin Books, 2005); and Gary Paul Nabhan and Stephen Trimble, *The Geography of Childhood* (Boston: Beacon Press, 1994).

22. Lane, *Loss of Happiness in Market Democracies*, 6, 9, 319–324.

   In 2006, sociologists reported that a quarter of Americans said they had no one with whom to discuss important matters, almost triple the number similarly isolated in 1985. Miller McPherson et al., "Social Isolation in America," *American Sociological Review* 71 (2006): 353. See generally Robert D. Putnam, *Bowling Alone: America's Declining Social Capital* (New York: Simon and Schuster, 2000).

23. Whybrow, *American Mania*, 4 (emphasis in original). Bipolar disorder diagnoses account for most of the 50 percent growth between 1996 and 2004 in American children diagnosed with psychiatric illness. See Andy Coghlan, "Young and Moody or Mentally Ill?" *New Scientist*, 19 May 2007, 6.

24. Bill McKibben, "Reversal of Fortune," *Mother Jones*, March–April 2007, 39–40. See also Bill McKibben, *Deep Economy: The Wealth of Communities and the Durable Future* (New York: Henry Holt, 2007).

25. David G. Myers, "What Is the Good Life?" *Yes! A Journal of Positive Futures*, Summer 2004, 15. See also David G. Myers, *The American Paradox: Spiritual Hunger in an Age of Plenty* (New Haven and London: Yale University Press, 2000).

26. See, e.g., Jean Gadrey, "What's Wrong with GDP and Growth? The Need for Alternative Indicators," in Edward Fullbrook, ed., *What's Wrong with Economics* (London: Anthem Press, 2004), 262; and Paul Elkins, *Economic Growth and Environmental Sustainability* (London: Routledge, 2000), 165.

27. Robert Repetto et al., *Wasting Assets: Natural Resources in the National Accounts* (Washington, D.C.: WRI, 1989), 2–3.

28. National Research Council, *Nature's Numbers: Expanding the National Income Accounts to Include the Environment* (Washington, D.C.: National Academy of Sciences, 1999).

29. See, e.g., U.N. Development Programme, *Human Development Report, 1998* (New York: Oxford University Press, 1998), 16–37.

30. Figure 3 is from Tim Jackson and Susanna Stymne, *Sustainable Economic Welfare in Sweden: A Pilot Index, 1950–2002* (Stockholm: Stockholm Environment Institute, 1996), available online at http://www.sei.se/dload/1996/SEWISAPI .pdf. On the ISEW generally and critiques of it, see John Talberth and Alok K. Bohara, "Economic Openness and Green GDP," *Ecological Economics* 58 (2006): 743–744, 756–757. See also Philip A. Lawn, "An Assessment of the Valuation Methods Used to Calculate the Index of Sustainable Economic Welfare (ISEW), Genuine Progress Indicator (GPI), and Sustainable Net Benefit Index (SNBI)," *Environment, Development and Sustainability* 7 (2005): 185.

31. See, e.g., Philip A. Lawn, *Toward Sustainable Development* (Boca Raton, Fla.: Lewis, 2001), 240–242.

32. Figure 4 is from Jason Venetoulis and Cliff Cobb and the Redefining Progress Sustainability Indicators Program, *The Genuine Progress Indicator, 1950–2002 (2004 Update)*, March 2004, available online at http://www.rprogress.org/ publications/2004/gpi_march2004update.pdf. See also Clifford Cobb et al., "If the GDP Is Up, Why Is American Down?" *Atlantic Monthly*, October 1995, 59.

33. William D. Nordhaus and James Tobin, "Is Growth Obsolete?" in Milton Moss, ed., *The Measurement of Economic and Social Performance* (New York: Columbia University Press, 1973).

34. Daniel C. Esty et al., *Pilot 2006 Environmental Performance Index*, Yale Center for Environmental Law and Policy (2006), online at http://www.yale.edu/epi.

35. Figure 5 is from Marque-Luisa Miringoff and Sandra Opdycke, *America's Social Health: Putting Social Issues back on the Public Agenda* (Armonk, N.Y.: M. E. Sharpe, 2007), 74.

36. University of Pennsylvania News Bureau, "U.S. Ranks 27th in 'Report Card' on World Social Progress; Africa in Dire Straits," 21 July 2003, available online with full analysis at http://www.sp2.upenn.edu/~restes/world.html.

   For an interesting review of a variety of measures, see Deutsche Bank Research, "Measures of Well-Being," 8 September 2006, available online at http://www .dbresearch.com.

37. Diener and Seligman, "Beyond Money," 1. See also Ed Diener, "Guidelines for National Indicators of Subjective Well-Being and Ill-Being," University of Illinois, 28 November 2005.

38. New Economics Foundation, *The Happy Planet Index* (London: New Economics Foundation, 2006), available online at http://www.happyplanetindex .org.

39. See Andrew C. Revkin, "A New Measure of Well-Being from a Happy Little Kingdom," *New York Times*, 4 October 2005, F1; and Karen Mazurkewich, "In Bhutan, Happiness Is King," *Wall Street Journal*, 13 October 2004, A14.

40. The measures listed here would respond to America's crisis of social inequal-

ity. See Kathryn M. Neckerman, ed., *Social Inequality* (New York: Russell Sage Foundation, 2004); Lawrence Mishel et al., *The State of Working America, 2006–2007* (Washington, D.C.: Economic Policy Institute, 2007); Mark Robert Rank, *One Nation, Underprivileged* (Oxford: Oxford University Press, 2004); David K. Shipler, *The Working Poor: Invisible in America* (New York: Alfred A. Knopf, 2004); Barbara Ehrenreich, *Nickeled and Dimed: On (Not) Getting by in America* (New York: Henry Holt, 2001); Barbara Ehrenreich, *Bait and Switch: The (Futile) Pursuit of the American Dream* (New York: Henry Holt, 2005); Louis Uchitelle, *The Disposable Americans: Layoffs and Their Consequences* (New York: Vintage, 2007); Jacob S. Hacker, *The Great Risk Shift: The Assault on American Jobs, Families, Health Care and Retirement—and How You Can Fight Back* (Oxford: Oxford University Press, 2006); Jonathan Cohn, *Sick: The Untold Story of America's Health Care Crisis—and the People Who Pay the Price* (New York: HarperCollins, 2007); National Urban League, *The State of Black America, 2007* (Silver Spring, Md.: Beckham, 2007); Frank Ackerman et al., *The Political Economy of Inequality* (Washington, D.C.: Island Press, 2000); Juliet B. Schor, *The Overworked American: The Unexpected Decline of Leisure* (New York: Basic Books, 1992); Juliet B. Schor, *The Overspent American: Why We Want What We Don't Need* (New York: HarperCollins, 1998); and Katherine S. Newman and Victor Tan Chen, *The Missing Class: Portraits of the Near Poor in America* (Boston: Beacon, 2007).

See also Report of the Task Force on Poverty, *From Poverty to Prosperity* (Washington, D.C.: Center for American Progress, 2007); Ross Eisenbrey et al., "An Agenda for Shared Prosperity," *EPI Journal,* Economic Policy Institute, Winter 2007, 1; *American Prospect,* special reports, "Bridging the Two Americas," September 2004, and "Why Can't America Have a Family Friendly Workplace?" March 2007; and Robert Kuttner, "The Road to Good Jobs," *American Prospect,* November 2006, 32.

Richard Layard discusses the need to tax income from excessive work. Layard, *Happiness,* 152–156. Robert H. Frank makes the case for a progressive consumption tax in *Luxury Fever,* 207–226. Harvard's Howard Gardner has proposed that no individual should be allowed to take home annually more than one hundred times what the average worker earns in a year and that no individual should be allowed to pass on an estate more than fifty times the maximum allowed annual income. See Howard Gardner, *Foreign Policy,* May–June 2007, 39.

Chapter 7. Consumption

1. Louis Uchitelle, "Why Americans Must Keep Spending," *New York Times,* 1 December 2003, 1 (Business Day).

2. Christopher Swann, "Consuming Concern," *Financial Times*, 20 January 2006, 11.

3. Kristin Downey, "Basics, Not Luxuries, Blamed for High Debt," *Washington Post*, 12 May 2006, D1.

4. Data are from *Grist*, 22 April 2005 (www.grist.org), and *Mother Jones*, March–April 2005, 26, and July–August 2007, 20.

5. See the discussion of U.S. environmental trends in Chapter 3.

6. See Benjamin Cashore et al., *Governing through Markets: Forest Certification and the Emergence of Non-State Authority* (New Haven and London: Yale University Press, 2004); and Benjamin Cashore, "Legitimacy and the Privatization of Environmental Governance," *Governance* 15 (2002): 504. See also Frieder Rubit and Paolo Frankl, eds., *The Future of Eco-Labelling* (Sheffield, U.K.: Greenleaf, 2005).

7. See William McDonough and Michael Braungart, *Cradle to Cradle: Remaking the Way We Make Things* (New York: Farrar, Straus and Giroux, 2002).

8. Joel Makower and Deborah Fleischer, *Sustainable Consumption and Production: Strategies for Accelerating Positive Change* (New York: Environmental Grantmakers Association, 2003), 2–3.

9. Wendy Gordon, "Crossing the Great Divide: Taking Green Mainstream" (presentation), *Green Guide*, 22 February 2007. See also Jerry Adler, "Going Green," *Newsweek*, 17 July 2006, 43; and John Carey, "Hugging the Tree Huggers," *Business Week*, 12 March 2007, 66.

10. Gordon, "Crossing the Great Divide."

11. Jonathon Porritt, *Capitalism as If the World Matters* (London: Earthscan, 2005), 269.

12. James Gustave Speth, *Red Sky at Morning: America and the Crisis of the Global Environment* (New Haven and London: Yale University Press, 2004), 125.

13. John Lintott, "Beyond the Economics of More: The Place of Consumption in Ecological Economics," *Ecological Economics* 25 (1998): 239.

14. Michael F. Maniates, "Individualization: Plant a Tree, Buy a Bike, Save the World?" *Global Environmental Politics* 1 (2001): 49–50.

15. See, e.g., Thomas Koellner et al., "Environmental Impacts of Conventional and Sustainable Investment Funds," *Journal of Industrial Ecology* 11, no. 3 (2007): 41.

16. Corporate Executive Board, Marketing Leadership Council, "Targeting the LOHAS Segment," Issue Brief, July 2005, 1. See also "New Green Advertising Network Launched," online at http://www.greenbiz.com/news/news_third.cfm?NewsID=34985.

17. See, e.g., Claudia H. Deutsch, "Now Looking Green Is Looking Good," *New York Times*, 28 December 2006; "More Firms Want to Market to Green Con-

sumer," Reuters, 5 March 2007; and Carlos Grande, "Consumption with a Conscience," *Financial Times*, 19 June 2007, 16.

18. Tim Jackson, "Live Better by Consuming Less? Is There a 'Double Dividend' in Sustainable Consumption?" *Journal of Industrial Ecology* 9 (2005): 19.

19. Jackson, "Live Better by Consuming Less?" 23.

20. See Chapter 6.

21. Tim Kasser et al., "Materialistic Values: Their Causes and Consequences," in Tim Kasser and Allen D. Kanner, eds., *Psychology and Consumer Culture: The Struggle for a Good Life in a Materialistic World* (Washington, D.C.: American Psychological Association, 2004), 11.

22. Quoted in Marilyn Elias, "Psychologists Know What Makes People Happy," *USA Today*, 10 December 2002. See also Tim Kasser, *The High Price of Materialism* (Cambridge, Mass.: MIT Press, 2002).

23. David G. Myers, "What Is the Good Life?" *Yes! A Journal of Positive Futures*, Summer 2004, 14.

24. Sheldon Solomon et al., "Lethal Consumption: Death-Denying Materialism," in Kasser and Kanner, eds., *Psychology and Consumer Culture*, 127. And see Ernest Becker, *The Denial of Death* (New York: Free Press, 1973).

25. Tim Jackson, "Live Better by Consuming Less?" 30. See also Gary Cross, *An All-Consuming Century: Why Commercialism Won in Modern America* (New York: Columbia University Press, 2000). And see Lizabeth Cohen, *A Consumers' Republic: The Politics of Mass Consumption in Postwar America* (New York: Alfred A. Knopf, 2003).

26. Hamilton, *Growth Fetish*, 84–85.

27. John de Graaf et al., *Affluenza: The All-Consuming Epidemic* (San Francisco: Berrett-Koehler, 2005), 173–174.

28. Center for a New American Dream, "New American Dream: A Public Opinion Poll," 2004, available online at http://www.newdream.org/about/PollResults.pdf.

29. See, e.g., Duane Elgin, *Voluntary Simplicity*, rev. ed. (New York: William Morrow, 1993); David G. Myers, *The American Paradox: Spiritual Hunger in an Age of Plenty* (New Haven and London: Yale University Press, 2000); Carl Honoré, *In Praise of Slowness: Challenging the Cult of Speed* (San Francisco: HarperCollins, 2004); Rick Warren, *The Purpose-Driven Life* (Grand Rapids, Mich.: Zondervan, 2002); and Richard Louv, *Last Child in the Woods: Saving Our Children from Nature Deficit Disorder* (Chapel Hill, N.C.: Algonquin Books, 2005).

30. See the extensive materials collected in "Resources for Citizens" in Speth, *Red Sky at Morning*, 231–256. See also www.CoopAmerica.org; www.Eco-Labels.org; www.TheGreenGuide.com; www.responsibleshopper.org; www

.Treehugger.com; www.stopglobalwarming.org; and www.campusclimate challenge.org.

31. Yvon Chouinard and Nora Gallagher, "Don't Buy This Shirt Unless You Need It," available online at http://metacool.typepad.com/metacool/files/10.02 .DontBuyThisShirt.pdf.

32. Anna White, "What Does Not Buying Really Look Like?" *In Balance: Journal of the Center for a New American Dream*, Winter 2006–2007, 1.

33. Leading works in consumption scholarship include Thomas Princen, *The Logic of Sufficiency* (Cambridge, Mass.: MIT Press, 2005); Thomas Princen, Michael Maniates, and Ken Conca, eds., *Confronting Consumption* (Cambridge, Mass.: MIT Press, 2002); Paul R. Ehrlich and Anne H. Erhlich, *One with Nineveh: Politics, Consumption, and the Human Future* (Washington, D.C.: Island Press, 2004); Juliet B. Schor and Douglas B. Holt, eds., *The Consumer Society Reader* (New York: New Press, 2000); and Ramachandra Guha, *How Much Should a Person Consume?* (Berkeley: University of California Press, 2006).

Broader in scope, and compelling, is Benjamin R. Barber's *Consumed: How Markets Corrupt Children, Infantilize Adults, and Swallow Citizens Whole* (New York: W.W. Norton, 2007).

34. See the works cited in notes 26–33 above and Naomi Klein, *No Logo* (New York: HarperCollins, 2000); Juliet B. Schor, *The Overspent American: Why We Want What We Don't Need* (New York: HarperCollins, 1998); Barry Schwartz, *The Paradox of Choice: Why More Is Less* (New York: HarperCollins, 2004); James B. Twichell, *Branded Nation: The Marketing of Megachurch, College Inc., and Museumworld* (New York: Simon and Schuster, 2004); John E. Carroll, *Sustainability and Spirituality* (Albany: SUNY Press, 2004); Bill McKibben, *Deep Economy: The Wealth of Communities and the Durable Future* (New York: Henry Holt, 2007); David C. Korten, *The Great Turning: From Empire to Earth Community* (San Francisco: Berrett-Koehler, 2006); Hazel Henderson, *Ethical Markets: Growing the Green Economy* (White River Junction, Vt.: Chelsea Green, 2006); Duane Elgin, *Promise Ahead: A Vision of Hope and Action for Humanity's Future* (New York: HarperCollins, 2000); Alan Weisman, *Gaviotas: A Village to Reinvent the World* (White River Junction, Vt.: Chelsea Green, 1998); and Carlo Petrini, *Slow Food Nation* (New York: Rizzoli Ex Libria, 2007). See also Dan Barry, "Would You Like This in Tens, Twenties, or Normans?" *New York Times*, 25 February 2007, 14.

35. Wendell Berry, *Selected Poems of Wendell Berry* (New York: Perseus Books, 1998).

Chapter 8. The Corporation

1. Adam Smith, *An Inquiry into the Nature and Causes of the Wealth of Nations*, ed. Edwin Cannan (New York: Modern Library, 1937), 800.

2. See Thom Hartman, *Unequal Protection* (Emmaus, Pa.: Rodale, 2002), 90–110.

3. Joel Bakan, *The Corporation* (London: Constable, 2005), 50. For a view that is somewhat more hopeful, see Bruce L. Hay et al., eds., *Environmental Protection and the Social Responsibility of Firms* (Washington, D.C.: Resources for the Future, 2005).

   Sometimes it seems there are no limits to the drive for profit. See, e.g., Brian Grow and Keith Epstein, "The Poverty Business: Inside U.S. Companies' Audacious Drive to Extract More Profits from the Nation's Working Poor," *Business Week*, 21 May 2007, 57; Heather Timmons, "British Science Group Says Exxon Misrepresents Climate Issues," *New York Times*, 21 September 2006; Tom Philpott, "Bad Wrap: How Archer Daniels Midland Cashes in on Mexico's Tortilla Woes," *Grist*, 22 February 2007; Caroline Daniel and Maija Palmer, "Google's Goal to Organize Your Daily Life," *Financial Times*, 23 May 2007, 1; Leslie Savan, "Teflon Is Forever," *Mother Jones*, May–June 2007, 71; and James Glanz and Eric Schmitt, "U.S. Widens Fraud Inquiry into Iraq Military Supplies," *New York Times*, 28 August 2007, 1A.

4. Bakan, *Corporation*, 60–61. See, e.g., John J. Fialka, "Oil, Coal Lobbyist Mount Attack on Senate Plan to Curb Emissions," *Wall Street Journal*, June 21, 2005, A4; and Robert Repetto, *Silence Is Golden, Leaden, and Copper: Disclosure of Material Environmental Information in the Hardrock Mining Industry* (New Haven: Yale School of Forestry and Environmental Studies, 2004).

5. Lou Dobbs, *War on the Middle Class* (New York: Viking, 2006), 37.

6. Robert Repetto, "Best Practice in Internal Oversight of Lobbying Practice," available online at http://www.yale.edu/envirocenter/WP200601-Repetto.pdf.

7. Lee Drutman, "Perennial Lobbying Scandal," www.TomPaine.com, 28 February 2007.

8. G. William Domhoff, *Who Rules America?* (Boston: McGraw-Hill, 2006), xi, xiii–xiv. See also Jeff Faux, *The Global Class War: How America's Bipartisan Elite Lost Our Future—and What It Will Take to Win It Back* (Hoboken, N.J.: John Wiley and Sons, 2006).

9. Edmund L. Andrews, "As Congress Turns to Energy, Lobbyists Are Out in Force," *New York Times*, 12 June 2007, A14.

10. These data are from Medar Gabel and Henry Bruner, *Global Inc.: An Atlas of the Multinational Corporation* (New York: New Press, 2003), 2, 7, 12, 28–29, 32–33, 132–133.

11. Gabel and Bruner, *Global, Inc.*, x.
12. There is, of course, a vast literature on globalization. For an environmental perspective, see James Gustave Speth, ed., *Worlds Apart: Globalization and the Environment* (Washington, D.C.: Island Press, 2003); Nayan Chanda, *Bound Together: How Traders, Preachers, Adventurers, and Warriors Shaped Globalization* (New Haven and London: Yale University Press, 2007); and Thomas L. Friedman, *The Lexus and the Olive Tree: Understanding Globalization* (New York: Farrar, Straus and Giroux, 1999).
13. John Cavanagh et al., *Alternatives to Economic Globalization: A Better World Is Possible* (San Francisco: Berrett-Koehler, 2002), 4.
14. Cavanagh et al., *Alternatives to Economic Globalization*, 17–20.
15. Cavanagh et al., *Alternatives to Economic Globalization*, 61, 8.
16. Cavanagh et al., *Alternatives to Economic Globalization*, 4–5.
17. Cavanagh et al., *Alternatives to Economic Globalization*, 122–124.
18. See, e.g., Sharon Beder, *Global Spin: The Corporate Assault on Environmentalism* (White River Junction, Vt.: Chelsea Green, 2002); David C. Korten, *When Corporations Rule the World* (San Francisco: Berrett-Koehler, 2001). See also John Perkins, *Confessions of an Economic Hit Man: How the U.S. Uses Globalization to Cheat Poor Countries out of Trillions* (New York: Penguin/Plume, 2004); and Carolyn Nordstrom, *Global Outlaws: Crime, Money, and Power in the Contemporary World* (Berkeley: University of California Press, 2007).
19. Fiona Harvey and Jenny Wiggins, "Companies Cash in on Environmental Awareness," *Financial Times*, 14 September 2006, 4.
20. Pete Engardio, "Beyond the Green Corporation," *Business Week*, 29 January 2007, 50, 53. See also Fiona Harvey, "Lenders See Profit in Responsibility," *Financial Times*, 12 June 2006, 1.
21. Francesco Guerrera, "GE Doubles 'Green' Sales in Two Years," *Financial Times*, 24 May 2007.
22. Daniel C. Esty and Andrew S. Winston, *Green to Gold: How Smart Companies Use Environmental Strategy to Innovate, Create Value, and Build Competitive Advantage* (New Haven and London: Yale University Press, 2006), 304.
23. The international survey was conducted for the University of Maryland's Program on International Policy Attitudes by GlobeScan. See http://www.globescan.com/news_archives/pipa_market.html. The U.S. survey was conducted by the Gallup Organization. See http://brain.gallup.com/content/Default.aspx?ci=5248 and http://brain.gallup.com/documents/questionnaire.aspx?STUDY=P0207027.
24. See generally Stephen Davis et al., *The New Capitalists: How Citizen Investors Are Reshaping the Corporate Agenda* (Boston: Harvard Business School Press, 2006).

25. See Andrew W. Savitz, *The Triple Bottom Line: How America's Best Companies Are Achieving Economic, Social and Environmental Success—and How You Can Too* (San Francisco: Jossey-Bass, 2006).

26. See Steven Mufson, "Companies Gear Up for Greenhouse Gas Limits," *Washington Post*, 29 May 2007, D1; Al Gore and David Blood, "For People and Planet," *Wall Street Journal*, 28 March 2006, A20; James Gustave Speth, "Why Business Needs Government Action on Climate Change," *World Watch*, July–August 2005, 30.

27. David Vogel, *The Market for Virtue: The Potential and Limits of Corporate Social Responsibility* (Washington, D.C.: Brookings Institution, 2005), 3–4 (emphasis in original). Some are more optimistic. See, e.g., Ira A. Jackson and Jane Nelson, *Profits with Principles* (New York: Doubleday, 2004).

28. Richard D. Morgenstern and William A. Pizer, eds., *Reality Check: The Nature and Performance of Voluntary Environmental Programs in the United States, Europe, and Japan* (Washington, D.C.: Resources for the Future, 2006), 184.

29. See, e.g., William J. Baumol, *Perfect Markets and Easy Virtue: Business Ethics and the Invisible Hand* (Cambridge, Mass.: Blackwell, 1991); Bill McKibben, "Hype vs. Hope: Is Corporate Do-Goodery for Real?" *Mother Jones*, November–December 2006, 52; Aaron Chatterji and Siona Listokin, "Corporate Social Irresponsibility," *DemocracyJournal.Org*, Winter 2007, 52; and John Kenney, "Beyond Propaganda," *New York Times*, 14 August 2006, A21. See also Thomas P. Lyon and John W. Maxwell, "Greenwash: Corporate Environmental Disclosure under Threat of Audit," available online at http://webuser.bus.umich.edu/tplyon/Lyon_Maxwell_Greenwash_March_2006.pdf.

30. See Kel Dummett, "Drivers for Corporate Environmental Responsibility," *Environment, Development and Sustainability* 8 (2006): 375.

31. See Common Cause et al., *Breaking Free with Fair Elections*, March 2007, available online at http://www.commoncause.org/atf/cf/{FB3C17E2-CDD1-4DF6-92BE-BD4429893665}/BREAKING%20FREE%20FOR%20FAIR%20ELECTIONS.PDF.

32. Repetto, "Best Practice."

33. See Robert Repetto and Duncan Austin, *Coming Clean: Corporate Disclosure of Financially Significant Environmental Risks* (Washington, D.C.: World Resources Institute, 2000).

34. Bakan, *Corporation*, 160.

35. Allen L. White, "Transforming the Corporation," Great Transition Initiative, Tellus Institute, Boston, 7 March 2006, 7–8. See www.gtinitiative.org. See also www.corporation2020.org. And see David C. Korten, *The Post-Corporate World: Life after Capitalism* (San Francisco: Berrett-Koehler, 1999).

36. White, "Transforming the Corporation," 12–17.

Chapter 9. Capitalism's Core

1. Gar Alperovitz, *America beyond Capitalism: Reclaiming Our Wealth, Our Liberty, and Our Democracy* (Hoboken, N.J.: John Wiley and Sons, 2005), ix.

2. Robert L. Heilbroner, *The Nature and Logic of Capitalism* (New York: W. W. Norton, 1985), 143–144.

3. Samuel Bowles et al., *Understanding Capitalism: Competition, Command, and Change* (New York: Oxford University Press, 2005), 531.

4. Bowles et al., *Understanding Capitalism,* 549.

5. Immanuel Wallerstein, *The End of the World as We Know It* (Minneapolis: University of Minnesota Press, 1999), 78–85. See also Immanuel Wallerstein, *World System Analysis: An Introduction* (Durham, N.C.: Duke University Press, 2004), 76–90.

6. John S. Dryzek, "Ecology and Discursive Democracy: Beyond Liberal Capitalism and the Administrative State," in Martin O'Connor, ed., *Is Capitalism Sustainable?* (New York: Guilford Press, 1994), 176–177. See also Matthew Paterson, *Understanding Global Environmental Politics: Domination, Accumulation, Resistance* (Basingstoke, U.K.: Palgrave, 2001).

7. Dryzek, "Ecology and Discursive Democracy," 185.

8. William Robinson, *A Theory of Global Capitalism: Production, Class, and State in a Transnational World* (Baltimore: Johns Hopkins University Press, 2004), 147.

9. Robinson, *Theory of Global Capitalism,* 171–172.

10. A notable exception is Amy Goodman's "Democracy Now" on Link TV. See www.democracynow.org.

11. Quoted in Robinson, *Theory of Global Capitalism,* 170.

12. Alperovitz, *America beyond Capitalism,* 1–4, 214.

13. Wallerstein, *The End of the World as We Know It,* 86.

14. The discussion here draws on Richard A. Rosen et al., "Visions of the Global Economy in a Great Transition World," Tellus Institute, Great Transition Initiative, Boston, 22 February 2006. See www.gtinitiative.org.

15. Mica Panic might fault this typology for failing to distinguish between the Continent's social democratic models (e.g., Sweden, Norway) and its "corporatist" ones (the Netherlands, Germany, France). See M. Panic, "Does Europe Need Neoliberal Reforms?" *Cambridge Journal of Economics* 31 (2007): 145. See also Pranab Bardhan, "Capitalism: One Size Does Not Suit All," *YaleGlobal,* 7 December 2006. And see Colin Crouch and Wolfgang Streeck, eds., *Political Economy of Modern Capitalism: Mapping Convergence and Diversity* (London: Sage, 1997).

16. Lawrence Peter King and Ivan Szelenyi, *Theories of the New Class* (Minneapolis: University of Minnesota Press, 2004), 242.

17. Hamilton, *Growth Fetish*, 211.
18. Hamilton, *Growth Fetish*, 212–214.
19. Alperovitz, *America beyond Capitalism*, 5.
20. William Greider, *The Soul of Capitalism: Opening Paths to a Moral Economy* (New York: Simon and Schuster, 2003), 22.
21. Greider, *Soul of Capitalism*, 33.
22. Greider, *Soul of Capitalism*, 65.
23. Jeff Gates, *The Ownership Solution: Toward a Shared Capitalism for the Twenty-First Century* (Reading, Mass.: Addison-Wesley, 1998).
24. Alperovitz, *American beyond Capitalism*, 88–89.
25. Peter Barnes, *Capitalism 3.0: A Guide to Reclaiming the Commons* (San Francisco: Berrett-Koehler, 2006).
26. See Stephen Davis et al., *The New Capitalists: How Citizen Investors Are Reshaping the Corporate Agenda* (Boston: Harvard Business School Press, 2006).

   In addition to the growth of fiduciary, pension fund capitalism, other changes in finance and ownership patterns sweeping through capitalism today present a daunting array of risks and opportunities. See, e.g., "Caveat Investor," *Economist*, 10 February 2007, 12 (private equity); Gerald Lyons, "How State Capitalism Could Change the World," *Financial Times*, 8 June 2007, 13 (state capitalism, sovereign wealth funds); and Martin Wolf, "The New Capitalism," *Financial Times*, 19 June 2007, 11 ("financial capitalism"). Meanwhile founding family ownership is still important (e.g., founding families own 18 percent of the equity in the Standard and Poor's 100 Industrials), and family firms are reported to have better environmental records on average. See Justin Craig and Clay Dibrell, "The Natural Environment, Innovation and Firm Performance," *Family Business Review* 19, no. 4 (2006): 275.
27. See, e.g., Stephanie Strom, "Make Money, Save the World," *New York Times*, 6 May 2007 ("Sunday Business," 1); Mary Anne Ostrom, "Global Philanthropy Forum Explores New Way of Giving," *San Jose Mercury News*, 12 April 2007; Andrew Jack, "Beyond Charity? A New Generation Enters the Business of Doing Good," *Financial Times*, 5 April 2007, 11.
28. A still valuable trove of ideas is Martin Carnoy and Derek Shearer, *Economic Democracy: The Challenge of the 1980s* (White Plains, N.Y.: M. E. Sharpe, 1980).

Chapter 10. A New Consciousness

1. Vaclav Havel, "Spirit of the Earth," *Resurgence*, November–December 1998, 30.
2. Quoted in Verlyn Klinkenborg, "Land Man," *New York Times Book Review*, 5 November 2006, 30.

3. Paul R. Ehrlich and Donald Kennedy, "Millennium Assessment of Human Behavior," *Science* 309 (2005): 562–563. See also Paul R. Ehrlich, *Human Natures: Genes, Cultures, and the Human Prospect* (Washington, D.C.: Island Press, 2000).

4. Paul Raskin et al., *Great Transition* (Boston: Stockholm Environment Institute, 2002), 42–43.

5. Peter Senge et al., *Presence: Human Purpose and the Field of the Future* (New York: Doubleday, 2005), 26.

6. Mary Evelyn Tucker and John Grim, "Daring to Dream: Religion and the Future of the Earth," *Reflections—The Journal of the Yale Divinity School,* Spring 2007, 4.

7. Erich Fromm, *To Have or to Be* (London: Continuum, 1977), 8, 137.

8. Thomas Berry, *The Great Work: Our Way into the Future* (New York: Bell Tower, 1999), 4, 104–105.

9. Charles A. Reich, "Reflections: The Greening of America," *New Yorker,* 26 September 1970, 42, 74–75, 86, 92, 102, 111. See also Charles A. Reich, *The Greening of America* (New York: Random House, 1970).

10. Robert A. Dahl, *On Political Equality* (New Haven and London: Yale University Press, 2007), 114–116.

11. For an interesting journey into behavioral psychology, see, e.g., Paul C. Stern, "Understanding Individuals' Environmentally Significant Behavior," *Environmental Law Reporter* 35 (2005): 10785; Anja Kollmus and Julian Agyeman, "Mind the Gap: Why Do People Act Environmentally and What Are the Barriers to Pro-Environmental Behavior?" *Environmental Education Research* 8, no. 3 (2002): 239; and Thomas Dietz et al., "Environmental Values," *Annual Review of Environmental Resources* 30 (2005), 335.

12. See Great Transition Initiative, online at www.gtinitiative.org.

13. Paul D. Raskin, *The Great Transition Today: A Report from the Future* (Boston: Tellus Institute, 2006), 1–2, available online at http://www.gtinitiative.org/default.asp?action=43.

14. Raskin, *Great Transition Today,* 2.

15. David Korten, "The Great Turning," *Yes! A Journal of Positive Futures,* Summer 2006, 16. See also David C. Korten, *The Great Turning: From Empire to Earth Community* (San Francisco: Berrett-Koehler, 2006).

16. The Earth Charter is available online at http://earthcharterinaction.org/ec_splash/. The site also describes the work of the Earth Charter Initiative.

17. See, e.g., Tu Wei-ming, "Beyond the Enlightenment Mentality," and Ralph Metzner, "The Emerging Ecological Worldview," both in Mary Evelyn Tucker and John Grim, eds., *Worldviews and Ecology: Religion, Philosophy, and the Environment* (New York: Orbis Books, 1994); Manfred Max-Neef, "Development and Human Needs," in Paul Ekins and Manfred Max-Neef, *Real-Life Economics:*

Understanding Wealth Creation (London: Routledge, 1992), 197; Thomas Berry, *Evening Thoughts,* ed. Mary Evelyn Tucker (San Francisco: Sierra Club Books, 2006; Stephen R. Kellert and Timothy J. Farnham, eds., *The Good in Nature and Humanity: Connecting Science, Religion, and Spirituality with the Natural World* (Washington, D.C.: Island Press, 2002); Carolyn Merchant, *Radical Ecology: The Search for a Livable World* (New York: Routledge, 1992); Mary Mellor, *Feminism and Ecology: An Introduction* (New York: New York University Press, 1998); Satish Kumar, *You Are, Therefore I Am: A Declaration of Dependence* (Totnes, U.K.: Green Books, 2002); Kwame Anthony Appiah, *Cosmopolitanism: Ethics in a World of Strangers* (New York: W. W. Norton, 2006); Bill McKibben, *Deep Economy: The Wealth of Communities and the Durable Future* (New York: Henry Holt, 2007); J. Baird Callicott, *In Defense of the Land Ethic: Essays in Environmental Philosophy* (Albany: SUNY Press, 1989); J. Baird Callicott, *Earth's Insights: A Multicultural Survey of Ecological Ethics from the Mediterranean Basin to the Australian Basin* (Berkeley: University of California Press, 1994); and Victor Ferkiss, *Nature, Technology, and Society: Cultural Roots of the Current Environmental Crisis* (New York: New York University Press, 1993).

18. George Levine, *Darwin Loves You: Natural Selection and the Re-enchantment of the World* (Princeton, N.J.: Princeton University Press, 2006), xvii.

19. William Wordsworth, "The Tables Turned," in *The Poetical Works of William Wordsworth,* ed. Thomas Hutchinson (London: Oxford University Press, 1895), 481.

20. Oren Lyons, address to delegates of the United Nations, 1977, reprinted in A. Harvey, ed., *The Essential Mystics: Selections from the World's Great Wisdom Traditions* (San Francisco: HarperSanFrancisco, 1996), 14–15.

21. Quoted in Lawrence E. Harrison, *The Central Liberal Truth: How Politics Can Change a Culture and Save It* (Oxford: Oxford University Press, 2006), xvi.

22. Harvey Nelsen, "How History and Historical Myth Shape Current Polities," University of South Florida (undated).

23. Thomas Homer-Dixon, *The Upside of Down: Catastrophe, Creativity, and the Renewal of Civilization* (Washington, D.C.: Island Press, 2006), 6, 109, 254.

24. Homer-Dixon, *Upside of Down,* 281.

25. Howard Gardner, *Changing Minds: The Art and Science of Changing Our Own and Other People's Minds* (Boston: Harvard Business School Press, 2006), 69, 82. See also James MacGregor Burns, *Transforming Leadership: A New Pursuit of Happiness* (New York: Grove Press, 2003).

26. See Chapter 7.

27. Bill Moyers, "The Narrative Imperative," TomPaine.CommonSense, 4 January 2007, 2, 5, available online at http://www.tompaine.com/print/the_narrative _imperative.php.

28. Thomas Berry, *The Dream of the Earth* (San Francisco: Sierra Club Books, 1988); Carolyn Merchant, *Reinventing Eden: The Fate of Nature in Western Culture* (New York: Routledge, 2003); Evan Eisenberg, *The Ecology of Eden* (New York: Vintage Books, 1998); McKibben, *Deep Economy*.

29. See the discussion of Robert E. Lane's *Loss of Happiness in Market Democracies* in Chapter 6.

30. Curtis White, *The Spirit of Disobedience* (Sausalito, Calif.: PoliPoint Press, 2007), 118, 124.

31. Mary Evelyn Tucker, *Worldly Wonder: Religions Enter Their Ecological Phase* (Chicago: Open Court, 2003), 9, 43.

32. See generally National Religious Partnership for the Environment, www.nrpe .org. See also Gary T. Gardner, *Inspiring Progress: Religions' Contributions to Sustainable Development* (New York: W. W. Norton, 2006); James Gustave Speth, "Protecting Creation a Moral Duty," *Environment: Yale—The Journal of the School of Forestry and Environmental Studies*, Spring 2007, 2; Bob Edgar, *Middle Church: Reclaiming the Moral Values of the Faithful* (New York: Simon and Schuster, 2006); Steven C. Rockefeller and John C. Elder, *Spirit and Nature: Why the Environment Is a Religious Issue—An Interfaith Dialogue* (Boston: Beacon Press, 1992); E. O. Wilson, *The Creation* (New York: W. W. Norton, 2006); James Jones, *Jesus and the Earth* (London: Society for Promoting Christian Learning, 2003).

33. See David Orr, *Earth in Mind: On Education, Environment and the Human Prospect* (Washington, D.C.: Island Press, 2004); and Orr, *Ecological Literacy: Education and the Transition to a Postmodern World* (Albany: State University of New York Press, 1992).

34. Stephen R. Kellert, *Building for Life: Designing and Understanding the Human-Nature Connection* (Washington, D.C.: Island Press, 2005).

35. See Alan Andreasen, *Social Marketing in the Twenty-first Century* (Thousand Oaks, Calif.: Sage, 2006).

Chapter 11. A New Politics

1. William Greider, *The Soul of Capitalism: Opening Paths to a Moral Economy* (New York: Simon and Schuster, 2003), 29.

2. Peter Barnes, *Capitalism 3.0: A Guide to Reclaiming the Commons* (San Francisco: Berrett-Koehler, 2006), 34, 36, 45.

3. Gar Alperovitz, *America beyond Capitalism: Reclaiming Our Wealth, Our Liberty, and Our Democracy* (Hoboken, N.J.: John Wiley and Sons, 2005).

4. Roger D. Masters, *The Nation Is Burdened: American Foreign Policy in a Changing World* (New York: Random House, 1967).

5. Kirkpatrick Sale, *Dwellers in the Land: A Bioregional Vision* (Athens: University of Georgia Press, 2000).

6. John Cavanagh et al., *Alternatives to Economic Globalization: A Better World Is Possible* (San Francisco: Berrett-Koehler, 2002). See Chapter 8.

7. William A. Shutkin, *The Land That Could Be: Environmentalism and Democracy in the Twenty-First Century* (Cambridge, Mass.: MIT Press, 2000), 128.

8. Ronnie D. Lipschutz, *Global Environmental Politics: Power, Perspectives, and Practice* (Washington, D.C.: CQ Press, 2004), 133, 242–243.

9. Lipschutz, *Global Environmental Politics*, 175.

10. See Sheila Jasanoff and Marybeth Long Martello, eds., *Earthly Politics: Local and Global in Environmental Governance* (Cambridge, Mass.: MIT Press, 2004).

11. Walter F. Baber and Robert V. Bartlett, *Deliberative Environmental Politics: Democracy and Ecological Rationality* (Cambridge, Mass.: MIT Press, 2004).

12. See, e.g., James Bohman, ed., *Public Deliberation: Pluralism, Complexity, and Democracy* (Cambridge, Mass.: MIT Press, 1996); James Bohman and William Rehg, eds., *Deliberative Democracy: Essays on Reason and Politics* (Cambridge, Mass.: MIT Press, 1997); and Iris Marion Young, "Activist Challenges to Deliberative Democracy" in James S. Fishkin and Peter Laslett, eds., *Debating Deliberative Democracy* (Oxford: Blackwell, 2003), 102.

13. Benjamin R. Barber, *Strong Democracy: Participatory Politics for a New Age* (Berkeley: University of California Press, 2003), 117, 151.

14. Barber, *Strong Democracy*, 152, 261 (emphasis in original).

15. David Held et al., *Global Transformations: Politics, Economics, and Culture* (Stanford, Calif.: Stanford University Press, 1999), 449–450.

16. Paul D. Raskin, *The Great Transition Today: A Report from the Future* (Boston: Tellus Institute, 2006), 5–6, available online at http://www.gtinitiative.org/default.asp?action=43.

17. See, e.g., "Is the U.S. Ready for Human Rights?" *Yes! The Journal of Positive Futures*, Spring 2007, 17–53; and George E. Clark, "Environment and Human Rights," *Environment* July–August 2007, 3. For an innovative rights-based approach, see Peter G. Brown, *Ethics, Economics and International Relations* (Edinburgh: Edinburgh University Press, 2000), 9–29.

18. See Chapter 6.

19. See the works cited in Chapter 6, note 40.

20. Robert A. Dahl, *On Political Equality* (New Haven and London: Yale University Press, 2006), x. Dahl believes that an alternative, hopeful outcome is also "highly plausible." "Which of these futures will prevail depends on the coming generations of American citizens," he writes.

21. Lawrence R. Jacobs and Theda Skocpol, eds., *Inequality and American Democracy* (New York: Russell Sage Foundation, 2005).

22. Jacob S. Hacker and Paul Pierson, *Off Center: The Republican Revolution and the Erosion of American Democracy* (New Haven and London: Yale University Press, 2005), 185–223. See also Al Gore, *The Assault on Reason* (New York: Penguin, 2007).

23. Common Cause et al., *Breaking Free with Fair Elections*, March 2007, available online at http://www.commoncause.org/atf/cf/{FB3C17E2-CD D1-4DF6-92BE-BD4429893665}/BREAKING%20FREE%20FOR%20FAIR %20ELECTIONS.PDF. See also www.democracy21.org.

24. Personal communication.

25. Steven Hill, *Ten Steps to Repair American Democracy* (Sausalito, Calif.: PoliPoint Press, 2006). See also David W. Orr, *The Last Refuge: Patriotism, Politics, and the Environment in an Age of Terror* (Washington, D.C.: Island Press, 2004). And see "Imbalance of Power," *American Prospect*, June 2004 (special report).

26. See generally Philip Shabecoff, *Earth Rising: American Environmentalism in the Twenty-First Century* (Washington, D.C.: Island Press, 2000); and Eban Goodstein, "Climate Change: What the World Needs Now Is . . . Politics," *World Watch*, January–February 2006, 25.

27. See Mark Dowie, *Losing Ground: American Environmentalism at the Close of the Twentieth Century* (Cambridge, Mass.: MIT Press, 1995), xi–xiv, 1–8, 205–257.

28. See Sidney Tarrow, *The New Transnational Activism* (Cambridge: Cambridge University Press, 2005); and Doug McAdam et al., eds., *Comparative Perspectives on Social Movements* (Cambridge: Cambridge University Press, 1996).

29. James Gustave Speth, *Red Sky at Morning: America and the Crisis of the Global Environment* (New Haven and London: Yale University Press, 2004), 197–198.

30. Paul Hawken, *Blessed Unrest: How the Largest Movement in the World Came into Being and Why No One Saw It Coming* (New York: Viking, 2007), 2, 186, 189. See also Katharine Ainger et al., eds., *We Are Everywhere* (London: Verso, 2003); and Tom Mertes, ed., *A Movement of Movements: Is Another World Really Possible?* (London: Verso, 2004).

31. See www.energyaction.net; www.climatechallenge.org; www.itsgetting hotinhere.org; and http://powershift07.org.

32. See Chapter 10, notes 31, 32.

33. See Mark Hertsgaard, "Green Goes Grassroots," *Nation*, 31 July–7 August 2006, 11.

34. See www.apolloalliance.org.

35. Joan Hamilton, "Man of Steel," *Sierra*, July–August 2007, 18.

36. See www.theclimateproject.org.

37. Nicola Graydon, "Rainforest Action Network," *Ecologist*, February 2006, 38.

38. See, e.g., Van Jones, "Beyond Eco-Apartheid," *Conscious Choice*, April 2007, available online at http://www.consciouschoice.com/2007/04/eco-apartheid0704.html; Michel Gelobter et al., "The Soul of Environmentalism," *Grist*, 27 May 2005; Hertsgaard, "Green Goes Grassroots," 11 (regarding Jerome Ringo).

39. Darryl Lorenzo Wellington, "A Grassroots Social Forum," *Nation*, 13–20 August 2007, 16.

40. See Jonathan Isham and Sissel Waage, *Ignition: What You Can Do to Fight Global Warming and Spark a Movement* (Washington, D.C.: Island Press, 2007); and Eben Goodstein, *Fighting for Love in the Century of Extinction: How Passion and Politics Can Stop Global Warming* (Burlington: University of Vermont Press, 2007). See especially www.stepitup2007.org and www.1skycampaign.org. See also Thomas L. Friedman, "The Greening of Geopolitics," *New York Times Magazine*, 15 April 2007, 40; and Mark Hertsgaard, "The Making of a Climate Movement," *Nation*, 22 October 2007, 18.

41. Hertsgaard, "Green Goes Grassroots," 14.

42. See generally Frances Moore Lappé, *Democracy's Edge: Choosing to Save Our Country by Bringing Democracy to Life* (San Francisco: Jossey-Bass, 2006).

43. Mark Kurlansky, *1968: The Year That Rocked the World* (New York: Random House, 2005), 380. See also Jon Agnone, "Amplifying Public Opinion: The Policy Impact of the U.S. Environmental Movement," *Social Forces* 85, no. 4 (2007): 1593 (finding that "a greater amount of federal legislation is passed when protest amplifies, or raises the salience of, public opinion on a given issue").

Chapter 12. The Bridge at the Edge of the World

1. Kenneth Brower, "Introduction," in Aldo Leopold, *A Sand County Almanac* (New York: Oxford University Press, 2001), 9.

2. Arundhati Roy, "Come September," in Paul Rogat Loeb, *The Impossible Will Take a Little While: A Citizen's Guide to Hope in a Time of Fear* (New York: Basic Books, 2004), 240.

Index

abundance, 162

acid rain: partial success against, 19, 71, 95; subsidies and, 54; threat from, 20(fig.), 37, 39, 75; valuation of damages from, 97

Ackerman, Franken, 99–100

advertising: and consumption, 47, 133–134, 159; and green consumerism, 155; restricting, 120, 145; and well-being, 160

Affluenza (de Graaf et al.), 161

Africa, 23, 30, 31

agriculture, 33, 38, 51, 54, 76. *See also* pesticides

air pollution, 57, 73, 74. *See also* greenhouse gas emissions

Alaska, 25

Alperovitz, Gar, 183, 188, 191–194, 219, 225

Amazon rainforest, 31. *See also* deforestation

American Lung Association (*2006* report), 74

amphibians, 37, 38, 76

Anderson, Fred, 93

Andrews, Richard, 78

Antarctica, 22. *See also* glaciers and ice sheets

anthropocentrism, 62

antiglobalization movement, 171–173. *See also* globalization

Arctic, 24. *See also* glaciers and ice sheets

Asia, 23, 123. *See also specific countries*

Audubon, John James, 2–3

Austria, 140(fig.)

automobiles, 50, 152

Baber, Walter, 221–222

Bakan, Joel, 167–168, 180

Barber, Benjamin, 221, 222–223, 225

Barbier, Edward, 97

Civil Rights Revolution (*1960s*), 231–232

Clean Air Act, 93, 95

Clean Water Act, 73–74, 84

climate change, 19–30; and biodiversity loss, 37; corporate concern about, 176; glaciers and ice sheets, 22, 24, 26; grounds for hope, 234–235, 237; international response needed, 27–28; other issues worsened, 39; projections, 22–25, 28–29; public awareness of, 233–234; reality of, 2, 19–22, 27; speed, 25–26; temperature increases, 21–22, 28–29; "tipping point," 25–26. *See also* desertification; drought; greenhouse gas emissions; Kyoto Protocol; sea level rise; weather

Collins, Robert, 121–222

communism, 48, 58, 183, 188

conflict, international/regional, 27, 33, 40

Congressional Research Service, 100

consciousness, transformation in, 10, 199–216; forces for change, 211–216; new worldview, 205–211; voices for change, 200–204, 235

consumerism, 7, 62, 147–164; environmental agenda and, 225; green consumerism, 10, 149–156, 174–176, 230; growing dissatisfaction with, 160–163; origins/causes, 157–160; in the U.S., 147–149; and well-being, 128 (*see also* well-being). *See also* advertising; consumption; materialism

consumption: as addiction, 133–134, 157–158, 236; challenging overconsumption, 160–164; and economic growth, 47; growth of, 50–51, 154; Hamilton on, 117; overconsumption, 92, 156–157; psychological underpinnings, 157–160; reducing, 148, 154, 156–160, 162–163; in the U.S., 147–149. *See also* consumerism; materialism

Convention on the Law of the Sea, 72

co-ops, 193

corals, 1, 23, 37

corporations: accountability, 152, 166, 178–179; characteristics affecting behavior of, 166–168, 178–181; corporate law, 166–167, 178–180; corporate social responsibility (CSR), 175–176, 177; economic and political power, 62, 83, 168–173, 179–180, 217–219; encouraging green practices, 151–152; externalization of costs, 7, 52–53, 60–61, 91–92, 167–168; and globalization, 170–173; good done by, 165; and the media, 79, 168; new ground rules needed, 120; resistance to regulation, 83, 175, 178; stock price, 61; transformation (greening) of, 173–182. *See also* capitalism, modern; economic growth; globalization

cosmopolitanism, 223

cost-benefit analysis, 98–99. *See also* valuation of environmental damages

Cronkite, Walter, 79

The Crucial Decade: The 1990s and the Global Environmental Challenge (World Resources Institute), 68–69

cultural change. *See* consciousness, transformation in

customer ownership, 192–193

employee ownership, 192

employment, 120, 123, 145

endocrine disrupting substances (EDSs), 35–36, 77

energy: co-ops, 193; energy efficiency, 29–30, 114, 155, 156; energy policy, 68, 100, 169–170; increased use/demand, 50; potential for productivity gains, 103–104; U.S. consumption, 75, 149, 152. *See also* fossil fuels; renewable energy

Environmental Defense, 71, 94, 239n2

environmental deterioration: books on coming crisis/collapse, 5–6, 241–242n21; capitalism's role, 6–8, 60–61, 82–83, 85–86, 111–112, 208–209 (*see also* capitalism, modern); change in consciousness needed to address (*see* consciousness, transformation in); consumerism's role, 147–148; driving forces, 6–8; economic costs, 40–41, 91–92, 117; economic growth's role, 7–9, 48–57, 111–112, 115–116, 172 (*see also* economic growth); and the end of capitalism, 185–188; first-generation issues, 18–19; global threats, 1–2, 20(table) (*see also* specific threats); globalization's role, 172 (*see also* globalization); grounds for hope, 234–235, 237; implications, 39–42; interactions, 39; possible responses, 42–45; response to threats slow, 115. *See also* market failure and the environment; *and specific issues*

environmental economics, 90–106; consumption not challenged, 148; economic growth imperative questioned, 117–118; market incentives, 93–95, 119–120; prices and environmental costs, 96–100, 148; public intervention, case for, 91–92

Environmental Grantmakers Association, 151–152

environmental organizations. *See* environmentalism

environmental performance measures, 141–144

Environmental Protection Agency (EPA), 70, 74

environmentalism: citizens' movement, 172–173, 220, 228–231; and consumption, 154–155; in the Earth Charter, 208–209; features and precepts, 68–71; future attitudes toward environment, 205–207; and human rights, 225–226; international movement/approach needed, 228–229; international results to date, 71–73; limitations and shortcomings, 9, 67, 79–86, 220–221; new environmental politics, 225–231 (*see also* politics: transformation of); opposition underestimated, 80; organization statistics, 230; and policy reform, 44–45, 68–70; and regulation, 93–94; in the U.S. (*1980s–2007*), 67–71, 79–82; working within the system, xii–xiii, 44–45, 69–70, 79–80, 85–86, 219

EPA, 70, 74

Estes, Richard, 142–143

Esty, Daniel, 141–142, 174–175

Europe, 28, 48–49, 151, 153. *See also* specific countries

extinction. *See* species extinction

Exxon, 170

Lovins, Amory, 11–12, 102–103
Lovins, Hunter, 11–12, 102–103
Lubchenko, Jane, 39
Lyon, Oren, 210–211

Maddison, Angus, 4
malnutrition, 23, 24
mammals, 2, 37, 38, 76. *See also*
    species extinction
Mander, Jerry, 171
Maniates, Michael, 154–155
"Manifesto" (Berry), 163–164
margarine, 160
market and market economy: in
    Bowles's analysis, 58; democratic
    government as counterbalance to,
    89; market fundamentalism vs.
    environmentalism, 81–82; Market
    World, 43, 44, 89, 111; place of,
    89–90, 105; proponents' faith in,
    43, 44. *See also* capitalism, modern;
    economic growth; market failure
    and the environment; market
    transformation
market failure and the environment:
    corporate transformation and, 177
    (*see also* corporations: transforma-
    tion of); environmental costs not
    reflected, 7, 8, 52–53, 60–61, 91–92,
    117, 167–168; environmental eco-
    nomics as answer, 90–106 (*see also*
    environmental economics); globali-
    zation and, 62, 170; perverse subsi-
    dies, 8, 54, 60, 91, 92, 100 (*see also*
    subsidies); and social regulation,
    105. *See also* market and market
    economy; market transformation
market transformation, 9, 12; attack-
    ing perverse subsidies, 100; in-
    creased resource productivity and

natural capital regeneration, 103;
    market incentives, 93–95, 101–102,
    119–120 (*see also* cap and trade sys-
    tems; "polluter pays" principal);
    need for, 105–106; political difficul-
    ties, 105; sustainability and, 103;
    valuation of environmental dam-
    ages, 96–100
Marx, Karl, 184
Maryland, 77
Masters, Roger, 219
materialism: growing dissatisfaction
    with, 160–163, 234; obsessive
    materialism, 117; and well-being,
    128, 137, 157–160 (*see also* well-
    being). *See also* consumerism;
    consumption
McKibben, Bill, 137, 213, 231
McMahon, Darrin, 126–128
McNeill, J. R., 4, 48, 50
Meadows, Dennis, 116
Meadows, Donella, 51, 116
meat consumption, 50, 51
media, 79, 82, 168
mercury, 36
Merwin, W. S., 235
methane, 21, 26
Meyer, Stephen, 36
migrations, human, 25
Mill, John Stuart, 125, 183–184
Millennium Ecosystem Assessment,
    40
mining, 18, 31, 83, 170
minority environmental leaders, 231
Miringoff, Marc and Marque-Luisa,
    142
Mishan, E. J., 116
momentum, 4–5
Mount Sinai School of Medicine,
    chemical toxin studies, 35–36

Moyers, Bill, 213
Moynihan, Daniel Patrick, 211
Myers, David, 137–138
Myers, Norman, 54, 100

natural capital, regeneration/
    conservation of, 103, 120
Natural Resources Defense Council,
    71, 74, 239n2
Nelson, Harvey, 211
Netherlands, 140(fig.)
New Jersey, 29
New Scientist, 33
New Sustainability World, 44, 45.
    See also sustainability
New York Times, 33, 49, 148, 169–
    170
New Zealand, 141–142
Newell, Peter, 72
1996 Human Development Report
    (UNDP), 109
nitrogen: fixed nitrogen, 2, 38;
    nitrogen oxide emissions, 21, 51,
    73 (*see also* acid rain)
Nordhaus, Ted, 80, 233–234
Nordhaus, William, 47–48, 49, 141
Norgaard, Richard, 103
nuclear energy, 54, 83

Oates, Wallace, 52–53, 90–91
oceans, 2, 23, 25, 26, 38. *See also*
    corals; fisheries, marine
OECD, 46, 49, 94, 123, 170
oil: vs. natural gas, 114; oil compa-
    nies, 169, 170; Santa Barbara
    spill, 215–216; U.S. consumption,
    75, 149; and U.S. growth, 46.
    See also fossil fuels; greenhouse
    gas emissions
Organization for Economic Coopera-

tion and Development (OECD),
    46, 49, 94, 123, 170
organized labor, 230
ownership alternatives, 192–194,
    273n26
ozone: ground-level ozone, 23, 74;
    stratospheric ozone depletion, 2,
    20(table), 71. *See also* greenhouse
    gas emissions
"Ozymandius" (Shelley), 158–159

Pacala, Steve, 84
Panayotou, Theo, 91–92
paper and paper products, 50, 51
passenger pigeons, 2–4
Patagonia (company), 162
Pearce, David, 97
performance measures, 141–144
performance standards, 93–95,
    119–120. *See also* regulation,
    environmental
persistent organic pollutants (POPs),
    35–36
pesticides, 35, 54, 76–77
Pierson, Paul, 227
plants, flowering, 76
Polanyi, Karl, 60
policy reform: corporate law and
    policy, 178–180; to correct market
    failure, 53–54; grants to promote,
    151; and green consumerism, 155–
    156; green growth belief, 112;
    Hamilton's proposal, 190; human
    welfare/well-being promotion,
    12–13, 145–146; proponents' faith
    in, 43–44; quantitative limits and
    performance standards, 93–95,
    119–120; today's environmentalism
    and, 44–45, 68–70. *See also* public
    policy

politics: challenge of market transformation, 105, 217; complexity of international environmental issues, 84; corporate power and, 62, 83, 168–173, 179–180, 217–219; and cultural change, 211; inability to address problems of capitalism, 217–220; political reform, need for, 227; postmodern politics, 64–65; transformation of, 10, 220–232. *See also* government; policy reform; public policy

"polluter pays" principal, 94–95, 101–102

pollution: air pollution, 57, 73, 74 (*see also* greenhouse gas emissions); and biodiversity loss, 37; cost not borne by producer, 53, 92 (*see also* market failure and the environment); of fresh water, 33, 73–74; Kuznets curve hypothesis, 56–57; market incentives to limit (*see* cap and trade systems; "polluter pays" principal); of the oceans, 34 (*see also* oceans); quantitative limits, 93–95, 119–120; taxes on, 96–97; toxic chemicals in humans, 35–36. *See also* regulation, environmental; toxic chemicals; *and specific pollutants*

population growth: acceleration, 4; as environmental issue, 77–78; fertility rates declining, 123–124; slowing, 234; statistics, 50, 51, 77–78, 123

Porritt, Jonathon, 153

Portney, Paul, 94

post-growth society, 120–125

Potomac River basin, 77

poverty: climate change and, 23 (*see also* disease; fresh water; sea level rise); and environmental deterioration, 6; growth and the alleviation of, 109 (*see also* social justice); responsibility of rich toward poor, 145

precipitation, heavy, 22

President's Council on Sustainable Development, 69

prices: curbing consumption through, 148; difficulties of incorporating environmental costs, 96–100; environmental costs not reflected, 52–53, 91–92; price signals muted, 103–104; and regulatory standards, 101, 102

privatization, 104

production: environmentally friendly production, 150–151; export-oriented production, 172; global increases (*1980–2005*), 50; over-production of depleting/polluting commodities, 92; producer responsibility laws, 151; resource productivity, 11, 55–56, 103. *See also* consumerism; consumption; economic growth

profit and growth motive, 7, 58–61, 82–83, 121–122. *See also* capitalism, modern; economic growth

property rights, 95, 218

public goods, 92

public policy: case for government intervention, 91–95; corporate power and, 62, 168, 169–170; energy policy, 68, 100, 169–170; today's environmentalism and, 68–70. *See also* policy reform

public trusts, 193

public vs. private sectors, 61–62

Raskin, Paul, 43, 201, 205–206, 224–225

rebound effect, 155

recycling, 110, 150, 151

Red Sky at Morning (Speth), 19, 71, 73, 154, 178, 229, 260n19

Rees, Sir Martin, 5–6

reflectivity of earth, 25

regulation, environmental: complexity and proliferation, 83–84; corporate resistance/fear of, 83, 175, 178, 218; limited shortcomings, 84–85; performance standards approach (quantitative limits), 93–94, 119–120; public views on, 175; standard-setting philosophies, 101–2

Reich, Charles, 202–204

relationships, importance of, 135–136, 263n22

religion and the environmental crisis, 214–215, 230, 234

renewable energy, 30

Repetto, Robert, 18, 139, 179–180

reptiles, 76

resources: commodification of, 104; depletion of, and GDP, 138–139; disproportionate use, 41–42; earth's capacity exceeded, 40–41; economic growth and resource use, 49–52 (*see also* economic growth); finite nature, 39, 116, 118, 208; growth rates of consumption, 50–51; market system inadequate to protect, 52–53 (*see also* market failure and the environment); resource productivity, 11, 55–56, 103; setting quantitative limits on use, 119–120; underpricing of, 92–93. *See also* *specific resources and issues*

Resources for the Future, 75

the right, 81–82

roads, 54, 76. *See also* transportation

Robinson, William, 186

Roy, Arundhati, 237

Russia, 48, 131(fig.)

ruthless economy, 49, 120, 144. *See also* well-being

Sagoff, Mark, 105

Sale, Kirkpatrick, 220

Samuelson, Paul, 47–48, 49

sanitation, 33

Santa Barbara Declaration of Environmental Rights, 215–216

satisfaction. *See* well-being

Scholte, Jan, 63

Scitovsky, Tibor, 157

sea level rise, 22, 23, 25

Seligman, Martin, 128–131, 133–134, 135, 143

Senge, Peter, 201

Shellenberger, Michael, 80, 233–234

shellfish, 23

Shutkin, William, 220

Sierra Club, 71, 230

Skocpol, Theda, 226–227

Smith, Adam, 166, 183

social democratic capitalism, 189

social greens, 44, 45

social health and development, 142(fig.), 142–143. *See also* human welfare; social values

social justice: environmental degradation and, 40, 225–226; international social movement for change, 186–188, 195, 235; social and economic inequality, 226–227. *See also* conflict, international/regional; human welfare

social movements: and consciousness

change, 214, 235; international social movement for change, 186–188, 195, 235 (*see also* Earth Charter)

social values: change needed, 12–13, 44, 199–216; culture war over, 80; current values, 62 (*see also* consumerism; materialism); in the future, 205–207; Keynes on return to, 107–109; and the sustainability worldview, 44, 120. *See also* well-being

socialism, 11, 183–184, 188–190

Southeastern United States, 24

Southwestern United States, 24, 31

species extinction, 36–38; contributing factors, 37, 40; effect of climate disruption on, 22–23, 26; freshwater species, 32; statistics, 1, 37–38; in the U.S., 2–4

spiritual change. *See* consciousness, transformation in

Stern Review, 29, 40–41

subsidies: eliminating perverse subsidies, 100, 105, 151; environmentally helpful subsidies, 68; fishing subsidies, 34, 251n16; perverse subsidies, 8, 54, 60, 91, 92, 100

sulfur dioxide, 50, 51, 73, 94–95, 102. *See also* acid rain

surplus product (profits), 58–59, 60. *See also* capitalism, modern: profit and growth motive

Susskind, Lawrence, 227

sustainability: consumer power and, 150, 151–152; corporations and, 175–176; encouraging sustainable business practices, 152; food production, 150; and market transformation, 103; setting quantitative limits, 119–120; strong vs. weak sustainability, 120; as worldview, 44, 45, 201. *See also* green consumerism

Sweden, 131(fig.), 140(fig.)

system, working within: belief in, 69–70; failure of, xii–xiii; limitations, 44–45, 79–80, 85–86, 219

Szelenyi, Ivan, 189

taxes: environmental taxes, 94, 96–97, 119; progressive taxation, 120

technology: availability of better technologies, 234; efficiency and resource productivity increasing, 55–56; new environmental issues, 83; for a new paradigm, 120; potential to compensate for growth, 112–115; and regulatory standards, 101

throughput, 56, 110, 111, 119–120. *See also* waste

Tietenberg, Tom, 96–97

Tobin, James, 141

toxic chemicals, 2, 35–36, 54, 76–77. *See also* greenhouse gas emissions; *and specific pollutants*

tragedy of the commons, 92, 95

transportation, 54, 76, 104–105, 172. *See also* cars; fossil fuels; oil

trust: in government, 79–81; importance of, 130–131, 173

Tucker, Mary Evelyn, 201, 214

unhappiness (depression), 130–131, 134

United Kingdom, 125, 132(fig.), 133, 140(fig.), 153

United Nations Environment Programme (UNEP), 69, 70

United States: air quality problems, 73, 74; consciousness transforma-

United States (*continued*)
tion, 203 (*see also* consciousness,
transformation in); consumption,
47, 147–149, 156 (*see also* consumerism; consumption; materialism);
democracy in, 217–219, 226–227,
231 (*see also* democracy; politics);
economic growth, 46, 49, 125;
energy consumption, 75, 149, 152;
energy policy and subsidies, 100,
169–170; environmental failures,
24, 75–78, 255n21; environmental
movement (*see* environmentalism);
environmental performance measures, 141–144; environmental
regulation, attitudes toward, 175;
environmental successes, 73, 75,
78; environmentalism today, 67–71;
fisheries loss, 35; government, 62–
63; green consumerism, 152; greenhouse gas emissions, 27, 75, 94–95;
greenhouse gas emissions, reducing, 29–30, 113–114; hazardous
waste, 36; inequality in, 226–227;
and international environmental
efforts, 47, 72, 73; market incentives in, 94–95; materialism,
attitudes towards, 162; natural
abundance (*pre-1900*), 2–4; pollution laws, results of, 73–75; population growth, 77–78; post-growth
society, 123–125; privatization and
government outsourcing, 104–105;
readiness for change, 65–66, 213;
subsidies, 100 (*see also* subsidies);
systemic crisis, 188; water issues,
33–34, 73–74, 75, 149; well-being
in, 130–133, 131(fig.), 132(fig.),
136–144, 140(fig.), 141(fig.),
142(fig.) (*see also* well-being)

valuation of environmental damages,
96–100
values. *See* social values
Virginia, 77
Vogel, David, 177

Wall Street Journal, 46
Wallerstein, Immanuel, 185, 188
Wal-Mart, 174, 179
Wargo, John, 76–77
waste: absorption capacity of environment, 118; eliminating, 11;
growth/increase, 6, 56, 76, 118.
See also throughput
water crisis, 32–34. *See also* fresh
water
weather, 22, 25. *See also* drought
Weber, Max, 128, 210
Weighted Index of Social Progress,
142–143
well-being (happiness, satisfaction):
components of subjective well-
being, 129; consumption/material-
ism and, 157–164; Earth Charter
on, 209; economic growth not
contributing to, 10, 116–117; in the
future, 205–207; and money (income), 128–134, 131(fig.), 132(fig.),
136–138; nature and history of,
126–128; and a new worldview,
205–206; policies to promote, 190;
and the possibility of change, 65–
66, 195, 213; reordering of priorities
needed, 144–146; social positioning
and habituation and, 133–134;
wellsprings (contributing factors),
134–138, 262–263n21. *See also*
human welfare
Westerfield, Brad, 17
wetlands: degradation/loss, 1, 18, 32,